PRAISE FOR *SCORING THE SCREEN*

"Undoubtedly the most important book on film scoring since On the Track."
—Derek Gleeson, director, MA in Scoring for Film
and Visual Media, Pulse College, Dublin

"Andy Hill has the ability to deconstruct and explain the process of writing film scores with extraordinary clarity, all the while imbuing the subject with a fervor that should, in my opinion, be reserved only for European football matches and Baptist revival meetings."
—John Powell, film composer

"You *must* read this—in the ever-growing pantheon of books on film music, this one is very special. While most analytical books are written by academics, Andy was right there in the thick of things as a member of the Disney music department, while the majority of the scores in the book were actually being recorded. Not to mention, it is so alive with his mad passion for film music."
—Christopher Young, film composer

"I calls 'em like I sees 'em, and this book is a home run."
—David Newman, composer/conductor

"With his book *Scoring the Screen*, Andy Hill has made an important and truly invaluable addition to an all-too-barren landscape of great literature about great film music. He presents his case that the finest composers to have worked in film over the last eighty years have contributed genuine masterpieces of music and drama to our culture. A film score must excel at both to be successful, and this is so beautifully illustrated in Hill's elegant prose. Part of the film composer's art is in fact to conceal the effort and the intellect that goes in to the creation of their scores. Hill thankfully lifts the veil. I am thrilled to see such a rare spotlight illuminating the artistry behind these masterworks."
—Robert Townson, film music producer (Varèse Sarabande)

"Finally, a book about composing for film from the perspective of the people who hire and supervise. Andy Hill has seen it all and brings to the table an experienced viewpoint of how it is done."
—Mark Watters, director, Beal Institute for Film Music and
Contemporary Media, Eastman School of Music;
six-time Emmy Award–winning composer and conductor

SCORING
THE SCREEN

music**PRO**
guides

SCORING THE SCREEN

THE SECRET LANGUAGE OF FILM MUSIC

ANDY HILL

ROWMAN & LITTLEFIELD
Lanham • Boulder • New York • London

Published in 2017 by Hal Leonard Books
An Imprint of The Rowman & Littlefield Publishing Group
4501 Forbes Boulevard, Suite 200
Lanham, MD 20706

Permissions can be found on pages 388–391, which constitute an extension of this copyright page.

Printed in the United States of America

Book design by John J. Flannery

Library of Congress Cataloging-in-Publication Data

Names: Hill, A. W. (Andrew Warren), 1951-
Title: Scoring the screen : the secret language of film music / Andy Hill.
Description: Montclair, NJ : Hal Leonard Books, 2017. | Series: Music pro guides
Identifiers: LCCN 2017013835 | ISBN 9781495073731 (pbk.)
Subjects: LCSH: Motion picture music--History and criticism. | Motion picture
   music--Analysis, appreciation.
Classification: LCC ML2075 .H53 2017 | DDC 781.5/42--dc23
LC record available at https://lccn.loc.gov/2017013835

www.rowman.com

CONTENTS

A Word on How to Use This Book.. ix

Acknowledgments.. xi

Foreword: The Greatest Gig in the World.. xiii

Introduction: Ancient & Modern: An Appreciation of James Newton Howard's *The Sixth Sense*........... xvii

One. From Among the Dead: Bernard Herrmann's *Vertigo*.. 1

Two. Boo Radley's Porch: Elmer Bernstein's *To Kill a Mockingbird*.. 23

Three. Signs and Meaning: From *Spellbound* to *Inception* 46

Four. *Perfume*: The Scent of Murder 78

Five. Carmen in Hell: David Newman's *The War of the Roses* 101

Six. Waltz for a Dead Girl: Christopher Young's *Jennifer 8*..130

Seven. Feed Your Head: Don Davis's *The Matrix*..160

Eight. Such a Long, Long Way to Fall: Danny Elfman's *Alice in Wonderland* 195

Nine. Surgical Precision: Alberto Iglesias's *La piel que habito* 228

Ten. The Strength of the Righteous: Ennio Morricone's *The Untouchables*....................................262

Eleven. Toward a New Aesthetic of Music for the Screen 300

Twelve. Through a Glass, and Darkly: Anatomy of a Cue from Jerry Goldsmith's *Patton*...................... 322

Thirteen. Stand Up! Two Cues from Elliot Goldenthal's *Michael Collins* 334

Fourteen. John Powell Slays a Dragon 350

Fifteen. Against the Odds: The Road to Kraków 382

Afterword.. 387

Music Permissions.. 388

A WORD ON HOW TO USE THIS BOOK

All of the score reductions created for *Scoring the Screen* have been indexed to scene timings derived from the downloadable versions of the feature films as available through online retailers, such as iTunes and Amazon. In most cases, these timings match or fall within a few seconds of the DVD timings. If you're a fan of film scores but don't read music, you can still derive enjoyment and a deeper appreciation of the score's dramatic function in cinema simply by following the text as you view the film critically.

If you're a composer, musician, educator, or musicologist, you'll find the greatest benefit comes from studying the text and reductions right at your DAW, with a keyboard at hand and the film (and the book, if you're using a digital copy) on your video display, just as if you were writing. The process is a little like "reverse scoring" the film: the work has been done, and now the mystery—and the learning—lies in discovering how it was done. Play along, sequence sections that particularly interest you, and have fun. All reductions are derived from the original concert scores used in recording, and all preserve the notational conventions used by the composer and his orchestrators, including chord spellings and pitch class. Unless otherwise noted, all scores are in C.

ACKNOWLEDGMENTS

A book like this is an improbability from the start. One might as well submit to publishers a manuscript titled *21st Century Falconry* or *Love Sonnets for Dummies* as one exploring the art of film scoring from a nonbusiness standpoint. And yet it's been evident to me for more than thirty years that such a book was needed, and that Roy Prendergast's classic *Film Music: A Neglected Art*, first printed in 1977, held a very lonely place on the library shelf. It is Roy—and the kindness that he and his ex-wife, Linda, extended to an eager but very green studio music executive in the mid-1980s—whom I want to acknowledge first. In these pages, I've tried to carry forward the passion and scholarship his work displayed. His book was my teacher when there were no others.

I was a first-timer to *Kickstarter*, and a skeptical one, when I launched the campaign that ultimately allowed me to shut out the world for the few months it took to gain serious traction with the manuscript. I owe a substantial debt of thanks to all 148 of my backers, and among them, a special shout-out to David Newman, John Powell, Mark Mancina, Bruce Broughton, Don Davis, Dan Carlin Jr., Paul Broucek, Mark Protosevich, David Lopez Tichy, Jami Striegel Orloff, and the family of Elmer Bernstein, not only for the level of their financial support, but for their encouragement throughout.

To my literary agent, Kimberley Cameron; my colleague in scientific detective work, Dr. Mani L. Bhaumik; and my daughter, Olivia Hill: thank you for the rocket fuel.

Finally, a text devoted to the works of contemporary film composers—most of them still very much alive—cannot possibly be compiled without the assistance and encouragement of music publishers (notably, John Cerullo, Lindsay Wagner, and Natalie Cherwin of Hal Leonard Music Publishing), production executives, music educators, and most important, the composers themselves. None of the scores examined within is yet in the public domain, and most are being presented for the first time in print to the public. In each case where the work of a living composer was studied, my research and the resulting chapter benefited from the insight and background provided by the composer himself.

And to violinist Nathalie Bonin, who did the last polish, *sul tasto*, with her bow.

FOREWORD

THE GREATEST GIG IN THE WORLD

A graduate student of mine, who had originally studied to be a concert pianist, told me that her undergraduate composition instructor had characterized film scoring as a form of prostitution. The only worthy use of great musical talent, he said, was in pursuit of great art. Why settle for *The Matrix* when *The Magic Flute* called? Thus, when she later confessed tearfully to him that all she really wanted to do was make music for the movies, she found herself branded—by his standards—not only a lesser artist, but a whore.

An eager student, belittled like that, may never entirely get over it. From every note written or played, there will always resound the slightest echo of doubt. Good teachers see each student as a deep well of possibility, and realize that, no matter how modest their own accomplishments, their position lends the power to inspire or to crush, to draw water or to seal the well. This book was conceived and written, in part, as a response to teachers who have sealed off wells of inspiration, and to their students, in hopes that those wells might once again be opened.

This is not to say that creating music for what is routinely described as "entertainment product" doesn't involve elements of artistic—and sometimes moral—compromise. It does. But so did writing for the eighteenth-century opera, and Mozart—for one—knew how to bend to the demands of the medium (and his patrons) and still deliver great music. That's the trick to making "assignment writing" an art: write interesting music both *within* and *in spite of* the limitations of form. Never use those limitations as an excuse to phone it in.

We'll stipulate that scoring for the screen is a form of popular art and that what's broadly called a film score is a form of *programmatic* music. We can concede that it's unlikely that any score crafted for a big-budget international action picture will ever rival *Le Sacre du printemps* for cultural impact. But let's also be clear about the fact that the good stuff—the music treated in this book—is programmatic music crafted to the most exacting standards and calling upon the deepest reservoirs of creativity and insight, and that its potential to reach people and reshape their sense of the world is nothing short of enormous.

Postmodern "pop culture scholars" have, in the last forty years or so, done a great deal to muddy the line between high art and low art, insisting that, say, *The Godfather* and a McDonald's commercial should both be regarded as expressions of "commercial art," and in that sense, have a kind of equivalency. I've done an informal but wide-ranging survey and discovered that nobody actually believes this nonsense. There is no cultural equivalency between *The Godfather* and a McDonald's commercial, or for that matter, between *The Godfather* and about 78 percent of Hollywood's typical yearly output. *The Godfather* is great popular art for one reason above all others: it aimed high and had the goods to reach its mark. This is true of most of the films (and all of the scores) treated in this book, and it can be just as true of a $100,000 indie film as a $100 million studio project. These are the projects that will put your career in motion, and if you are lucky enough to land one, you have a solemn duty to your craft to give it all you've got. This book is an examination of how that is to be done.

The cynicism and snobbery implicit in the teacher's comments about the artistic merits of film music are endemic and contagious. They spill out of the ivory tower and into the profession. Behind the swagger and beneath the vanity of many working in the commercial film and video industries is a secret fear that "we're all turning tricks for the idiots in the audience." In the years since the passing of such seminal artists as Elmer Bernstein, John Barry, and Jerry Goldsmith, too many contemporary film composers have bought into this self-abasement and turned in scores that lower the bar for those that follow. But the real secret is that quality triumphs in the end, even if it's sometimes hard to see that amid an onslaught of garbage. There are millions of discriminating listener-viewers out there, waiting for music that touches both mind and heart, and they can make your career. Write for them. The others will follow eventually.

At the time of this book's writing, big changes are occurring in the way we receive and appreciate "serious music." Radio still exists, and probably will in some form as long as people drive cars, but otherwise—to borrow a term from the drug industry—the "delivery systems" for music are being revamped. As in all periods of rapid change, there are those who want to ride the change and those who want to buck it, and a whole lot who feel an uneasy ambivalence. Critics bemoan the fact that fewer people go to the concert hall, and almost no one seems to sit down and listen to a complete "album" anymore, whether it's a symphonic work or a pop release. Music seems at risk of becoming completely incidental.

But there is a time *when* and a place *where* we do absorb and digest seriously composed music for ninety minutes or more at a stretch, and that is when we are under the spell of the screen. The "cinema" these days is wherever we are able to fall into that spell-state, whether in a state-of-the-art theater or on an iPod with earbuds in a crowded room. And this media mindspace is also, in many ways, the new concert hall. With less coughing, clearing of throats, and without the stiff attire and comportment. You, the composer, have been given a captive audience for the length of the viewer's entrancement by the film, television program, or video game. What a shame it would be not to play to it with all your heart.

On what's now known as the Eastwood Scoring Stage at Warner Bros.

Studios, I once witnessed a moment of pure joy. Composer David Newman, son of Alfred, brother of Thomas, cousin of Randy, had just recorded an especially great take. The name of the film isn't important. What is important is that Newman had written his heart out and nailed the cue and that the orchestra recognized this with an ovation. David, who is not known for being balletic, leapt three feet in the air and cried out, "This is the greatest gig in the world!" When you get it right, it is.

INTRODUCTION

ANCIENT AND MODERN: AN APPRECIATION
OF JAMES NEWTON HOWARD'S *THE SIXTH SENSE*

Ah me! Ah me! All brought to pass, all true! / O light, may I behold thee nevermore! / I stand a wretch, in birth, in wedlock cursed, / A parricide, incestuously, triply cursed! [Exit OEDIPUS]

Photograph by Wim Lippens

James Newton Howard

Not to worry. Despite the loftiness of opening a book about film music with a line from Sophocles's *Oedipus Rex*, possibly the greatest of the Greek tragedies, this will not be a dry, academic dissertation on the history of dramatic music. Movies, when they *move* us, are anything but dry. They affect us because they have slipped past rationality and into one of the oldest parts of the brain, the moist, dark center where such emotions as terror, dread, anxiety, desire, reverence, wonder, and awe reside. The principal task of film music is to both clear and light the way into that ancient chamber.

In the scene excerpted above, King Oedipus of Thebes, the man who solved the Riddle of the Sphinx, realizes in a (literally) blinding flash that he is guilty of both patricide and incest. Unknowingly, but in accordance with a prophecy, he has murdered his father and married his mother. Throughout the play, which is spoken in verse, Oedipus plays the part of detective in his own crime story, trying to root out the cause of the plagues that have afflicted his state—plagues that are the wages of his own sin. The character of the detective, the solitary and often damaged man who seeks the truth, may be drama's most essential protagonist, and certainly its greatest gift to a film composer. We're going to meet a lot of them.

The key thing is that, until things begin to unravel, Oedipus has no idea that the man he killed at the crossroads years ago was his own father, or that the woman who has borne him two daughters is the same woman who gave birth to him. He has misunderstood the prophecy, and the drama in the story—still a nail-biter after nearly 2,500 years—comes from the slow but inexorable way the awful truth comes home to him. Sophocles may have created the world's first noir.

In *The Sixth Sense*, M. Night Shyamalan's remarkable 1999 feature debut, Bruce Willis plays the tragic protagonist, Dr. Malcolm Crowe, a man suspended between the living and the dead. Like Oedipus, he is unaware that the hand of fate has already dealt him his cards, and similarly, his sense that something has gone wrong leads him to investigate his own history. In this case, Malcolm, a celebrated child psychologist, is the victim rather than the perpetrator of a heinous crime, but otherwise the dramatic tension derives from the same relentless unraveling. He is dead. He just doesn't know it, and it takes him a moody, terrifying, and beautifully crafted two hours to figure it out.

Both stories begin with their protagonists at the center of the labyrinth, and both stories develop as they attempt to backtrack to knowledge of how they came to be there. Both stories conclude with a tragic epiphany: the character learns the truth, but it's not the truth that he'd hoped for. Both *Oedipus Rex* and *The Sixth Sense* rely for their power on heavy doses of guilt, dread, and portentous turns of event—all elements that play to that ancient core of the brain.

I've chosen to kick off this study of the film composer's art with these narratives not just because they share certain dramatic values, but because they come as close as any I know to model candidates for great scoring. In fact, if after studying the craft, you can't score a man coming to the realization that his fate is out of his hands, you may want to consider an alternative career path.

PRECEPTS

We know how James Newton Howard rose to the challenge of handling this primal drama, because we have his *Sixth Sense* score as evidence, and we can and will examine aspects of how he did it. Film scoring is fundamentally about *solving dramatic problems* in the same plodding way detectives solve mysteries, and there's no better way to learn this craft than to study the successes—and failures—of those who've practiced it before. Scoring for the screen now embraces forms as diverse as video games and PSAs, and you may wonder what the plights of Oedipus or Malcolm Crowe have in common with a character in a digital dungeon preparing to face a boss with sixteen fire-breathing heads. The answer is: *plenty.*

At a minimum, your video game avatar will have to figure out how to defeat the sixteen-headed boss and get out of the dungeon alive. A *protagonist* + an *antagonist* = *conflict*, and conflict is the soul of drama. We've all had dreams of pursuit and narrow escape, and some would assert that the emotional meat of these dreams comes from a distant genetic memory of being on the savannah with a hungry predator at our heels. That is certainly what they *feel* like. Another universal dream involves being surrounded, as if by a pack of wolves, and feeling that "things are closing in on us." That feeling might also describe the drama of your video game character, as well as that of both Oedipus and Malcolm Crowe. Things are "closing in" on all of them, and the increase in tension has a definite musical shape in terms of line, harmony, timbre, and dynamics.

Dreams don't come with packaged soundtracks, but they do come with all the tonal values of a good *cue.* Imagine that we could take dictation in a dream state, or wake and go immediately to the keyboard while still in the emotional grip of the dream. Assuming we had the requisite technical skill, we would most likely end up after a couple of hours with a very useable sketch. This isn't very different from the "sense memory" exercises that some actors practice to get into character, and the dramatic composer is very much like an actor, or perhaps more accurately, a *medium.* It doesn't matter whether you're scoring an A-level feature film, a backyard indie, episodic TV, or a video game. Your job, in large measure, is to occupy a *point of view* and employ your compositional skills to map the emotional terrain as experienced from that perspective. There are exceptions, of course, and alternative approaches, but in most of the cases examined in this book, that's essentially what the composer has done.

We can't know exactly what the music composed for *Oedipus Rex* sounded like when it was first performed in 429 BCE, but we know from the historical record that there *was* music, and that it played an important role. Certainly, it wouldn't have been *underscore* in the sense exemplified by masters from Wagner to Goldenthal, but it wouldn't have been background filler, either. Instrumentation would have been sparse: a seven-stringed lyre, maybe a kithara or a double-reeded *aulos*, and of course, the Greek chorus performing its *stasimons*, the "scene-break" compositions that summed up for the audience both text and subtext of the drama. Until relatively late in the classical period, the Greeks did not notate their music in any way that's decipherable to scholars, but we can get an idea of what a typical melodic line sounded like from such pieces as the second-century BCE composition, the *Seikilos Epitaph* (which is as Mixolydian as anything by Thomas Newman). The music was homophonic, modal, and rhythmically simple, but we can make a reasonable guess that it met the following three requirements:

• It entered and exited the scene at dramatically appropriate times.
• It was tonally appropriate (in the sense of both mode and color).
• It supported rather than intruded upon or conflicted with the story.

These remain, more than two millennia later, the basic criteria for dramatic music. If your music hasn't met all of them, you can be sure that any director who knows what he or she is doing will object. But knowing this and doing it are very different things, and even after reading this book and all the others available, it may still take you a few thousand hours of scoring before you get the hang of it. Careful study of the scores excerpted here can save you a few hundred of them.

Others, including Aaron Copland, Sergei Prokofiev, and such film music scholars as Royal Brown and Claudia Gorbman, have weighed in on the proper function of music in cinema (we can use the European term *cinema* because it simply means "moving pictures" and can therefore refer to any of the forms we discuss in this book). In coming chapters, we'll consult them all. These and similar aesthetic guidelines tell you what your music needs to *do*, but they don't tell you a great deal about what you, the composer, need to *know* to be able to write an effective cue. One of the most incisive sum-ups comes to us courtesy of Rolfe Kent, a longtime collaborator of director Alexander Payne. Rolfe has scored such films as *Election, Up in the Air,* and *Gambit*. Rolfe contends that there are three things a composer must know before he or she sits down to tackle a scene:

• What is the point of view? (Whose perspective/experience does the music embody? It could conceivably be the director's!)
• What is the energy level the music must convey? (Will it work with or against the pace of the scene and the editing? Is it active or passive?)
• Does the music need to tell us something that the picture does not?

With these three considerations in mind, along with the first three criteria, we're ready to take a look at how a contemporary composer handles the drama of a character whose fate is closing in on him—a man whose time has run out. This will be a brief preview of the sort of in-depth analysis that will occur in the remaining pages of this book, a "hermeneutic" of film music that has served my students very well, and which I believe holds the key to a practical understanding of the craft. Hermeneutics, by the way, is a particular kind of study: the study of *interpretations*. It's an ancient word that, fittingly enough, goes back to the Greeks and their god of communication, Hermes, and originally had to do with the correct way to interpret an oracle. Now it is used in the field of semiotics to describe a way of interpreting the meaning of signs in both verbal and nonverbal communication. Since it's my contention that film music is a language of signs, it seems a good way to look at scores. The fact that great film music often speaks in a tonally and harmonically ambiguous language akin to that of oracles is just one of those weird and happy coincidences!

MALCOLM IS DEAD

Let's run our two story threads in parallel: Oedipus is about to discover that he is guilty of unspeakable acts, and Malcolm Crowe is about to discover that he's dead. For Oedipus, the truth is cinched when he is finally able to question the Herdsman who took him as an infant from his mother's arms, and knows that those arms belonged to Jocasta, Oedipus's present wife. It is the sudden confluence of past and present that sparks realization. For Malcolm, there's a similar confluence. He comes home, late at night, from a harrowing odyssey, to tell his neglected wife that she is first in his heart. He finds her curled up, asleep, in an armchair before the fire, oblivious to his physical presence but murmuring, "Why did you leave me?" on her vaporous breath. When he sits down to insist, "I never left you," her clenched fingers open to reveal his wedding ring—the ring he was sure was still on his own hand . . . *until he checks his ring finger*. This is where James Newton Howard's "Malcolm Is Dead" cue delicately enters the scene. An instant later, Malcolm stands and staggers back, experiencing a flood of flashbacks that seal the truth that—for the entire length of the story—he has been wandering in that strange land between the living and the dead, and now, it's time to let go. This, famously, is as much a surprise to the audience as it is to him.

The cue enters at approximately 1:37:46 into the film with ascending harmonies in high strings and flutes that begin at a dynamic marking of *pp* and swell slightly to *p* on each rise before falling back. This movement in the flutes and first violins is parallel, moving in alternating major and minor thirds in bars 1–4 from an A-flat minor chord through E minor, E major, and E-flat major harmonies, but *always against the constant A-flat minor chord* in the second violins. This creates a sequence of striking "harmonic poles" that effectively portray Malcolm's disorientation. Bars 1–4 are seen in Figure 0.1, in a reduction for flutes, horns, orchestra bells, celesta, violins, and cellos. Omitted are oboes and clarinets, trumpet, and the choir that enters in bar 4. These largely double the flutes and strings.

Figure 0.1. *The Sixth Sense,* 6M2, "Malcolm Is Dead," bars 1–4

This broad movement occurs against shimmering ostinatos in the glock-enspiel and celesta that create further harmonic ambiguity by appearing to toggle between E major and E minor (but note that an E major chord and an A-flat/G-sharp minor chord have two common tones). Without wanting to be too literal in our hermeneutics, it's fair to describe this rising line as the beginning of Dr. Crowe's "dawning realization." This is a pretty good example of *isomorphism,* a musical shape used to *signify* meaning. The orchestrational choices are also telling: glockenspiel and celesta are both delicate, ethereal textures that suggest a dream state, particularly against the muted violins and soft winds. In fact, everything about these first four bars, right down to the subtle, breathlike crescendos and decrescendos connotes the idea of a man who is "beginning to see the light."

What happens harmonically in these introductory measures can't really be described as a "chord progression," nor do the pitch stacks really lend themselves to identification as the sort of embellished chords we hear in a jazz chart. A chord progression is, almost by definition, *going somewhere*, and usually leads us either away from or toward a tonic. That doesn't happen here.

The four "chords" in bars 1–4 move by *chromatic inflection* from a nominal key center of A-flat minor to a crescendo on its dominant chord, but we're not returned to the key center. Instead, we shift in bar 5 via *two* common tones to a new ascent beginning with a G minor chord, as seen in bar 5 of Figure 0.2. The moving lines in flutes and first violins continue to ascend sequentially in thirds through passing chords, but again, *always* against the G minor harmony in the lower voices. Second violins and celesta have steadfastly maintained that foundation. They are the stone against which the ax of Malcolm's epiphany is ground.

This harmonic movement makes a lot more sense if we look at each four-bar phrase as the prolongation of a single chord: A-flat minor for the first four and G minor for the second four. What seem to be complex passing chords created by motion in the flutes and top violins are actually a result of "rubs" created as the principal lines ascend against a static harmony, creating incidental polychords. Incidental doesn't mean accidental. For example, Newton Howard, a sophisticated writer, was certainly aware that the mediant shift from A-flat minor to E minor in measures 1–2 was one of film music's classic "supernatural" *memes*.

A meme is the socio-cultural equivalent of a gene, an idea or notion that spreads virally through the information grid and replicates and mutates just like a gene. Its origin, also, is Greek, from *mimema*, something imitated. A *museme*, a term coined by scholars of the psychology of music, is its musical counterpart: a melodic, harmonic, or rhythmic gesture that composers "imitate" when they want to get an idea across.

This particular museme—a shift of minor triad roots by the interval of a major third—is one whose cinematic origins can be traced to the legendary Bernard Herrmann, who alone may be responsible for more of them than all the other film composers combined. And that brings up another notable thing about Newton Howard's writing. He is very much aware of—even reverential toward—the legacy of his craft. This cue is full of what the semioticians call *intertextual references*; that is, allusions to other film scores of the same genre. The harmony recalls Herrmann, the use of ostinatos to activate the harmonies recalls Jerry Goldsmith's *Basic Instinct* (which was itself an homage to Herrmann), and the use of delicate struck and plucked textures to play deepest mystery evokes not only these two predecessors but Saint-Saëns and Ravel, who influenced them both! In this sense, Newton Howard's cue carries three generations of lineage, and yet remains entirely his own invention. Not a bad way to make sure you get your point across.

But there are more interesting things going on here than the composer's awareness of film music vocabulary. For one, the blunt-force harmonic movement from A-flat minor to G minor across the first eight bars of the cue prefigures the dramatic revelation shown in Fig 0.2.

Figure 0.2. *The Sixth Sense*, 6M2, "Malcolm Is Dead," bars 5–9

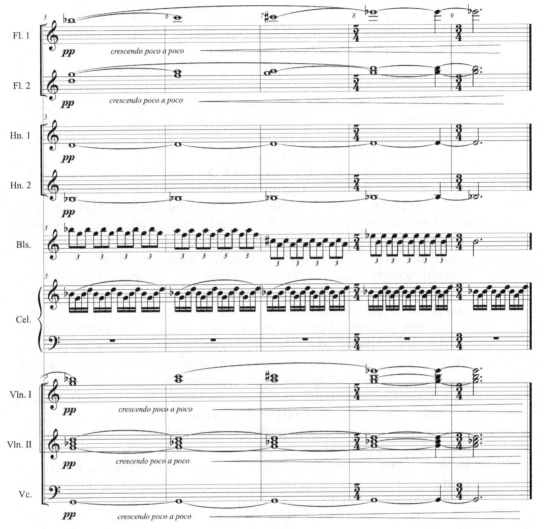

In measures 13–15, Newton Howard and his orchestrator, Brad Dechter, show themselves to be adept at the kind of extended techniques and quasi-aleatoric writing that have become so strongly associated with the horror and fantasy genres. Note that the effect they're after is that of noisily humming bees, and that they're leaving the creation of this sound, in part, to the players by instructing them to ad lib. On screen, Malcolm is staggering toward the stairwell, clutching his mortal wound, backing away from the awful truth of his death. A big glissando in the chorus takes us (and him) up the stairs and to the climax of the cue.

Figure 0.3. *The Sixth Sense*, 6M2, bars 13–16, score excerpt

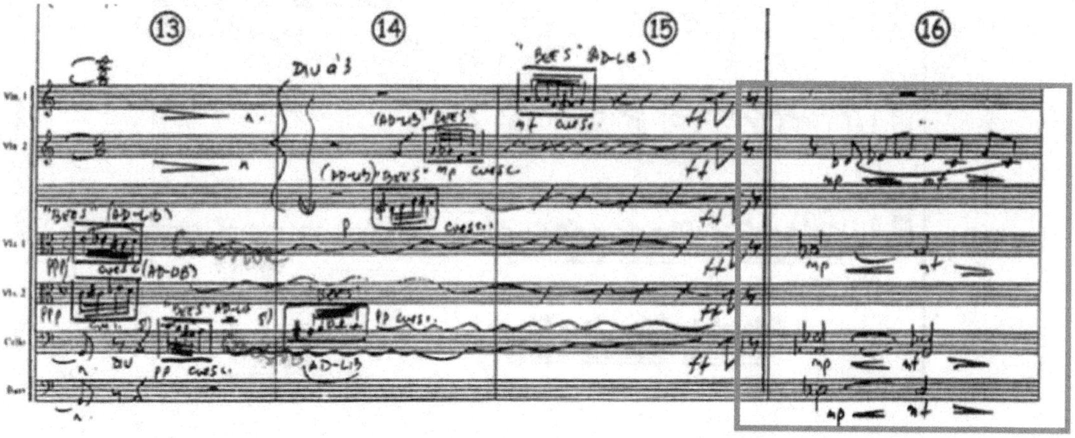

Here is a reduction of this section, with most of the ad lib pitch sets written out, just to show the importance of the staggered entrances and the use of the choir. The choral parts are also reduced to the core inner parts. A passage such as this would never be written out fully, since the whole idea is randomness.

Figure 0.4. *The Sixth Sense,* 6M2, "Malcolm Is Dead," bars 13–15

The seven-bar section shown next in Figures 0.5 and 0.6 is justly considered one of the most masterful passages of underscore for one of the boldest dramatic gambles in the commercial cinema of the late (very late) twentieth century. Second violins double the horn line, while the supporting harmony is a very dramatic block D-flat minor to C minor change utilizing raw parallel fourths and fifths (prefigured, as mentioned, by the A-flat minor to G minor in bars 1–8). Block shifts of a semitone are rare, rarer still with chords of the same mode, but in this case, the primal drama warrants them. The use of this very dark (but entirely triadic) harmonic plunge gives the cue a sort of monumental gravitas.

Figure 0.5. *The Sixth Sense*, 6M2, "Malcolm Is Dead," bars 16–19

Figure 0.6. *The Sixth Sense*, 6M2, "Malcolm Is Dead," bars 21–23

In fact, one of the few musical forms in which we might hear this kind of thing is the funeral dirge. The horn melody, repeated four times, has an inexorable quality: Malcolm Crowe is not going to escape his fate. The high violin and trumpet figures in measures 17 and 19 are full of anguish and provide the sole element of dissonance: that E-natural suspended over the yawning chasm.

Malcolm's final epiphany comes at measure 23, after an almost Wagnerian harmonic sweep—with full-octave leaps in trumpet and violins and a machine gun blast of accented sixteenth-notes in brass, percussion, and low strings—takes us literally to the sound of the gunshot that killed him just ten minutes into the film. The funereal drive of the preceding four bars has given way to a B major chord that feels transcendent and then leads to a temporary plateau of E-flat minor, once again requiring a shift of only one chord tone by a semitone.

TONALITY AND MEANING

A careful look at just this much of the *Malcolm Is Dead* cue reveals not only ambiguity as to *key*, but elements of bitonality. Wandering key centers are common in film music, and although most cues have a "practical tonality," you'll almost *never* see a key signature on a concert score. *Malcolm* goes a bit further. Throughout the examples in this book, we're going to see hints of clashing key centers (see especially chapter 12, on *Patton*). In most cases, it won't be the outright bitonality of Stravinsky or Ives, but something more *incidental*. Bitonality became attractive to screen composers not just because it was a hip, modernist device, but because drama is rife with situations where two different versions of the truth (sometimes, even two different realities) are present. This is especially true in film noir and psychological thrillers. "Who *really* is this man who seems to be my husband? Who *really* is this woman who pretends to be my wife? And if he/she loves me, why is he/she trying to kill me?" Splitting the key center doesn't always work to reflect this *cognitive dissonance*, but it's a valuable tool to have ready.

In both the *Oedipus* story and *The Sixth Sense*, there is conflict in the protagonist's mind between *the man he thought he was* and the man he turns out to be. Look at the voicing in Newton Howard's measure 6. The low strings and brass hold down a G pedal. The rest of the brass section, as well as chorus and second violins, fill out a G minor chord—which as we've said, is the "prevailing harmony." But flutes, first violins, and even glockenspiel have notes that spell an F major chord. If we isolate the bar and look at this like a jazz chart, I suppose we could call it a Gm9sus4, but that wouldn't make sense in either musical or dramatic context. The placement of this harmony occurs just as Malcolm's first flashback comes, following a reprise of the film's famous line, "I see dead people." Whether by instinct or design, the composer chose this moment to use a *polychord*—two chords, reflective of two different realities, superimposed.

That whole question of *instinct versus design, intuition versus intellect*, by the way, is one I'd like to comment on before going further. Books that engage in analysis of artistic works often make presumptions about artistic intent that miss the mark, sometimes in absurdly and unintentionally ridiculous ways: *"The composer depicts a quiet day of fishing by liberally quoting from Schubert's 'Trout Symphony,' albeit in retrograde and by way of clever inversions of the melody!"* This sort of thing serves more to point out the analyst's cleverness than the composer's. When we are in the throes of creative effort, focused on task, our process is the opposite of analytical. We may find ourselves making "Schubertian statements," but this will rarely be because we've said to ourselves, "I think it's time for a Schubertian statement!"

James Newton Howard's cue works so well precisely because he has so effectively and *unconsciously* integrated the vocabulary of his craft. His quotes or allusions, when they occur, feel completely natural, like the speech of someone who has mastered a dialect well enough to pass as a native. This is what composers of music for drama (and by drama, I mean all forms of dramatic expression) should aim for: not originality for its own sake, but an original use of the vocabulary. Not an entirely new language (though if you can create one that works, more power to you!), but a development of the shared language in service of the story you have been asked to assist in telling.

MUSIC AS NARRATIVE

And that brings us to the closing note of this opening chapter.

It's the story.

It's the story.

It's the story.

That's your mantra. Your "Hail, Mary." If your music is helping to tell the story the director (or whoever holds the reins) wishes to tell, then it will be successful, no matter how offbeat or idiosyncratic it is. Your choice of harmonic language, instrumentation, and style must all be rooted in story. Don't make the mistake of assuming this means that a present-day production of *Oedipus Rex* needs to be scored for lyre, kithara, and chorus (though it might be an interesting way to go, especially if the production is a contemporary take on the myth à la Julie Taymor). Literal translations don't usually work in the dreamland of cinema, and intellectual rationalizations for your choices can mean certain downfall. The Greeks didn't use the lyre because it was Greek; they used it because it was their most expressive instrument. If they'd had access to *granular synthesis*, and it served to make the plight of Oedipus more poignant, they'd have utilized it in a heartbeat. There are indeed "circles of permissibility" and "acceptable parameters" in dramatic scoring, beyond which you may be on thin ice stylistically. But in general, anything goes if it serves the story.

This total, selfless focus on *narrative*, on functioning as a codramatist, will also relieve you of experiencing anguish every time you have to revise, rewrite, or throw out a cue you've just spent thirty-seven sleepless hours working on. The measure of a film cue's success is its dramatic *effectiveness*, and after enough experience, you'll develop an ability to separate yourself from your own creation and be as discerning and demanding a judge as any. Music created for visual media is, broadly speaking, a high form of "popular music." It is meant to be experienced as a communal event, and there is a kind of alchemy that occurs when a successful fusion of music and image is achieved. Everyone can feel it. Similarly, there's a distinctly "empty" vibe in the room when a cue isn't working. At some point—probably many points—in your career, you'll experience that emptiness. Learning how to recognize both alchemy and emptiness will be as much a factor in your success as technique, and aiding you in that is one of this book's reasons for being.

James Newton Howard relates a conversation he had with *Sixth Sense* director M. Night Shyamalan shortly after the film—but not the score—had received an Academy Award nomination. "Why do think they overlooked the score, Night?" he asked (or words to that effect). Shyamalan pondered the question and then said, "Maybe because you did *too much*. Awards voters seem more likely to vote for you when you do *one* thing." There may have been wisdom in that answer, but for my part, I doubt this exceptional film would have had anywhere near the emotional complexity it does if the composer had taken a stingier approach. By using the vocabulary of film music to its fullest, James Newton Howard has left us a treasure trove of knowledge.

ONE FROM AMONG THE DEAD

BERNARD HERRMANN'S *VERTIGO*

Bernard Herrmann

It may or may not be a coincidence that *Vertigo*, the first full score we'll put under the microscope, flows from a film whose characters, like those in *The Sixth Sense*, seem to occupy a space somewhere between life and death. Ghosts have always haunted the cinema. In fact, one of the early arguments advanced for having music in cinema at all was to dispel the "ghostly effect" of seeing apparently living but disembodied people wandering around on the flickering silver screen. Hanns Eisler, a pupil of Arnold Schoenberg's and a collaborator of Bertolt Brecht who himself earned two Oscar nominations in the 1940s, wrote with Theodor Adorno in *Composing for the Films* (Bloomsbury Academic, 1947), "Motion picture music corresponds to . . . whistling in the dark," and "the magic function of music consisted in appeasing the evil spirits unconsciously dreaded (by the viewers)."

I'm inclined to agree with film music scholar Roy Prendergast, who in his incisive (and sometimes acerbic) *Film Music: A Neglected Art* (W. W. Norton, 1992) dismisses Eisler's theory as overthink, but there is something to the idea that a movie theater is a natural habitat for ghosts and ghost stories. Cinema isn't "live" theater, nor is it "dead" painting, but somewhere in between, and its projected images remind us a little of why indigenous tribesmen in remote areas may once have refused to have their photographs taken, for fear the camera would "steal their soul."

The uncanny quality of filmed images makes the story of *Vertigo* a perfect subject for cinema, because it revolves around a woman who is not what she appears to be.

If you were exiled to a desert island for a year with nothing but your composing rig and orders to learn the craft of film scoring, and were allowed to take with you only one score for study, Bernard Herrmann's score for Alfred Hitchcock's *Vertigo* would be a strong contender. It's a "touchstone" score, not only defining a genre (the glossy, labyrinthine psychological thriller) but seeding the vocabulary of the craft with so many now familiar musical expressions that hearing it for the first time is a bit like finding an old photograph of your great-great-grandfather and saying, "Ah . . . now I know where my nose comes from." Herrmann was one of a precious handful of genuine originators in the field of film music, and quite possibly the greatest of them all. These days, even the most perfunctorily composed made-for-TV thriller score owes a debt to that cantankerous and uncompromising soul that his collaborators once knew as Benny Herrmann.

Entire books have, and probably *will be* devoted to Bernard Herrmann and his impact on motion picture art. Among the most notable are Steven C. Smith's definitive biography, *A Heart at Fire's Center* (University of California Press, 1991) and David Cooper's score studies of *The Ghost and Mrs. Muir* and *Vertigo* for, respectively, the Scarecrow Press *Film Score Guide* series and Greenwood Press (the latter is out of print but can still be found on the Web). This book, as a collection, won't aim to treat either Herrmann's life or his work as comprehensively, but as a "founding father," he'll get his due.

Before entering Herrmann's world and plunging into the musical vortex that is *Vertigo*, let me state one of this book's critical assumptions: not all music composed (or assembled) for use in films is "film music." Film music as a distinct form developed over roughly a quarter of a century from the early talkies to its first maturity in the mid-1940s. The first generation of film composers, such men as Max Steiner and Erich Wolfgang Korngold, sprang directly from the European late romantic period and the salons and opera houses of Vienna. If not for the dark currents of history that swept over Europe in the 1930s, many—if not most—of them would have enjoyed celebrated concert careers in Europe rather than taking flight to New York and, ultimately, Hollywood. Because film was an entirely new form of entertainment, no signposts existed to guide them as to how music should make its way through the story, and so these early composers turned most-ly to opera—and to the programmatic music of such mentors as Richard Strauss—for guidance. The scores they created, though often stirring and memorable as music in its own right, were—by today's standards—orches-trationally overrich and overwritten. Even the great Alfred Newman and Dimitri Tiomkin, who came along just a little later, largely stayed faithful to the aesthetics of concert and theatrical music. This is understandable. New aesthetics don't appear overnight.

Experts will differ on precisely where the breakpoint occurred and film music began to sound like *film music*, but I might argue that the baby spoke its first full sentence in 1945—the year that Miklós Rósza delivered the score for Hitchcock's *Spellbound*—and was having complete conversations by 1950, when Franz Waxman scored *Sunset Boulevard*. Bernard Herrmann, one of those kids who "doesn't play well with others," was present throughout this developmental stage, from *Citizen Kane* in 1940 to *The Man Who Knew Too Much* in 1956, but he burst from the pack in 1958 with *Vertigo*, and the movies have not been the same since.

Why they have never been the same and *what* Herrmann did to make it so are the subjects of this chapter and, in a broader sense, this book, for we'll trace the birth of the film score as we know it to the theatrical release date of *Vertigo*. Herrmann's score not only met and exceeded the standards set in this book's foreword, it also entirely satisfied film music scholar Claudia Gorbman's[1] insistence that effective film music should "lower the threshold of belief" and allow the audience to experience a loss of bear-ings that in the rational, waking world might be considered dissociative. Great film music not only aids in storytelling and stirs our emotions, it can effect a kind of altered state of consciousness. As another scholar, Royal S. Brown, has argued, Bernard Herrmann created for Alfred Hitchcock a "music of the irrational."[2]

MUSIC AND MYTH

Herrmann's approach to the challenge of scoring *Vertigo* is a textbook exam-ple of the composer functioning as codramatist. The script is a reasonably faithful adaptation of *D'entre les Morts,* a French *policier* written by Pierre Boileau and Thomas Narcejac (1954) and published in the United States as *The Living and the Dead*. The title translates literally as "From Among the Dead," which was, in fact, the working title of *Vertigo*. It also references the underlying source material for the story, the classical myth of Orpheus and Eurydice, and, in a less overt sense, the Celtic legend of Tristan and Iseult.

Like the tragedy of Oedipus, the Orpheus and Eurydice story is one of mankind's foundational myths, psychologically rich enough to have earned countless studies. And also like Oedipus, it's a progenitor of the detective

1 Claudia Gorbman, *Unheard Melodies* (Bloomington: Indiana University Press, 1987).
2 Royal S. Brown, *Overtones and Undertones* (Berkeley: University of California Press, 1994).

story, in this case the variant that has the detective looking for a girl in trouble, a girl who is invariably not just a girl, but a hidden aspect of the detective himself. Briefly, the myth relates how Orpheus, son of Apollo and the most gifted of all musicians, descends to the underworld in hopes of resurrecting his beloved Eurydice, who has succumbed to a snake bite while being pursued through a field of flowers by a would-be rapist. With the aid of his lyre, Orpheus charms the gods of the underworld into allowing Eurydice a second life, on the condition that he not turn around to gaze at her beauty until they have returned to the surface. But Orpheus isn't able to resist the temptation, and Eurydice *dies a second time*—this time, for eternity. Things just get worse for Orpheus from there on.

Tristan and Iseult (or Isolde) is a tale of illicit love, born from the great trove of Arthurian lore. Iseult is promised in marriage to King Mark, but finds herself smitten with the dashing Tristan, who has been entrusted with her care. On the eve of the wedding, a powerful love potion intended as a marital aid for the newlyweds is instead consumed by the two young lovers, after which they are passionately—and hopelessly—attached. The mere sight of Iseult drives Tristan to distraction, and because their union is impossible, he sails away to a distant shore, marrying a substitute, *also named Iseult*, in hopes of forgetting the original. But nothing can break the shackles of obsession, and to cut to the chase, a tragic misunderstanding causes Tristan to kill himself. Upon discovering this, Iseult takes her own life, and the two lovers are finally joined in death. If that sounds familiar, yes, even Shakespeare borrowed from myth.

Mythical sources aren't always openly acknowledged, but in the case of *D'entre les Morts*, Orpheus and his subterranean bride are clearly embodied by the main characters of Roger Flavières and his quarry, the mysterious Madeleine. The novel's action is in Paris, where Flavières is on medical leave from his job as police investigator after having suffered a severe attack of vertigo that resulted in the falling death of a fellow officer. While nursing his psychic wounds, he receives a call from a wealthy former classmate who asks him to take on an off-the-record private assignment: tailing his beautiful and death-haunted young wife as she moves about Paris apparently in a hypnotic trance and convinced that she has incarnated both the spirit and the tragic fate of her grandmother, who committed suicide when she was precisely Madeleine's age. True to the form of the psychological mystery, the nominally "rational" protagonist, Flavières, assumes that Madeleine is suffering from some sort of mental disorder and can no longer distinguish between her true self and the persona she has adopted, while we the readers are invited to consider more supernatural reasons for her strange and self-destructive behavior. This toggling between the rationally explainable and the truly fantastical is what makes the story a natural for the movies, and doubtless why Hitchcock, who was fascinated by aberrant psychology and the landscape of nightmares, snatched it up. After a series of screenwriters made contributions, he finally had a shooting script.

In *Vertigo*, Roger Flavières becomes Scottie Ferguson (James Stewart), but Madeleine remains very much Madeleine (Kim Novak, half Stewart's age). The action has moved to San Francisco and Madeleine's ill-fated ancestor is now Carlotta Valdes, a Hispanic beauty from the age of the California missions, but the story of possession that sets Scottie's surveillance in motion is very much the same, as is the crippling vertigo that makes every step in Scottie's pursuit one likely to lead him over the edge and into the abyss. Madeleine is the Eurydice he must attempt to redeem from the underworld of her delusional state, and it is the very fact of her downward spiral toward death that exerts such a powerful attraction. He isn't on the case for a day before he finds himself falling head over heels in love with her. She's also his Iseult (or, in this case, his Isolde, since it's the German/Wagnerian version of the heroine that Herrmann chose for his own muse), as she is another man's wife, and he'll never truly be able to possess her. To summarize an intricate puzzle of a plot, Scottie's investigation leads to a rescue from drowning, a brief but torrid love affair, and a double tragedy of a depth and weight we rarely see in the movies—much less in commercial films. In the end, Scottie will be no better off than Orpheus, and just as "dead to the world" as Tristan.

Underpinning all this modern mythology is a fairly straightforward crime plot, a gambit to commit the perfect murder. Scottie is being played, both by Madeleine's ostensibly worried husband and by Madeleine herself, and all this is revealed in good time, but the mechanics of a murder plot have very little to do with the way Hitchcock directs the film, and nothing to do with the way Bernard Herrmann chose to score it. Both men opted to mine the psychological gold of the story's mythical framework.

HERRMANN'S *LIEBESTOD*

Bernard Herrmann lacked neither artistic ego nor an original voice. On the contrary, his certainty about the rightness of his approach could boil over into arrogance and inconsiderateness on occasion, and the musical choices he defended so vociferously were nothing if not profoundly innovative (and usually correct). Indeed, Herrmann never plagiarized anyone but himself (he had a fondness for recycling his best ideas). Therefore, his choice to infuse the *Vertigo* score with the harmonic DNA of Wagner's *Tristan und Isolde* (in particular, the Prelude and the *Liebestod*, or "Love-death" from the third act) was the act of a storyteller who—far from wanting to assert his own artistic primacy—realized that the "right score" for the film had, in a sense, already been written. *Tristan* is often described as the genesis of modern harmony. Its composer—himself not exactly an easygoing fellow—asserted that "having never in (his) life enjoyed the true happiness of love," he would "erect a memorial to this loveliest of all dreams," and having finished, "cover himself over—to die." Herrmann, who considered himself, like Wagner, an expert on the subject of unrequited love, found his Madeleine in Isolde.

Whether or not *Tristan und Isolde* fathered modern harmony, as some critics think, there's no question that it has influenced the development of film music's language as much as any single piece in the classical repertoire. Its fervent chromaticism, always reaching but never quite grasping the object of its desire—was imitated (often badly) in melodrama right through the 1940s, so much so that it had become a cliché by the time Herrmann stepped up to do it justice. A more lasting effect was its expression of heightened emotion as an unresolved chain of *suspensions*, leading to unexpected places harmonically. Wagner's dramatic vocabulary has stayed with us, notably in the work of composer Elliot Goldenthal. [And Lars von Trier's broodingly beautiful *Melancholia* (2012), another love poem to death, used the *Tristan* Prelude exclusively as its score.]

For many music theorists, the harmonic heart of the *Tristan* Prelude (and of the *Vertigo* score, as well) is the so-called Tristan chord, which is a half-diminished seventh (or m7flat5 in jazz parlance), voiced 1–flat5–7–3 from bottom to top. It is the first chord to appear in the *Tristan* score, following the statement of the opening leitmotif.

Figure 1.1. Wagner, *Tristan* Prelude

The half-diminished seventh chord has an astringent quality that makes it especially good for evoking the "sting" of frustrated desire. Because its axis is a diminished fifth, it is very unstable and will never serve as a chord of resolution. Likewise, its "spelling" makes it highly ambiguous: all four of its tones are the same as those of the minor sixth chord whose root lies a minor third above, an enharmonic kinship that Herrmann made great use of in many scores.

The most exposed—and affecting—use of the Tristan chord in *Vertigo* occurs at just under forty-four minutes into the film, in a cue that Herrmann called "Sleep." In the previous scene, Madeleine, possessed by the spirit of her great-grandmother, has taken a suicidal leap into San Francisco Bay, and Scottie has rescued her and taken her back to his apartment to recover. The music, scored for strings only (8-8-4-4, with no contrabass, all in mutes) enters at *pp*, as Scottie tosses a log on the fire. Hitchcock's roaming, voyeuristic camera reveals that in the background, Madeleine sleeps fitfully in Scottie's bed, relieved of her wet clothes and whispering cryptically from a troubled dream. It's important to note that the camera's point of view is not Scottie's, but Hitchcock's—and ours. We arrive at the bedroom door before Scottie does, and are allowed a moment to admire Madeleine's form beneath the sheets and to hear her ghostly utterances. It's a shivery and unsettling moment, and Herrmann's music informs us that trouble lies ahead.

Figure 1.2. Bernard Herrmann, *Vertigo*, "Sleep" excerpt

The violins are marked "Div A4" in Herrmann's autograph score, so firsts and seconds each occupy a system of their own. I've collapsed them in the foregoing example to make Herrmann's voicing of the F half-diminished seventh and C minor chords more apparent. Herrmann was a master at making the same chord or chords sound like a new harmony through exchange of voices, inversion, and registral shifts, a technique he used to great effect in *Psycho*. The two-chord pattern shown in the first four measures (Figure 1.2) repeats itself in successively lower registers until it finally comes to rest in the violas and celli (the latter with a C below the bass clef) on a final C minor chord the sounds both ominous and serene, like a body at last being laid to rest.

At barely forty-five seconds in length, "Sleep" is nonetheless one of the most indelible cues in film music history. The inside joke, or if you like, the "intertextual reference," lies in the fact that the F half-diminished seventh chord that opens it is, in fact, exactly the same harmony that opens *Tristan und Isolde*, pretty much right down to the voicing.

The second element of Wagner's opera that Herrmann adapted to his own devices in *Vertigo* is the gorgeous, never consummated gesture that figures so importantly in Isolde's dying pledge of eternal love, the *Liebestod*. Herrmann paid homage to both the melodic shape and harmonic tension of Wagner's motif, but did so in an ingeniously original way that insured that its familiarity would pull the desired emotional levers without sounding like slavish imitation or cribbing. In doing so, Herrmann showed himself to be the first great film composer to grasp the fact that the power of cinema lies in its ability to resonate with shared experiences, memories, even subconscious content. If Hitchcock played on our common fears, then Herrmann proved a worthy accomplice, working his magic behind the curtain, striking chords of both desire and dread.

First, here is a reduction of Wagner's *Liebestod* motif:

Figure 1.3. Wagner, *Liebestod* motif (excerpt)

The key is B major, which makes the chord progression IV–ii–I, not in itself unusual. The beauty and urgency of the tune comes from the sequence of falling seconds, two of them beginning on appoggiaturas: a nonchordal C-sharp over the E major chord (resolving to B); A-sharp to G-sharp over the C-sharp minor sixth chord; a nonchordal G-sharp over the B major chord (resolving to F-sharp), followed by that chromatic triplet run-up to the repeat. (see sidebar) The dotted rhythm on beat two, combined with the triplet on beat four, lend a feeling of triple meter, and this is what Herrmann felt, too.

But Herrmann, mischievous boy that he was, did not, in fact, use the *Liebestod* melody, with its only mildly dissonant sixths, as the model for his own love theme, but a similar idea, stated just a couple of times in the Prelude as a foreshadowing of events to come, and carrying the more striking dissonance of an augmented fourth: B-natural falling to A over an F major chord (in the first case) and D-sharp falling to C-sharp over an A major chord (in the second). These "Lydian" moments (see sidebar) in the Prelude have sometimes been labeled by theorists as the

Composer's Sidebar: APPOGGIATURAS

An appoggiatura is a nonchordal tone heard on a downbeat; for example, a D-natural in the melody line over an F major chord. Classically, it's approached by skip and resolves to a chord tone by step. The fact that it's approached by a skip and decidedly accented makes it entirely different from any kind of passing tone. It's a melodic device, and often one used to evoke longing or deep feeling. An astonishing number of the most memorable melodies in both the classical and film repertoires (not to mention popular song) are characterized by well-placed appoggiaturas.

"Tristan's Anguish" motif, and whether or not Wagner intended them as such, the label fits. As we will see, Herrmann clearly felt that this particular "anguish" described the way Scottie felt when he gazed at Madeleine.

Figure 1.4A. Wagner, Prelude to *Tristan and Isolde*: "Anguish" motif

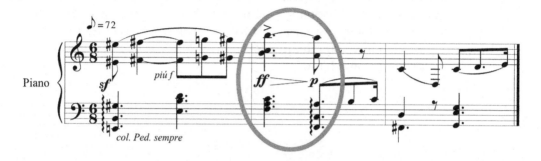

Figure 1.4B. Wagner, Prelude to *Tristan and Isolde*: "Glance" motif

The *Vertigo* love theme, most fully realized in a cue titled "Scene d'Amour," is a gorgeously orchestrated marriage of the *Liebestod* and "Anguish" motifs, and in this case, the combination yields a piece of music that, while recalling the source in all its mythical depth, is also entirely new—and so iconic that it provided the musical centerpiece for the 2011 film *The Artist*, and arguably helped to win both that film and its score Oscars. In Wagner's Prelude, the "Anguish" motif is left hanging as soon as the augmented fourth resolves. It's an incomplete phrase—barely a motive. A "be still, my heart" gesture.

Composer's Sidebar: LYDIAN MODE

If appoggiaturas are common features of enduring melodies, among the most affecting is the one used by Wagner in the "Anguish" motif: the augmented fourth characteristic of the Lydian mode, the archaic "church mode" originally based on pitch "F" (or solfege Fa) of the C-diatonic pitch set (a major scale with a raised fourth, or a tritone between the first and fourth scale degrees). The brief dissonance heard before an augmented fourth resolves to the third of the chord is one of the great gifts "the Devil's interval" has given to music. In the chapter on *To Kill a Mockingbird*, we'll explore Lydian mode further.

By choosing this undeveloped idea as his starting point, Herrmann pulled off a couple of neat tricks. First, he took the *masculine* point of view, i.e., Tristan/Scottie (the *Liebestod* melody is associated with Isolde/Madeleine), which is appropriate, as this is the perspective from which the movie unfolds. Second, he set himself up to "complete" Wagner's unfinished melodic statement on his own terms: by opening the melody on the more astringent augmented fourth dissonance, he ensured that the score would never veer into grand romance, or succumb to the overblown style then current in Hollywood, but would remain a monument to the agony of impossible love. Here it is in his own hand:

Figure 1.5. *Vertigo*, "Scene d'Amour" (excerpt)—autograph score courtesy of the Library of Congress and the Bernard Herrmann Papers collection at University of California, Santa Barbara

Herrmann's classic scores, curated by University of California, Santa Barbara, and archived on microfilm by the Library of Congress, aren't easy to read. He had a pinched, almost childlike hand, that of a man whose fevered brain was way ahead of his pencil. Beyond that, the microfilm has deteriorated over time, leaving frustrating gaps in the scores. Nonetheless, I've included it here because there is something wonderful about seeing work in the author's hand, and especially the work of a mind like Herrmann's.

The excerpt shown is the climax of the cue and the "false climax" of the film. At nearly two hours in, with barely fourteen minutes left, Scottie—it seems—may finally achieve his goal of possessing Madeleine, though he has had to go to hell and back to accomplish it. She materializes in a ghostly light after a full makeover at the beauty parlor, and the theme based on "Tristan's Anguish"—never fully realized until now—bursts forth at bar 60, marked *"Molto Largamente e Appassionato"* and *"tutti."* But Herrmann, who was incapable of insincerity, makes no false promises of happily ever after. As lush as the orchestration is, harmonically speaking, the cue offers no foundation to build a happy ending on. To illustrate Herrmann's musical storytelling, I've cheated a bit by using bars 60–63 as written and tacking on bars 6 and 7 from the beginning of the cue, which are variations on the theme. This sequence is used often in his presentation of the melody.

Figures 1.6A and 1.6B. *Vertigo*, "Scene d'Amour" (excerpt/reduction)

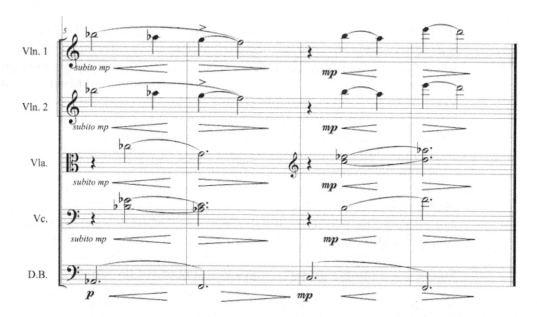

Take a look at what he's done. The descending melodic phrase (D–C–B–E) is harmonized with an A-flat major chord under the D–C descent, creating a Lydian dissonance on the downbeat that then resolves to the third of the chord. The second half of the phrase, dropping a P5 from B to E, falls over an A minor harmony, giving us that most anguished of jazzy rubs on the downbeat: a minor triad with a major second ("add 9") wedged in between its root and third. We are already quite a long way from the unbridled romanticism of the *Liebestod*. But Herrmann isn't done wringing out the anguish. His variation of the theme in the consequent phrase retains the A-flat pitch center but shifts to the parallel minor, and then even more boldly to an F minor chord. The melody reaches its highest point most astringently in its final statement, over a C major seventh to D diminished change. No conventional tonality can accommodate such a progression, but neither have we left tonality behind. Herrmann is utilizing a form of mode mixing that became one of the most characteristic elements of his signature and led to a brand of extended tonality that is a hallmark of film music and will recur throughout this book.

Again and again in Herrmann's music—most strikingly in his sci-fi and fantasy scores—we hear progressions that include block movement of minor chords whose roots are either a major or minor third apart. Theorists can argue about whether this means that he was consciously employing scales based on symmetrical divisions of the octave. It's not clear that Herrmann ever felt himself bound to any compositional rules other than the rules of drama, story, and musical coherence. He simply discovered that the harmonic grid best suited to the depiction of shifting emotional states was less about classic root movement by fifths than about harmonies arrived at by chromatic inflection—harmonies linked by common tone, yet offering a striking clash. Since this approach to harmony had been with him from his very first film score, *Citizen Kane* in 1940, it's possible it had taken shape during his days with Orson Welles at the Mercury Radio Theater, where he'd learned that it not only conveyed dramatic ambiguity and psychological realism more precisely, but did so in a way that called less attention to itself than the more florid melodrama utilized by his contemporaries. Herrmann was the first to truly understand that film music required a harmonic language of its own, distinct from both the nineteenth-century romantic tradition and twentieth-century modernism.

To illustrate, play an A minor triad in root position. Then, while maintaining the third of the chord (C), "spread" each end by a semitone (dropping A to A-flat and raising E to F). The common tone C now becomes the fifth of a second inversion F minor chord. This is one of the most common examples of the "Herrmann effect."

Figure 1.7. Example of Herrmann's use of mediant harmonies

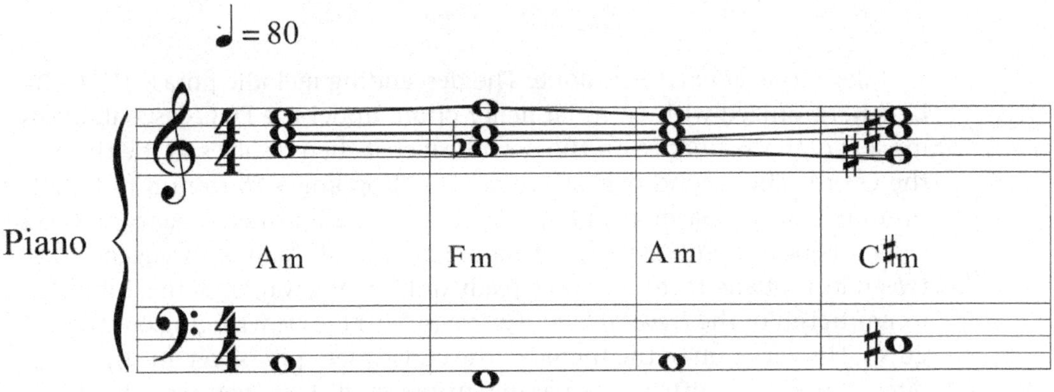

It's interesting to hear how strongly the sense of an A minor "key center" is maintained here, even though we are clearly looking at "nonfunctional" harmony. Each two-chord unit behaves a little like a phantom cadence. The F minor chord behaves like a very strange sort of substitute dominant, its A-flat (enharmonic G-sharp) *rising* as a "leading tone" and its F-natural *falling* in the manner of the seventh in either a dominant seventh or *vii* chord. The second change is more ethereal, but feels a bit like an alien *plagal* cadence, with the C-sharp having a "tendency" to fall back to its original position, the way the fourth scale degree falls to the third. And this points to something quite important: the sense of "function" and harmonic intent in a sequence of chords is not dependent on conventional diatonic or even extended voice leading. As long as the *contextual relationship* between adjacent chords includes pitch affinities like those shown in Figure 1.7, we will have a sense that the chords are taking us somewhere. None of Herrmann's signature scores can be considered atonal, since despite the absence of conventional harmony, there is always a de facto key center. Herrmann was a savvy enough psychologist to know that audiences at sea need an anchor.

Those with extensive knowledge of the classical repertoire will be able to point to any number of works in which this kind of harmony occurs incidentally or for dramatic effect. Root movement by thirds is not something Herrmann invented. But only in film music do we hear these harmonies so exposed and central to composition. In film music vocabulary, the chromatic "slipping" of pitches around one or more common tones has become the staple form of harmony. Among the reasons for this are that film music must be both "otherworldly" and extremely stealthy—sometimes almost to the point of aural invisibility. It must "sneak in and out" of scenes and curl like smoke around dialogue. The language of extended and ambiguous tonality was tailor-made for cinema.

VERTIGO'S MUSICAL MIRRORS

Typical of film music, none of the cues in the *Vertigo* score have key signatures, and in this case (given the movie's final chord), that may truly mean that the score is "in C"! It doesn't mean, however, that we hear anything resembling a tonic chord often—if at all. Harmonically, *Vertigo* is all over the map. We now look at its "Prelude," a cue that launched a thousand careers.

Bernard Herrmann died on Christmas Eve 1975, so it isn't possible to ask him whether, as a child, he had a fascination with mirrors, puzzles, or palindromes. Steven C. Smith's otherwise very fine biography, *A Heart at Fire's Center*, doesn't probe that deeply into his skull. But after getting to know the architecture of his music, it's hard not to believe that he perceived the concert score as a domain in which the arrow of time pointed both forward and backward, where anagrammatic spellings of the same complex chord could produce entirely different shades of meaning, and where the mirror image of a line of music could serve as its counterpoint. He was fond of symmetry and balance, but not necessarily of a restful kind. (The diminished chord, arguably his harmonic signature, is perfectly symmetrical, but hardly serene) As messy as his hand was, his scores often have the visual design of a madman's mosaic or an agitated mandala. They are perfectly organized, and there is never one note more than necessary. He enjoyed counterposing opposites—just as his directors did—and was able to find dramatic consonance even in clashing key centers. His lifelong championing of the music of American eccentric Charles Ives suggests that he heard music, far ahead of his time, as a kind of "sound design," the auditory counterpart of a film in which the familiar is constantly juxtaposed with the utterly alien. He was a marriage of opposites, and we are the luckier for it.

Ever since film musicologist Royal S. Brown gave it a name, much has been made of Herrmann's "Hitchcock" chord, a minor-major seventh chord (a minor triad with a major seventh) that in the work of Bartók was labeled *hyperminor*. Its most iconic use is as the very first sonority in the *Psycho* score, where it looks like this:

Figure 1.8. The "Hitchcock" chord

In a jazz chart, the chord would be labeled a B-flat mM7, but that is in itself such a strange breed of "chord" that it practically begs to be looked at from an alternate angle, especially given Herrmann's mischievous way with chord spellings. It works just as well as an open voicing of a B-flat minor triad overlaid with an D-flat augmented triad, and toggling back and forth between those two harmonies does evoke the schizophrenic quality of the cue that follows. The film is, after all, *Psycho*. But is it truly a polychord? Let's reserve judgment until we see what Herrmann did in *Vertigo*.

In the plot synopsis, we learned that the protagonist, Scottie Ferguson, suffers from the title affliction, *vertigo*, which may be best described as a fear of falling *overlaid* with a terrible desire to fall. Hitchcock, ever the meticulous storyteller, makes sure to show us the origin of Scottie's fatal weakness in a prologue that involves a rooftop pursuit and the death of Scottie's partner. Scottie, hanging onto the storm gutter for dear life, makes the mistake of looking down, and it is at this moment that we hear what has become known as the "Vertigo" chord. Here it is:

Figure 1.9. "Vertigo" chord

This chord, first heard in measure 58 of the cue entitled "Rooftop," amid swirling harps and in conjunction with Hitchcock's famous "dolly back/zoom forward" camera technique, is in some ways a condensation of the score's key ideas, a kind of harmonic fractal. It's a stack of thirds spelled as an E-flat minor triad surmounted by a D major triad. Opposing modes, a semitone apart. Now, look back at Figure 1.6, the reduction of the *Vertigo* love theme from "Scene d'Amour." The chords underlying the four-bar theme are A-flat major and Am. Opposing modes, a semitone apart. Let's take a look at the cell that opens the Prelude, heard over the Saul Bass–designed Main Title sequence.

Figure 1.10. *Vertigo* Prelude

What we're looking at here appear to be broken E-flat minor (sixth) and D augmented (seventh) chords in mirrored opposition. All of the notes utilized derive from an E-flat melodic minor scale, but their arrangement in opposing tetrachords strongly suggests conflicting key centers in the same way that the mM7 "Hitchcock chord" that opens *Psycho* did (in another musical "fractal," the four tones of an E-flat mM7 chord are embedded in this sequence). To make his moving mirror work, Herrmann has altered a pitch in the "Vertigo" chord (E-flat minor/D major) by raising the fifth in the D major chord (shown as enharmonic B-flat in the score) and inserting a C-natural at the top of the E-flat minor broken chord, creating a nasty little M2 rub when the two opposing lines meet. Chords in posttonal music can be chimeras, and both fully diminished and augmented chords can masquerade via inversion. It's possible to look at the entire sequence as derived from an E-flat minor tonality, but that's not how it *feels*. Accentuated by the visual spirals in the Saul Bass title design and the matching violin trills, it feels as if it is going *up and down* at the same time. Reaching for love, descending to the grave. Both *vertigo* and *Liebestod*. Hitchcock's masterpiece is nothing if not deep.

In the bass clef of the example (Figure 1.10), I've added the simple but ominous D to C drop that is heard in the brass and bassoons in the full orchestration. Like all of Herrmann's choices, this one is absolutely deliberate. It further blurs any sense of a stable E-flat minor key center and draws our ears to the conflict in tonality instead.

David Cooper's now out-of-print *Bernard Herrmann's* Vertigo, *A Film Score Handbook* (Greenwood, 2001) offers a full-blown analysis of the score, and it deserves no less, but we have much ground to cover in this book, so we'll leave *Vertigo* with just three more examples, each of which typifies Herrmann's distinctive approach. The first, simply titled "Madeleine," plays at just over 17:00, under the scene in which Scottie is "stung" by his first glimpse of her. Madeleine's husband has arranged the "chance encounter" to occur at a swank San Francisco restaurant, and Scottie is seated at the bar when Madeleine makes her stunning exit. As the melody hits its climax, she turns just slightly toward him. We will hear the tune only a couple of times, but its traces linger like perfume. Here's a piano reduction. Notice that the "sighing" intervals on the downbeats of measures two and three have the same shape as the four pitches of the love theme, and the same triple meter feel.

Figure 1.11. *Vertigo*, "Madeleine" @ 17:19 (excerpt/reduction)

The next scene—and the next cue—come immediately on the heels of this love struck moment, though there's a *time cut* to the next morning. Hitchcock and Herrmann want to let us know that their man is hooked. "Madeleine's Car" commences at 18:28, just as Scottie begins to tail his quarry through the roller coaster streets of San Francisco. In this and so many other cues, Bernard Herrmann elevates the humble ostinato from a device for sustaining motion to a means of maintaining dramatic continuity and suspense across shifts in time and place. Here, the rhythmic pattern of the ostinato is a habanera, a popular Latin dance rhythm chosen to evoke Madeleine's psychic connection to the tragic history of Carlotta Valdez. As you'll see, the shape of the violin line, although elongated, links to that of the "Madeleine" melody, ensuring continuity of story and feeling from the night before. And through this linkage, Herrmann projects forward, once again, to the grand love to come. It's done so subtly, we hardly see the kinship of the three, but it's there.

Figure 1.12. *Vertigo,* "Madeleine's Car" @ 18:28 (reduction)

The harmony spelled out by the ostinato is basically a B-flat7 chord with-out a fifth, although an E-natural in the cello (nominally a sharp eleventh) creates an uneasy quality. This example (and all others in this book) is no-tated in concert pitch, so you can see just how low the clarinets are. In this range, they can't play much louder than the indicated *piano.* Throughout the ensuing scene, which goes on for nearly twelve minutes, Herrmann achieves a remarkable degree of tension simply by raising the "key" of the ostinato and the accompanying melody a semitone at a time. And the melo-dy, superficially as basic as can be, is what makes the cue linger in our mind and suggests that Hermann is once again exhibiting a tonal split personal-ity. As mentioned, the habanera figure is a B-flat7 chord, but the melody, played here by the first and second violins, pulls in another direction, giv-ing us the Phrygian flavor of Spain (the B and F-naturals) and another sug-gestion of clashing key centers.

In classic dramatic form, more like a playwright than a concert com-poser, Herrmann has introduced his "love object" with a clearly and briefly stated melody in "Madeleine," and then drawn its silk thread out across a lengthy and mesmerizing scene.

THIS IS WHERE I DIED

The strangest cue in *Vertigo*—and one of the strangest in all of film music—is the one called "The Forest." It occurs at the very heart of the film—just shy of the halfway point at 58:20. It's the day after Madeleine's leap into the bay and Scottie's rescue, and they're already acting like lovers. Now wise to Scottie's surveillance, Madeleine concedes that he might as well follow her at closer quarters, and invites him to "wander" with her up the Pacific Coast Highway and into a dark forest of giant sequoias. Just as in classic fairy tale, the forest is a place of both wonder and terror, and even more so when the trees stand like the columns in an enormous cathedral. Madeleine hasn't chosen this place by accident. She is weaving a love-death spell that will keep Scottie suspended in his dizzy delirium for the rest of the story.

Sorceresses of myth and legend knew that when they gave the hero a love potion, they were most likely spelling his death, for the love object was almost always unattainable. Because this scene is an enchantment of that sort, Herrmann plays it *almost* as horror—not of the melodramatic or grip-the-armrest kind, but the horror of finding oneself in an utterly alien place with feelings that can't be controlled. Anyone who's ever run off with a stranger knows this combination of thrill and dread. The lovers come across a felled sequoia whose tree rings, preserved in amber, have been labeled by the Park Service with significant dates in world history. As Madeleine, the sorceress, traces out the map of her imaginary life as "Carlotta," isolating the moment of her death a hundred years before, Herrmann casts his own spell with some highly unusual potions.

Figure 1.13. *Vertigo*, "The Forest" (excerpt) @ 58:20

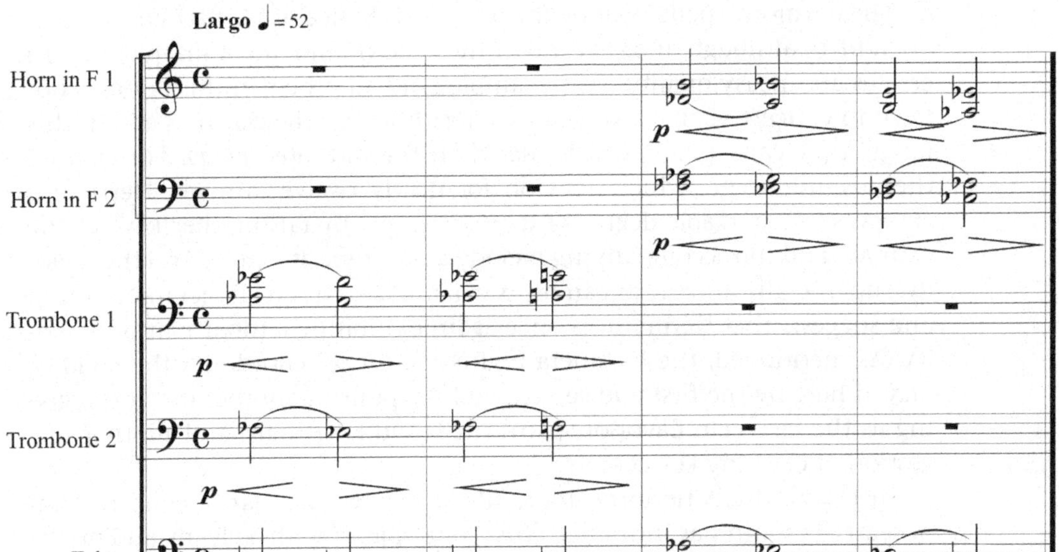

It's hard to get a handle on exactly what's happening here in terms of harmony, but it seems fair to say that we are once again dealing with a "smeared" tonal center and a number of *vagrant chords* (chords with multiple "meanings" and enharmonic spellings). There isn't any orthodox voice-leading scheme that will help us understand what sort of "chord progression" occupies the bizarre first four bars of this cue, except to say that the movement of the voices is largely parallel and could be described as *planing* (i.e., moving from chord to chord with voices in the same relationship and pitch hierarchy). Taking Herrmann's chord spellings literally, what we are looking at in bars 1–2 is a brass choir playing second inversion major seventh chords with the following spellings: F-flat M7–E-flat M7–F-flat M7–FM7.

The horns enter antiphonally in measure 3, and the harmony is altered in a subtle but striking way. In measure three, horns 2 and 4 (in the bass clef) have descending parallel major thirds (4s in posttonal language), opening to a P4 (5s) on the second half-note of bar 4, while horns 1 and 3 (in the treble clef) have augmented/diminished intervals (6s), also descending in parallel by semitone, then opening, respectively, to P4 and P5 in measure 4. Notice that the outer voices are descending by consonant tenths (with tuba doubling the lowest horn part). It's the inner voices that create the strident dissonance. It's probably a foolish exercise to try and give names to these chords. They'd be full of sharp elevenths and other artifacts. They are textural and mood-evoking rather than functional in any typical sense. Measure 4 does have a weird kind of functionality, because it allows Herrmann to come full circle back to his opening F-flat major7 (enharmonic E major seventh), by way of a pseudo-cadence (notice the "resolution" by descending half-step).

The progression to this harmonic closure (to call it resolution would certainly stretch the meaning of that term) is accomplished with the absolute minimum of movement—what theorist Richard Cohn calls *voice-leading parsimony*. Only one voice shifts by an interval larger than a major second (horn 3 in measure 4), and most move only by semitones. The architecture is simple, but the effect is far from that. If I seem to be making too much of this brief passage, that's because I know of no instance in commercial cinema where a director and composer have so determinedly attempted and achieved a sense of the *uncanny*.[3] Like the increasingly humanlike robots in Masahiro Mori's "Uncanny Valley" theory, the music is both familiar and alien. And as with "Sleep" (Figure 1.2), which has a very similar design, a whole world is contained within a few bars of music. When the Hammond organ enters at bar 25—at an hour and sixteen seconds into the film—as Madeleine mysteriously vanishes behind a massive tree trunk, we are spellbound, just like Scottie.

Everything in Bernard Herrmann's body of work extends backward and forward from *Vertigo*. Every real artist should have a kind of *summa*, a touchstone work that somehow encapsulates everything he or she is in a single opus, and for Herrmann, this is the one. And as mentioned earlier, we've barely scratched its mirrored surface here. The score has been the subject of dozens of erudite analyses, and I haven't set out to surpass them in this brief chapter. But as you explore the rest of his enormous contribution, from

---

3 For an especially insightful treatment of musical depictions of the uncanny, see Richard Cohn, "Uncanny Resemblances: Tonal Signification in the Freudian Age," *Journal of the American Musicological Society* 57, no. 2 (Summer 2004), 285–323.

the better-known (and far more frequently analyzed) *Psycho* score to his marvelous science-fiction and fantasy scores (*The Day the Earth Stood Still, Journey to the Center of the Earth*, etc.) and those later works of dark romanticism, such as *Obsession* and *Taxi Driver*, you'll see the same musical tropes, tics, and quirks identified here appear in entirely different contexts. Always, the worldview is bittersweet (though never cynical) and the sense is of the airless emptiness that follows the end of love or the passing of something equally beautiful. And always, the music gives eloquent voice to the life of the psyche, Herrmann's bailiwick.

Herrmann was a man who knew what he wanted to say, and found a way—through each and every one of the assignments he took—to say it. This thematic consistency is the mark of an artist, and a signpost to finding a place in his lineage.

TWO   BOO RADLEY'S PORCH:
ELMER BERNSTEIN'S *TO KILL A MOCKINGBIRD*

Elmer Bernstein and John Sturges

Photograph courtesy elmerbernstein.com

What is it like to experience the adult world—a world of contradiction and conflict, where evil presents itself in the guise of community standards and good is often forced into the shadows—with the eyes of a child? Describing this ephemeral perspective through music was basically the challenge that Elmer Bernstein set for himself when, at the age of thirty-nine, he was asked to compose the score for *To Kill a Mockingbird*.

Like *Vertigo*, Bernstein's *Mockingbird* was a standard-setter and quickly became iconic. In this case, the prototype being assembled was that of the lyrical, "personal" score that wistfully evokes a time and a world that can never come again. And in this case, the musical godfather of the score was not Wagner, but Aaron Copland, and the musical geography was distinctly American. Copland had, in fact, been a mentor to Elmer Bernstein, recognizing his talent at an early age and recommending his first real teacher. Yet there is far more going on in this score than homage. There are influences ranging from Erik Satie and his protégé, Francis Poulenc (and the other members of Les Six, including Darius Milhaud) to Indonesian gamelan and Appalachian folk, and like *Vertigo*, it transcends its influences to become thoroughly original.

Elmer Bernstein was, in fact, as much an originator of film music vocabulary as Herrmann, though his influences—despite his classical training—tended to come more from the American (and Parisian) street and folkways than from the concert hall. He put his signature on at least four distinctive genres of underscore: the western (*The Magnificent Seven*), the A-list action picture (*The Great Escape*), the jazz score (from *The Man with the Golden Arm* all the way to *The Grifters*), and the poetic, personal "chamber score," of which such efforts as *My Left Foot* and *Da* are late career examples. *To Kill a Mockingbird* belongs to this last one, but is almost a genre in itself.

TO KILL A MOCKINGBIRD AND ITS TIME

The film was released in 1962. The novel, published just two years earlier, had won a Pulitzer Prize and been a critical and popular success—a rare accomplishment in any era. Its overriding theme was tolerance, but not the easy tolerance that predominates in the early years of the twenty-first century so much as the hard-earned tolerance that comes from learning to look at the world directly and without social filters. The agent of this perspective is the narrator, Jean Louise "Scout" Finch, whose character channels the small town, Depression-era memories of the author, Harper Lee. The film faithfully captures the book's voice and spirit, and its key gesture may be the quizzical cock of the head and soft smile of recognition given by Scout when, at the movie's end, she finally stands face-to-face with her shadowy protector, Boo Radley, and says, "Hey, Boo."

It's not possible to examine Elmer Bernstein's musical choices without knowing something about both the historical period and Bernstein's place in it. In 1962, John F. Kennedy, himself a target of provincial intolerance, was president of the United States, and the civil rights movement—the long-delayed affirmation of equal protection under the law to American negroes—was in full flower. The nation seemed ripe with promise, but that promise was threatened at every turn with ugliness and peril. The Beat Generation of the repressed 1950s had handed the anarchic baton to the new hipsters of the Swinging Sixties, and in a Liverpool basement club, the Beatles were getting ready to invade, but reactionary impulses bristled like the nuclear missiles aimed east and west across the planet. Amid this social upheaval, Elmer Bernstein made his way untimidly as an ally of what were deemed "left-wing causes," and earned the enmity of Senator Joseph McCarthy's goons in the process.

Perhaps more than at any time since, the world of the early sixties seemed to teeter precariously between hope and cataclysm, just as the drama in *Mockingbird* is stretched tautly between its antagonists: Atticus Finch, the enemy of "cruel ignorance," and Bob Ewell, its embodiment. Ewell falsely accuses a local negro man, Tom Robinson, of raping his daughter, Viola (appropriately named), and Atticus, a widower who is also the town's only qualified attorney, is appointed to defend the black man before a jury of white males. The action is set in the hard-times 1930s, against the passage of a year in the "tired old town" of Maycomb, Alabama, and the witnesses to Atticus's stalwart attempt to see justice done are his six-year-old daughter, Scout, her older brother, Jem, and a neighbor boy, Dill, who visits for the summers and was based upon a childhood friend of Harper Lee's, Truman Capote. The trial of Tom Robinson, although in many ways the story's central act, occurs largely "in the background" and almost entirely without music. It is also the only element not perceived from the children's point of view.

The framing narrative, and the aspect of the film most remembered by viewers, involves the children and is what's now called a coming-of-age story. Scout and Jem are growing up without a mother, and although Atticus is the most loving of fathers, he cannot weave the weblike circle of protection from life's darker edges that a mother can. Over the long year, the children will begin to perceive shades of gray between the poles of good and evil and discover that things are not always what they seem to be. Neighbors will become strangers and strangers will become friends. This metamorphosis occurs not only as a consequence of the trial's outcome, but through what is revealed by and about another neighbor, the mysterious Boo Radley. Boo is the neighborhood bogeyman, never seen but always present, whispered to be a murderous mental defective "chained in the basement" of the ramshackle Radley house at the end of the street, a house on whose plank porch a rotted swing creaks eerily in what seems a perpetual autumn breeze. This house, and the children's ambivalent feelings about it and its reclusive resident, set the tone for the film and for its score, and that tone conjures expertly the way we experienced the adult world as children: with an awe that was equal parts *wonder* and *terror*.

THE EYES OF A CHILD

Bernstein, who died in 2004 among family at his home in the enchanting Southern California town of Ojai, has said in a number of interviews that he did not get a handle on what the score of *To Kill a Mockingbird* ought to be until he had adopted the children's perspective. Once he'd settled on this, he felt it needed to be present from the very beginning of the film, and indeed, it is. In fact, the film's Main Title sequence, with its ticking pocket watch, listlessly rolling marble, and soft humming underscored by Bernstein's musical poetry can be read almost as an incantation that invites us to enter the mind and world of the young narrator. Bernstein has said the opening piano melody—unaccompanied by the left hand—was conceived to suggest the way a child picks out a tune one note, and one key, at a time. But it holds other secrets, as we'll see. Here is the solo piano heard over the film's very first images. One of the most interesting things about it is that it isn't the "A" section of the main thematic period, but the "B" half, so in a sense, we are coming into the melody already "in progress."

Figure 2.1. *To Kill a Mockingbird* **piano opening**

The pitch selection and shape of the tune strongly suggest the key of C major, but that seems to have been a choice dictated by Bernstein's desire to make the line sound more "childlike," and as we'll see from the sophisticated design of the Main Title as a whole, there is no single key center, but a sequence of "Lydian periods" whose raised fourth acts as a leading tone pushing the second eight-bar phrase up a perfect fifth to start a new cycle. In other words, if Bernstein had chosen to open the film with the "missing" first eight measures of the theme, this is what they would have looked like:

Figure 2.2. *To Kill a Mockingbird* **"phantom opening"**

I've added the broken second inversion F major chord in the left hand to reveal the tune's harmonic anchor and to show why it's typically described as Lydian (the B-natural in measure two is the giveaway, as it forms an augmented fourth with the pedal F). Bernstein's haunting melody, however, will never be heard in the film in this key except as this "phantom antecedent." When the piano actually enters, the dissonant fourth is gone and the harmony has resolved to C major. The rest of the Main Title music follows the same scheme, with the "A" melody stated for eight bars in a Lydian setting and then resolving down a P4 for the second eight to what feels more like the genuine (if temporary) key center. *Genuine* in the sense that the pitch group in the "A" melody is completely diatonic to the key center of the

"B" melody, which calls into question whether it's accurate to say, as often is, that Bernstein's famous theme is "in Lydian mode."

Not to put too fine a point on it, but it's questionable whether anything can really ever be in Lydian mode, since Lydian, by its nature, is an ambivalent mode that wants to be something other than what it is—specifically, the major scale a P5 higher. Our ears cannot help but hear the augmented fourth degree of the scale as a leading tone. This is just one of the reasons Bernstein's choice is so brilliant. Like the children in the story, seesawing between a child's perception of the world and the harsher adult reality, that augmented fourth is like the rusty hinge between two different worlds.

Since we're on the film's opening, it should be noted that eleven bars of Bernstein's Main Title music wound up on the cutting-room floor. After the solo piano opening (Figure 2.1), bars 9–19 were cut from the film's theatrical release to allow the audience to hear the voiceover of Scout (Mary Badham), humming to herself (in what seems a not entirely accidental pitch relationship to the music) as she picks through the cigar box of "treasures" that Boo Radley has secretly left for the children in the cleft of a neighborhood tree. Following this, the filmmakers cut directly to the first statement of the Lydian theme in D. But these missing bars can be heard on all available recordings of the score, and they're well worth listening to because they affirm Bernstein's intent to use a range of musical "dialects" and devices to evoke the world of children. The first four bars (9–12 in the score) of the missing passage are a lyrical flute solo over harp runs and trilling violins. Here is a reduction:

Figure 2.3. *To Kill a Mockingbird*, Main Title, missing section (bars 9–12)

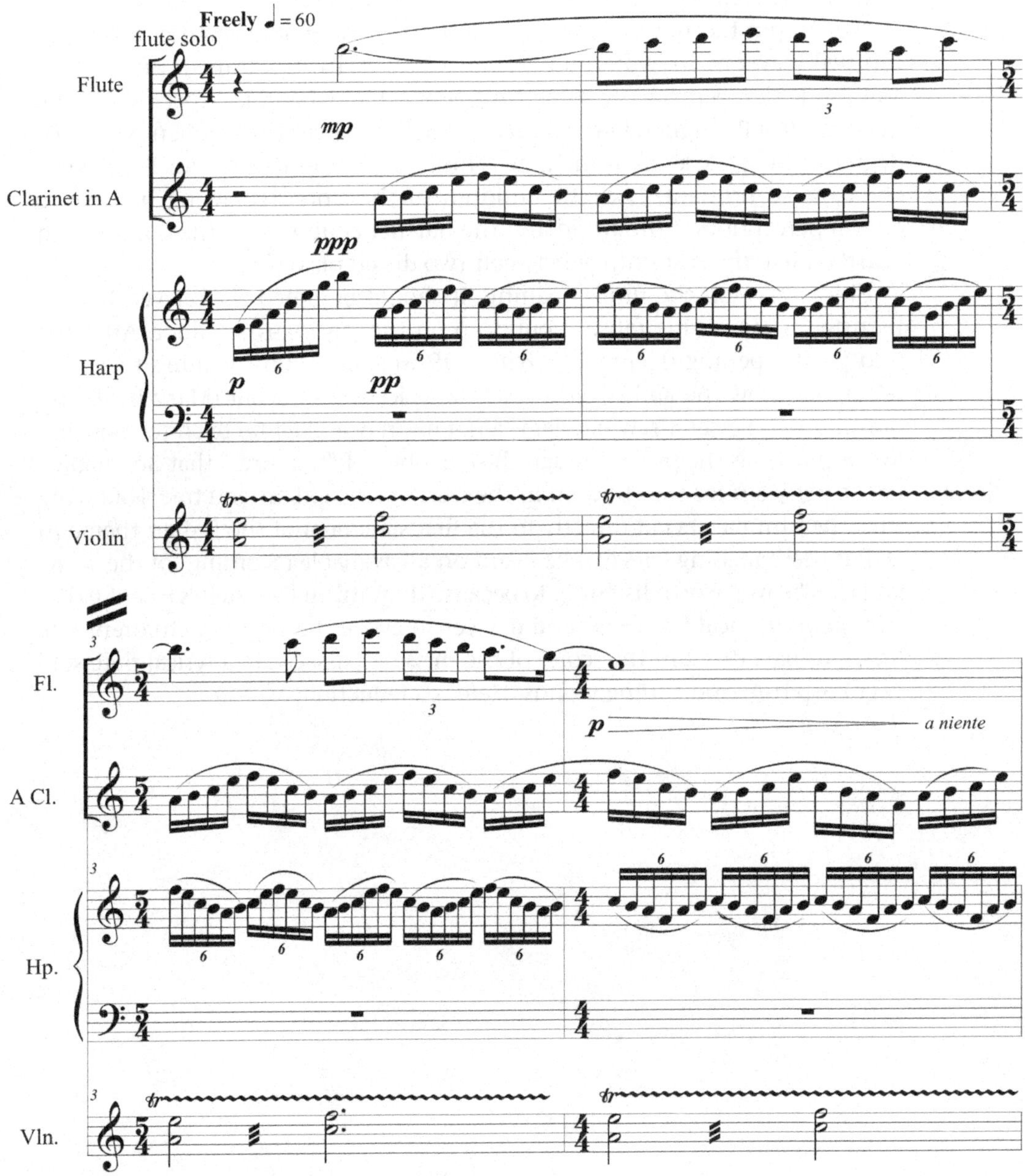

The first thing we become aware of when hearing this passage is its "exotic" quality. Unlike some of the more Coplandesque cues in the score, there is nothing particularly "American" about the sound, and certainly nothing regional. A sense of continually flowing motion is created by the straight sixteenth-note runs in the clarinet beating against the sextuplet sixteenths in the harp and the trills in the violins, with the flute solo gliding freely above it all like a Chinese wren. We will see and hear this motion elsewhere in the film whenever Bernstein wishes to capture the presence of magic and mystery, especially in the autumnal air (think of a pile of dry leaves lifted and spun into a vortex by a gust of wind). But there is more going on.

The pitches throughout are all common to the natural minor mode in the key of A, and indeed, the key center feels like it lives mostly there. But if we look at those violin trills, which appear to be toggling back and forth between the I and vi chords of that mode, we see that the third of the chords is provided only by the "blurring" effect created by the rapid trilling, creating an ambiguity of harmony that winds up splitting the difference between A minor and F major, yielding a hazy Fmajor7 hue. (If you play an A major triad with an F major triad on top, you'll hear the sonority.)

This bimodal wash of pastel color evokes Asia more than Mississippi, and for anyone familiar with Indonesian music, the flavor of gamelan. Did Bernstein, in his search for a language to capture the innocence and mystery of childhood, derive inspiration from the same music that such composers as Debussy and Britten had found so enchanting? Take a look at the clarinet part. Notice that the fourth and seventh degrees of the A minor scale are nowhere to be found, a characteristic of the pentatonic modes we associate with Asia. Equal-tempered instruments can't replicate the unique sound of Indonesian gamelan's hand-hammered bronze, but the effect here is a bit like a westernized *pelog* (the actual second scale degree would be between a minor and major second). The sextuplet runs in the harp part add the pitches of G and B-natural, further blurring tonality.

The flute solo, which ought to help solve the mystery, only deepens it by opening on and circling around the pitch of B-natural. Every note the flute plays could be read as outlining a Cmajor7 harmony, and yet the underlying bed is clearly minor. This is what gives the solo its ethereal, "floaty" quality. It is part of and yet independent from the rest of the ensemble. Only in the following section of the Main Title (not shown) do we land clearly in A minor for seven measures before commencing with the famous "Lydian" theme.

After having established the film's haunting subtext with the Main Title, Bernstein could easily have reverted to more conventional Hollywood form and depicted Maycomb, Alabama, using the harmonic language of Copland or even Samuel Barber. Doing so, however, would have violated the brief he'd already given himself: to score the place as the children saw it. No town, however small, *seems* small to a child. On the contrary, the streets we grow up on contain entire worlds. Likewise, the characters who inhabit our neighborhoods—particularly those who are "different" or socially set apart—seem bigger than life, and even commonplace events can be laden with drama and mystery. To have scored these things with the (relative) musical sophistication typical of Hollywood in the 1960s would have diminished the children's experience of them.

THE SCORE

The first piece of underscore occurs nearly nine minutes into the film, and the cue is entitled "The Meanest Man." The title refers to Jem's characterization of Boo Radley's father, Arthur Radley Sr., who walks by as the children gather around the tire swing in the Finch's front yard and prompts the film's first discussion of Boo. Despite its title, the ensuing cue is more about the children's mythical perception of Boo and the mystery of the ramshackle Radley house, with its haunted porch swing and flapping shutters, than it is about the father. "There goes the meanest man who ever took a breath of life," says Jem. "Why is he the meanest man?" asks Dill, the new kid in town. "Well, for one thing," Jem replies, "he's got a boy named Boo he keeps chained to a bed in the basement."

There's the Southern Gothic recipe in a nutshell. And in the cue, we will hear all of the most distinctive tropes of Bernstein's score in a nutshell, as well. In effect, he displays his musical palette, and it is immediately different from anything that had been heard in the cinema up to that time. For one thing, it was not *symphonic*, and for another, it was more French than Austrian in the way it lived inside the movie. In our present era, it's become almost obligatory for film composers to attempt to integrate music with the film's broader sound design, but this wasn't the case in 1962, when the score was distinctly a thing apart. In *Mockingbird*, Bernstein proved himself once again—and not for the last time—a pioneer by using what might be called *musical onomatopoeia* to achieve a synthesis of score and sound effects ahead of its time.

To Kill a Mockingbird is a film of evocative sounds and images: long shadows, rustling leaves, the creak of rusty springs, footsteps in the dark, and schoolhouse pianos left too long in the damp, all of them perceived through the mesh of nostalgia, since the story is narrated retrospectively by Scout as a grown woman. But rather than using, for example, the ragtime chromaticism of early twentieth-century popular song, or even the Baptist hymnal, to evoke the Deep South as Scout remembers it, Bernstein creates a vocabulary of musical gestures that sound like what they depict: for the violins, shuddery whole-step trills in two voices that "valve" open and closed between M3 and m6, suggesting the shivers provoked by a childhood spook story; piano figures that "scamper" the way children scamper and creep the way they creep; an accordion, wheezing between P5 and M3 as its bellows fill and empty, reminiscent of an organ grinder or a summer carnival's carousel. String chords, voiced to sound like a pipe organ, moving in parallel from Am to E-flat minor as we catch our first glimpse of the haunted Radley house. None of these devices is the least bit naturalistic. They are, instead, *impressionistic* (see sidebar), and this choice was perhaps Elmer Bernstein's greatest contribution to the art.

The excerpt shown in Figure 2.4 is a re-creation of Bernstein's "conductor score," a four-line reduction of the full score (I've increased it to five to make it less cluttered and to accommodate music notation software). This reduced version is the one that Bernstein presumably used at the podium, as it incorporates his timings, streamer markings, and every note that he wrote—but in a highly condensed form that eliminates the need for the frequent page turns involved in working from a full score. It wouldn't work for a Wagnerian or Mahlerian orchestration, but for a "chamber score," it's perfect.

Figure 2.4. *To Kill a Mockingbird*, "The Meanest Man," bars 1–8 (@ 08:50

Composer's Sidebar: IMPRESSIONISM

Ever since film music historian Roy Prendergast identified Wagner, Puccini, and (Richard) Strauss as the formative influence on "Golden Age" film scores in his seminal text *Film Music: A Neglected Art* (W. W. Norton & Co., 1992), it's been customary to link movie music with the romantic tradition, and this remains the correct reference for such composers as John Williams. But contemporary film composers may be better served by studying the work of the impressionists, and even the later expressionists. Ravel's *Ma Mère l'Oye* and String Quartet in F Major, Debussy's *Images pour Orchestre*, Saint-Saëns's *Carnival of the Animals*, and Messiaen's Éclairs *sur l'Au-dela* are more apt today than Strauss's *Also sprach Zarathustra*. Bernstein once told me that he'd been going through a "Poulenc period" when he wrote *To Kill a Mockingbird*. Most contemporary film music is more "French" than Austro-German. Listen to Alexandre Desplat's score for Ang Lee's *Lust, Caution*.

There are, of course, doublings, as indicated above the staves. The simple rising semitone motive on line 3 is played by piano, celeste, and marimba. Harp doubles the flute and oboe octaves at the beginning of line 1. The horn reinforces what appears to be the fifth of an implied C-sharp minor chord bracketed by the cellos (more on that in a moment). But otherwise, every voice is represented here, and each one works in exquisite counterpoint to the dialogue, which consists essentially of Jem's relating the legend of Boo Radley to his new friend, Dill.

Writing beneath and between lines of dialogue, known as underscoring, is the film composer's greatest challenge, and it quickly separates the pikers from the pros, and the show-offs from those whose interest truly lies in supporting story. These are the moments in poorly or cheaply made TV drama (and even in some high-profile contemporary feature films) when we hear the endless low pedal D, or where the composer sets his dreamy pad to loop and goes for coffee. And truth be told, there are occasions when this is all that's necessary, and all the director wants to hear. But when we hear what a master like Bernstein did, we begin to understand that music can also be an eloquent form of storytelling.

"The Meanest Man" is something of an oddity, even today: a genuinely posttonal (as opposed to atonal) piece of music written to evoke the imaginal world of young children. Bernstein wasn't the first to treat kids with such respect. Such works as Debussy's *Children's Corner* are marvelously sophisticated while true to the vision of a child, and some works by Satie are "childlike" without being the least bit infantile. A child's perceptions aren't "childish," nor are they necessarily best expressed in strictly diatonic language. This cue, like so many of Bernard Herrmann's, gives us a sense of "wandering tonality." Wherever we happen to be in the piece, we feel the stability of a key center, but no sooner do we try and identify it than it vanishes. One good reason for this may be found in the mirroring lines for solo piano (line 3, measure 4) and bass clarinet (line 5, measure 6).

The pitch set common to both lines appears to derive from a B-flat *octatonic scale*. Technically, any eight-note scale is octatonic, but what's generally meant by the term is what in jazz theory is called a *diminished scale,* an alternating whole step—half-step pattern that yields a scale that is completely symmetrical. An octatonic scale has two modes: the first mode begins with a whole step followed by a half-step, and continues that pattern. The second mode simply shifts the pattern to half-step–whole step. Either way, the complete pitch set comprises two diminished chords balanced like a seesaw on the fulcrum of a tritone. Another way to look at it is as a sequence of nested minor thirds. This symmetricality lends itself to all sorts of interesting harmonic possibilities for film music. It offers balance with the uneasy feeling of imbalance, and because there is no dominant-tonic relationship to provide resolution, the scale suits the emotional ambiguity of cinematic drama particularly well.

The octatonic scale became so closely associated with the Russian composer Nikolai Rimsky-Korsakov and his cohort that in some circles it was known as the Korsakovian scale. Music theorists hear evidence of it in the earlier works of his student Igor Stravinsky, though Stravinsky consistently denied that his work could be tagged by any tonal system other than that generated by his own ear. No artist likes to have his or her work classified.

Here are the two modes of the B-flat octatonic collection. Bernstein seems to be drawing from both modes (or, as is always possible, simply using his ear):

Figure 2.5A. Octatonic scales in B-flat

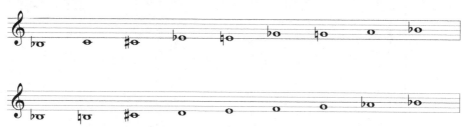

And here, in isolation, are the two passages:

Figure 2.5B. Octatonic passages in 1M2, "The Meanest Man"

Olivier Messiaen called symmetrical sets like the diminished and augmented scales "modes of limited transposition," and strictly speaking in terms of pitch classes, there are really only three bona fide octatonic collections: those based on the pitches E-flat, D, and D-flat. But this need not keep film composers from experimenting. We'll explore other "exotic" scales in later chapters.

Figure 2.6. *To Kill a Mockingbird*, "The Meanest Man," bars 9–12, ⟨ 09:18

In the following eight bars, things get even more interesting. On screen, Jem leads Dill and Scout across the street to get a better look at the Radley house. As they scamper to find cover behind a tree trunk, a two-measure passage of piano-harp counterpoint pushes the cue closer to genuine atonality. It's a little caprice, and perfectly captures—*but does not ape*—the mischief of children. In measure 1 (Figure 2.6), the piano initially flirts with a broken D minor harmony as the harp accompaniment, while rhythmically straightforward in the style of second species counterpoint, feels a semitone lower in its tonal orientation. Then, just as the piano seems to fall toward the harp's C-sharp minor locus, the harp wanders off completely, leaving the piano alone for its final, functionally unrelated statement. This is as close to a modernist approach as we'll see in the score. But the composer is simply sticking to his brief: this is the sound of children crossing the boundary from talk to action, and from fun to danger.

As Jem says, from a vantage across the street, "See . . . he lives over there," Bernstein introduces for the first time what he describes in his conductor score as "organ strings." A chamber group–size string section plays a very widely voiced A minor chord with an empty middle, as might be played on a pipe organ (the top note for the violins is actually an "A" five spaces above the treble staff, not shown in my reduction). Why "organ strings"? Because this is the sound of the almost reverent awe that Jem feels when describing Boo Radley. The Radley house is taboo, but remember that the term *taboo* originally had a connotation of holiness as well as peril. The chord is held for ten full beats, while harp breaks the harmony into triplets and piccolo and clarinet run in parallel octaves to a gently unsettling augmented fourth over the chord. In measure 7, as Jem describes Boo's nocturnal wanderings, the cue offers its most dramatic gesture: a bold shift from A minor to E-flat minor, and simultaneously from *forte* to *piano*. The motion of the voices is entirely parallel, and the effect, again, is to evoke both fear and wonderment. This gesture is a Bernstein signature.

As the strings slowly diminish, and Dill asks aloud, "I wonder what he does in there," the harp reenters almost tenderly with triplet figures based on Lydian E-flat, linking Boo for the first time with the score's main theme and major trope. It's an important moment in a very important cue, one often overlooked in studies of *Mockingbird*.

The next cue we'll examine occurs at the film's midpoint, when all major story elements are in play. As happens in life when big and deeply affecting events swirl around us (e.g., things like war, the civil rights movement, the AIDS crisis, 9/11), there is "emotional crosstalk" between the community and the individual, and children are the most receptive. These are the times of night terrors and imaginary friends. The central drama in *Mockingbird* is the trial of Tom Robinson, and although Atticus is the most at-risk for his decision to defend a black man against a white man's accusation, we sense that he is no stranger to small-town bigotry and its potential for terrible violence. His children, however, largely have been insulated from the hatred in their midst, and its sudden manifestation in the person of Tom Ewell is disturbing at the deepest level.

In the semirural South of the 1930s, poor whites and poor blacks lived side by side in a shotgun shack and cinderblock milieu dripping with tension and animosity. Jem accompanies Atticus on a drive to speak with Tom Robinson's wife about his defense, and while Jem waits in the car, he is confronted by a snarling Tom Ewell, stumbling drunk. When Atticus emerges from the house, Ewell spits in his face and calls him a "nigger lover." The threat of violence is as palpable as the smell of moonshine, and we see in Jem's eyes that he has glimpsed the hideous side of the white man's dominion. Arriving back home after dark, Atticus asks Jem to watch over Scout while he drives the Finch's housekeeper home, saying, "There's a lot of ugly things in this world, son. I wish I could keep them all away from you. But that's never possible."

Jem settles apprehensively into the old porch rocker, the full moon casting tendrils of undulating shadow on the clapboard exterior. He is alone, the man of the house, but he has brought something back from the encounter with Tom Ewell: a sharp sense that the world is no longer the safe place it was before. In fact, the night air is alive with peril. The sound of a passing car and the screech of a hawk are suddenly ominous. Jem leaps from the porch and begins running down the sidewalk in the direction of the Radley house, calling, "Atticus! Atticus!" And then, something magical stops him.

About :30 into the cue titled "Jem's Discovery," at measure 31 of the conductor score, everything stops to allow muted violins to enter with a staggered G augmented chord articulated in ghostly trills.

Figure 2.7. *To Kill a Mockingbird*, "Jem's Discovery," bars 31–40, ⟨ 49:26

We now begin to see the recurrence of key ideas. Some, like the clarinet/accordion figure in measure 3 (bar 33 in the actual conductor score) are just motives, but still important. Remember that we first heard this when Mr. Radley passed by and Jem introduced the subject of Boo. The G-natural at first glance looks like an appoggiatura, given the pedal A-flat in the upper parts and the trumpet. But we also have pedal G's in the strings and brass, creating a very deliberate "rub." Only when the piano melody enters in measure 5 (bar 35 in the score), clearly in the key of C major, do we begin to see what's going on. This entrance coincides visually with a shot, from Jem's point of view, of the Radley's "haunted porch swing," set in motion by a summer evening's sultry breeze. Everything about the Radley house is dilapidated, broken, off-center. It's a house that has not seen life in many years, and yet there is a life inside. This contrast is what Bernstein is playing.

In measure 9 (39 in the score), the flute (with piccolo an 8ve above) takes up a line we haven't heard before, but which is reminiscent of the octatonic piano runs in "The Meanest Man." (In fact, if we look at the harp and vibraphone as outlining a diminished E chord, then the flute melody is derived from an E octatonic scale of the first mode.) Two four-note chromatic runs, a tritone apart, bring the perfume of Baghdad into the Mississippi night, but it's not any common Middle Eastern mode. The sound is more akin to the whimsical exoticism of Satie, particularly when you look at the counterpoint. What's happening on screen is a transformation of Jem's world—a transformation that is as much spiritual as emotional. In the midst of fear, he finds something marvelous. Once again, Bernstein has utilized impressionism to convey the mysteries of growing up.

THE LONGEST JOURNEY

The closing act of *To Kill a Mockingbird* has held its own as one of the most satisfying dénouements in American cinema. The Tom Robinson story has ended tragically, the long summer has passed, and the Finch children have glimpsed the sometimes menacing world that lies beyond the garden gate. But their greatest lesson is still to come, and it is delivered in barely fifteen minutes of screen time that compresses two hours of a single October night, "their longest journey together," in Scout's words. Jem has been charged with escorting Scout home from a Halloween pageant in the school auditorium, in which she has been costumed in full-body papier-mâché as a smoked ham. The walk home takes them through the woods, and as Scout is unable to get her cumbersome costume off quickly enough to suit Jem's impatience, she's able to see only through the narrow eye slit, and therefore only directly in front of her. This, of course, makes her more vulnerable, but it will also serve as our point of view of what is to come.

The music that underpins the entire sequence is divided into four cues, "Footsteps in the Dark," parts 1 and 2, "Assault in the Shadows," and "Boo Who?" By the time the last note is played, everything will have changed. It begins with a recapitulation of the Main Title theme, the first time we've heard it fully stated since the beginning of the film. It's in "D Lydian" over the same second inversion broken chord in the harp that we've heard before, but now we know the reason for the inversion. Bernstein is using the augmented fourth of Lydian mode as a leading tone for resolution to the key a P4 below, only this time, he delays that resolution by moving directly from D Lydian to A Lydian rather than settling into A major, and then using the transitional C-sharp minor to land mysteriously on the same tonally ambiguous i/VI fulcrum (this time, G-sharp minor/E major) that has been present from the beginning, here voiced by his "organ strings." Only the high strings linger before diminishing when Jem hears "footsteps in the dark." A harp enters gently.

Figure 2.8. *To Kill a Mockingbird*, "Footsteps in the Dark," bars 43–53, ⟨ 01:53:29

At first glance, there seems to be nothing here we haven't seen already. It's the way the elements are combined that makes the cue distinctive. And until Bernstein had done it, I'm not sure that any film composer had ever treated a scene of this type in quite this way. On the face of it, it's a scene about children in physical danger, being stalked by a demented alcoholic whom we've already learned is capable of savage violence. So, why, when Jem and Scout turn to look into the rustling foliage that conceals their attacker, do we hear the lyrical rise and fall of the "bitonal" harp line in measures 1 and 2? Because those bushes also conceal the children's rescuer: the guardian angel who has been watching over them from the beginning. First-time viewers of the film, however, don't know this (although there have been plenty of hints), so Bernstein took a chance in playing the moment so delicately. It could have undercut the danger.

Later in this book, we'll discuss Christopher Young's score for a dark thriller called *Jennifer 8*, another game-changer. Briefly, it's a film about a serial killer who has already claimed the lives of seven young women. The "Jennifer" of the title is to be the eighth. But Young scored the film to feature a moody, romantic, and strikingly pretty piano melody that has since become a style model for thrillers of this sort. The haunting beauty of the melody actually made the heroine's peril more intense and more poignant. He took a chance, as well, and might not have done so without Bernstein's prior example.

We've previously examined Bernstein's use of nonfunctional harmony and carefully placed dissonance to portray ambiguity and the "seesawing" between the magical world of childhood and the far more dangerous world of adulthood. Here we see three examples of it laid back to back. The harp arpeggio traces an arc between G-sharp minor 7 and E major 7/9, the same mediant relationship heard in the "Main Title" cue. An accordion enters, wheezing or "valving" between A-flat minor (enharmonically identical to G-sharp minor) and B-flat major—an even more striking contrast. Finally, the piano enters with the main theme now in E-flat Lydian, its accompaniment provided by an accordion with the Lydian fourth (A-natural) as an appoggiatura on beat 2, perhaps the score's most memorable museme.

Now we come to the film's major revelation, the source of its title and its greatest mystery, and in many ways, the cue that all those before have been preparing us for. The cue is called "Boo Who?" and the wordplay is fitting for a piece of music that puts the final puzzle piece in place.

We're in Jem's bedroom following the assault on the children by a drunken, rabid Bob Ewell. They've come through it intact, but Jem has had his arm broken in the struggle and now lies unconscious on his bed, the doctor having made him a splint. Atticus and Scout are at his side when Sheriff Tate comes in to report that Ewell's body has been found in the woods "with a kitchen knife stuck up under his ribs." "He's dead, Mr. Finch," says Tate. "He's not gonna bother these children anymore."

A question hangs in the air. Whose knife? And who drove it home with enough force to kill a grown man? Was it Jem? The sheriff turns to Scout, saying, "Miss Jean Louise, do you suppose you could tell us what happened out there?" Throughout these moments of suspense, the score is silent. Scout relates the narrative of the attack as seen through the narrow eye slit in her "baked ham" costume. She's in mild shock, and the memories return slowly. "And then," she says hesitantly, "I saw someone carrying Jem home." "Well, who was it?" asks the sheriff. Scout searches first in the shadows of her memory, then in the shadowed corners of the room, and her eyes widen. "Why there he is, Mr. Tate," she says in wonderment, as the cue enters with the same rising step gesture we've heard whenever Boo's spirit is present. "He can tell you his name."

What follows is the loveliest moment in the film, and one of the most touching in American cinema. No one says a word, but the camera reveals what Scout has seen: that in the shadows behind the open door, cowering against the wall, is a grown man with the demeanor of a mistreated child. A pale, ghostly face that has rarely seen sunlight—a face that we've never seen before and yet know. The accordion creaks on the musical hinge between B major 7 and E minor, then toggles from E minor (add9) to F-sharp minor before a brief oboe line takes us by way of the common tones of B and D to the new key of G major.

After two bars of harp introduction, a sweetly played solo violin enters with a new melody—or, to put it more accurately, a melody we have heard only as a suggestion, never fully realized until now. "Hey, Boo," Scout says to the gentle man behind the door, and it is as if she is welcoming an old friend home. The violin melody is Boo's theme, and it's the first time that Bernstein has landed us in an unambiguous key center, although again, not in a conventional fashion. (The key of G major will close the cue, as well, but not without some remaining tonal ambiguity. The outcome is happy, but the world remains a place created from fabric of both light and dark.) Here is a reduction of the cue from measures 1–12.

Figure 2.9. *To Kill a Mockingbird*, "Boo Who?" bars 1–12, ℗ 02:00:15

And here is an excerpt (somewhat compressed) from the second half of "Boo Who?" It begins with a hymnlike gesture in the strings that I can only describe as a polychordal cadence.

Figure 2.10. *To Kill a Mockingbird*, "Boo Who?" bars 30–42, ⓡ 02:01:34

Violins and violas play what is clearly spelled as a C major to E minor descent, while the low strings ascend from C major to F major. There is no way to read the resulting voicing as a single highly embellished chord—it is E minor over F major. The harmony congeals in measure 3, when all voices move from C major to F major via a gorgeous descending top line (particularly affecting on beat 2, where there is a G-natural appoggiatura over the F major harmony). Meanwhile, low strings support the C to F cadence. In measure 6, there is a final hymnlike restatement of the gesture, setting up a kind of plagal cadence which brings us to an entirely new variation on the Main Title theme, for the first time in C Lydian. (I've omitted the two bars of introduction in the new meter of 6/8 to economize on page space, but they appear as bars 36/37 in the score and are identical to the arpeggiated figures seen in the harp and celeste.)

The wrap-up of the film occurs after Sheriff Tate reveals (albeit obliquely) that it was Boo who delivered the fatal stab wound, but that his official conclusion will be that "Bob Ewell *fell* on his knife." He counsels Atticus to let it stand that way, despite his lawyer's inclination to let the truth be known, for to announce to Maycomb that Boo Radley was the children's rescuer would "drag him into the limelight," and to do this to a character as shy and reclusive as Boo would be a grave sin. Atticus assents, but it's Scout, not him, who is first to see the deeper truth: that to expose a gentle soul like Boo to the harsh light of notoriety would be "like shooting a mockingbird," that is, harming a creature that does nothing but bring beautiful music into our lives.

The "End Title" music enters as Scout walks Boo Radley home, and begins under the voice of Scout, as a grown woman, delivering the film's benediction. Immediately following, we hear the loveliest of many renditions of Bernstein's Main Title theme, this time—initially—in Lydian D. As in the Main Title, the theme will undergo a series of "Lydian modulations," again using the augmented fourth scale degree as a leading tone to the key a P5 above: from Lydian D to A major, and from Lydian A to a delicate (and unambiguously resolved) closing on E major. The children have come successfully through their harrowing rite of passage, an injustice has been—in some measure—rectified, and in Scout's words, "Boo Radley has come out."

Here is a reduction, again from Bernstein's conductor score, of measures 20–43 of the "End Title." Notice that the simple "carnival organ" accompaniment—second inversion D major chords alternated in accordion and clarinets/horns—is unchanging throughout, as is the harp arpeggio. A delicate crescendo begins at bar 20, followed by a slight rallentando at bar 24, just before the tutti orchestra picks up the transcendent theme.

Figures 2.11A and 2.11B. *To Kill a Mockingbird*, End Title, bars 20–43

THREE SIGNS AND MEANING
FROM *SPELLBOUND* TO *INCEPTION*

ou are on a two-lane rural highway on a moonless night, doing about 75 mph on blacktop and listening to weepy country music on the only available radio station. A flash of light up ahead causes you to brake and lean forward to peer through the dirty windshield. You make out the silhouetted figure of a man in the middle of the road, waving his arms frantically, clearly trying to signal. Is he hailing you for assistance, warning you away, or simply asking you to slow down? Has there been a serious accident, or just a flat tire?

If you react as most people do, you slow down, both as a precaution and to get a better read on what the man is trying to tell you. Because he can't speak to you telepathically, he is using the language of signs. Arms waving above the head are a signifier, and the thing being signified can range from a simple alert (*there's trouble ahead*) to a panicked plea for help, depending on a number of factors: the speed *(tempo)* with which he is waving his arms; the force and urgency *(dynamic and accent/emphasis)* of the waving; and perhaps most important, the look on his face (*expression, degree of dissonance, modality*).

The scene I've described could easily be like one you're assigned to score. Many things will determine how you approach such a scene musically. Do we know the character behind the wheel? The man in the road? Do we have strong feelings, positive or negative, about them? Do we have reason to be suspicious of either? And as we approach the source of that flash of light, do we see the police? A stalled car with its hazard lights blinking? Flames from an overturned vehicle with a passenger trapped inside? Or only a reflection?

Whatever the case, we—like the man in the road—will make use of signs to direct the audience to read the scene in a way that supports the agreed upon dramatic objective. Our signals can be clear and forthright (*there's been a terrible accident and someone is badly hurt*), uncertain and ambiguously sinister (*something is happening here, but we don't know what it is*), or even purposefully neutral and noncommittal (*this looks innocent enough . . . but wait . . . maybe it's a trap*). Each of these choices will involve the making of musical *gestures*. They will affect tempo and tonality, rhythm and accent, instrumentation, and particularly the amount of tension we bring to bear through dissonance. If, for example, *we know* that the man in the road is an escaped convict—perhaps a serial killer—whereas the driver approaching the scene doesn't have a clue, our approach will be entirely different from the one we might take if driver and audience share the same state of knowledge.

Human beings communicated with signs and physical gestures long before they communicated with formalized language. Language, in fact, can be seen as a codification of signs—a kind of shorthand that gets the message across more quickly and precisely than pantomime or physical expression. The most highly developed prose can make even the most difficult ideas comprehensible. But music, despite its great expressiveness and sophistication, is not prose. It cannot *denote* a specific thing, such as "the room is red" or "the girl is blind," but it can most definitely *connote* things; for example, "this is the sound I associate with a stark winter landscape," or "these timbres suggest a rural, backwoods setting." It's critically important for composers to understand the distinction between denotation and connotation, because if we try to use music to denote something specific, we will most likely fail—or at least, be accused of "mickey-mousing." This is not how music works best. Music must work through metaphor, association, juxtaposition, and most of all, *connotation*, as in: *I connote those low, tremolando strings to mean that something wicked is coming this way.*

The principal question this chapter—and in part, the rest of this book—asks is whether we can now say, after a hundred years of movie music, that some of these connotations have become truly universal. To what degree is film music a global language?

MUSICAL MIMESIS

In recent years, as the field of musical semiotics has evolved and attracted such scholars as Philip Tagg and Eero Tarasti, semioticians have begun to pay more and more attention to the concept of musical *gestures*. A musical gesture is like a physical gesture (a lifting of the eyebrows, a shrug of the shoulders, a finger drawn across the throat). It is a succinct, and usually short, expression of meaning or sentiment. And as with physical gestures, different cultures and social groups can infer different meanings. This used to present far greater problems than it does now. The ubiquity of mass entertainment gives us, to an ever-increasing degree, a shared language of gesture. An iconic character, such as James Bond, reads just as potently in Singapore as he does in Chicago, or the franchise would never have become so hugely successful internationally.

Because visual signs are grasped more quickly than aural signs, the universality of musical gesture in cinema lagged behind the purely visual/physical, and so did the study of it. And again, many scholars were slow to believe that music could be "about" anything at all. Slowly but surely, this is changing. If it were not, it would be very difficult to teach a college-level course in composing for the screen.

Composer's Sidebar: MUSICAL SEMIOTICS

The study of signs and meaning is called semiotics, or in Europe, semiology. It emerged in the late nineteenth and early twentieth centuries from the field of linguistics, and its pioneers included such people as Ferdinand de Saussure, Charles Peirce, and Roland Barthes. The foundational premise of semiotics is that a sign consists of a signifier (the symbol, metaphor, or gesture used to communicate meaning) and a signified (the thing or meaning the signifier is pointing to). When the signal is sent and received, the sign is complete. But if something goes wrong at either end, you have miscommunication, or *codal incompetence*. Yes, if you, as a composer, fail to communicate your meaning via use of the right signs, you will be judged incompetent. Some signs are simple and direct. An octagonal red road sign tells us to stop. In most cultures, a lateral shaking of the head—especially if forceful—means no. In the visual language of cinema, worldwide urban audiences have come to recognize a wide range of signs based on lighting (e.g.,

high key and low key), camera angles and lenses, editing/montage, and what is known as mise-en-scène, the arrangement before the camera of all the elements of the scene. But music communicates meaning more obliquely. In fact, the specialized field of musical semiotics was held up for decades by the widely shared belief that music, in and of itself, could not mean anything. But that belief may have reflected a modernist bias toward music as pure sonic architecture: self-sufficient, nonreferential. Art for art's sake. The composer of music for movies does not write music for music's sake: he or she writes to support, animate, illuminate, and enhance the story. The music must mean something—even if that something is a total uncertainty, a suspended reality. From here on, I will employ (not excessively, I hope) some of the terminology of semiotics—such words as signifier, signified, gesture, target, and sometimes percipient for a member of the audience: one who perceives. Most of these terms are easily relatable to music.

In the field of language studies, a *morpheme* is the smallest possible unit of meaning. If so much as one letter is taken away, the meaning changes. *Cat, dog, Ma*, and *Pa* are all morphemes, but so are prefixes and suffixes, such as *un-* (meaning "not"), *-er* (meaning "more"), and *-ish* (meaning "resembling"). The musical equivalent of a morpheme is a *museme*, a term coined by Philip Tagg. Unlike morphemes, a museme generally requires more than one musical "syllable" (i.e., beat, note, pitch, etc.), though I'm sure there are examples of monosyllabic musemes! The shortest good examples I can cite are the rising perfect fifth and the falling minor third. The first is a call to arms—a summons—and the second is almost universally a sign of ridicule, mockery, or perhaps fate (as in Copland's *Billy The Kid* or John Powell's *The Bourne Identity*), at least in the Western world.

These semiotic terms—signifier, gesture, museme—can sometimes be used interchangeably. The rising fifth, for example (especially if played on a horn), would seem to be an example of all three. Usually, however, there are important distinctions. If we make the statement "Use of the Lydian mode in film music evokes wistful feelings of childhood and/or wonderment," we are probably talking about the Lydian mode as a *signifier*. Likewise if we say, "The oboe takes the solo after Mary loses the baby." The oboe, used as a solo

SIGNS AND MEANING

instrument, often signals a shift to a plaintive tone. If we say, "That ascending harp glissando was a little hackneyed, don't you think?" we are most likely describing a *gesture*. Same thing with a big brass hit or a jazzy *doink*. But if we describe a major seventh chord as limpid or "mellow," or a tritone in the low woodwinds as "ominous," or the interval of a minor sixth on a musette as "French," we are most likely describing musemes. I'll try to keep the distinction clear, but just to maintain a little wiggle room, all of them fall under the heading of *signs*.

A BRIEF HISTORY OF CINEMUSICAL SIGNS

For the rest of this chapter, we'll examine a number of film music *signifiers*, beginning with developed thematic statements, and then moving down to the fine grain where we can spot gestures and musemes. To start with, if you have access to a keyboard, play the simple triads below at a tempo of about 120 bpm.

Figure 3.1.

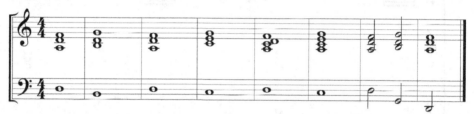

Chances are, if you stayed to the tempo, some of you recognized the piece as soon as you heard the first inversion G major chord in measure two. Others will pick it up at the C major chord in bar 4. And if it hasn't hit you by the final cadence from G major to D minor, then it certainly will when you play the melody line:

Figure 3.2. Ennio Morricone, *The Good, the Bad and the Ugly*, Main Title reduction

This is, of course, a bare-bones reduction of Ennio Morricone's immortal opening statement from the best remembered of Sergio Leone's spaghetti westerns, *The Good, the Bad and the Ugly*. If you haven't listened to it in a while, it's well worth doing, because it is one wild piece of music, and is a veritable field guide to what film composers must do to create indelible impressions. It also lends itself beautifully to both musical and semiotic analysis. The entire eight-bar period is Morricone's *theme*. Each two bar unit is a perfect example of a melodic *phrase*. And the sixteenth-note to tied quarter-note figure (circled in Figure 2) is one of the best *motives* ever created for film. It's also one of the three or four best exemplars of a museme that movie music offers. It's featured in cell phone ring tones, comedy sketches, and Quentin Tarantino movies, and along with the *Jaws* shark motif, the first bar of the *Love Story* theme, the machine gun blast of the James Bond theme's iconic guitar lick, and of course, the *Psycho* string stabs, resides in the nuclear core of film music *signifiers*.

The antecedent, or "A" half of each phrase is heard first as voiced by an ocarina, and later by a male voice (yodeling in what must have seemed to Morricone cowboy style), and a whistler. The consequent, or "B" half, works like an echo, and is heard on both Morricone's signature harmonica and by the same male voice imitating a harmonica ("mwah-m*wah*-mwah"). The over-the-top arrangement includes a tape-delayed tom-tom, twangy guitar, male chorus, "sword and sandal"–style orchestration, and some manic *pasa doble* brass, all of it recorded in spectacularly grungy mono.

A big part of what gives to this theme its epic character is that both melody and harmony utilize the medieval European version of *Dorian mode* (see sidebar), as does much of the world's most stirring folk music, from the Hindustani raga known as *kafi* to British folk songs (e.g., "Scarborough Fair") and a great deal of Celtic and Appalachian melody. What gives Dorian such a unique flavor is that it is a minor mode with a *raised sixth degree*. That altered scale step allows the IV chord—the Dorian subdominant—to be a major chord. That makes a huge difference. Just cadencing back and forth between D minor and G major will put you into an epic space, on high, windy steppes with armies or star-crossed lovers in a standoff, and the chord change is arguably a signifier in and of itself.

Let's turn back to Morricone's museme. For any musical gesture, statement, or shape to be a genuine signifier, it must have *meaning* to those who hear it. It must signify *something*. In what ways does *The Good, the Bad and the Ugly* motif qualify? Or not?

By 1960s standards, the audience for Sergio Leone's spaghetti westerns was huge. The films made Clint Eastwood (*The Man with No Name*) an international superstar, and like

Composer's Sidebar: DORIAN MODE

This is the name now commonly assigned to the interval set ascending from D to D on the white keys of the piano (or any transposition of the same interval series). As mentioned, it is a natural minor mode with a raised sixth. It was the first of the eight church modes derived in sixth-century Europe for the composition and performance of plainsong, a.k.a. Gregorian chant, but it has a counterpart in virtually every developed folk music system on the planet. This is because it gets both its name and its intervallic sequence from the original Greek modes, or tonoi, of more than twelve centuries earlier—although the names were scrambled! The Dorian mode that Plato referred to as the most ennobling and virile of the tonoi ran diatonically in descending sequence from E to E, thus corresponding to what we now call *Phrygian mode*: a minor mode with a lowered second degree. And what the Greeks of the sixth century BCE called Phrygian is what Pope Gregory—and we—call Dorian. Some scholars think the medieval churchmen got it mixed up because they didn't realize that the pitches of the Greek modes ran in descending order, or perhaps did not understand how the Greeks employed tetrachords. In any case, Dorian is now what the Church made it, and has an easy mnemonic as D = Dorian. Plato liked this mode, as well. The one he wasn't crazy about (he thought it would "soften the male virtues") was Lydian, which in another medieval flip-flop is the mode the Church called Ionian, known to us since the sixteenth century as the major scale!

the James Bond franchise (we'll look at that later in this chapter), had an appeal that was transcultural. They were tales of the American West shot in Spain by an Italian director with an international cast and a visual style and moral tone that was both biblical in its archetypal clarity and Asian in its deliberate obscurity of meaning.

Morricone's music was so closely wedded to audience perception of the films that few people were able to think of one without the other. In the ocarina/vocal figure in *The Good, the Bad and the Ugly*, we are looking at one of the most primal of aural signifiers. It is a *call*: a summons, an alert, even a warning. It mimics birdsong in its shape and repetition, just as so many of the most ancient human calls did. It is simultaneously (1) a *clarion call* (i.e., a demand for action); (2) the war cry of an avenging angel (*he's coming, he's badass, and he's going to put things right*); and (3) a hero's fanfare (in this case, an antihero's, since it wasn't always easy to tell Clint Eastwood from the bad guys).

Heard on its own (as it often is in the film), this wild whoop of a motif functions almost *diegetically* (see chapter 1: the *diegesis* is the imaginary world on the screen, so "source music" is usually considered diegetic, whereas underscore is described as nondiegetic because it comes from *outside* the world on the screen). The film's characters (especially the villains) almost seem to "hear it." As wild as it is, in the context of Morricone's arrangement, it has a strange beauty and symmetry. This is both due to the Dorian setting, and because Morricone uses the most venerable musical form as its vehicle: the call and response, or antiphony. The theme is a perfectly balanced eight bar statement, resolved modally in a satisfying way. This points up one of the few rules about writing memorable music for movies that seems to be axiomatic:

If you're going to do something bold or stylistically risky, do it in a form (such as rondo, canon, ABAB, AABA, etc.) that is tried and true, and with techniques (e.g., ground bass, imitative polyphony, continuous "motor" rhythm) that are familiar. It's a bit like the famous Trojan Horse: disguise the strange within the familiar.

On the other hand, if you're going to do something conventional, such as a waltz or a big, lush love theme, it may be best to dress it up in something harmonically or rhythmically unconventional. Why do I say this?

The Russian formalists of the early twentieth century had a wonderful term for this defamiliarization of the commonplace. They called it *ostranenie*, or literally, "making strange," and it is a key concept in such forms as surrealism and science fiction. You can hear it at work in two marvelous early works for the cinema by Sergei Prokofiev: The "Battle on the Ice'" from *Alexander Nevsky*, and the entirety of *Lieutenant Kijé*.

Our senses crave the familiar but respond to the different. Think about the sensation of frisson, known in American vernacular as goose pimples. (Every composer knows that the highest compliment is to be told that his/her music gave us goose pimples). Frisson arises from difference: slipping into a hot bath on a winter's night, or feeling suddenly that there is another presence in the house when you thought you were alone. A familiar hand on our arm—a parent, friend, or longtime partner—will not raise goose-flesh, but the touch of a desirable stranger will cover our skin with bumps. And though frisson is associated at some primal level with fear or surprise, it is almost universally described as a pleasurable sensation. This is a paradox of sorts, one that I'll refer to as the *familiar-unfamiliar*. It's very much at play in Morricone's theme.

Another paradox active in the theme is what we might call the *ancient-modern effect*: creating something *new* by reaching back to the distant past. The *tintinnabulum* of the Estonian composer Arvo Pärt is a very good example of this (just listen to his best-known piece, *Fratres*, which has been tracked into any number of contemporary films, and try not to get the chills). Morricone uses a ninth-century church mode as the setting of his cowboy melody, complete with tubular bells! We'll encounter the ancient-modern effect again in later chapters and other scores.

There are some musical semioticians who contend that *meaning* arises only when our *expectations* (such as a perfect cadence or functional harmony) are *not* met. In other words, if you want people to pay attention to your message, you have to surprise them a little. Ennio Morricone has been surprising us throughout his long career, and he had one more surprise in store for diehard fans of the classic Hollywood western: electric guitar.

Figure 3.3. *The Good, the Bad and the Ugly* guitar

Of course, no Fender Telecasters were around in 1860. And one of the five cardinal rules laid down for film composers by no less than Aaron Copland was to "create a convincing atmosphere of time and place." To introduce instruments, sonic textures, and styles not reasonably "native" to the period and setting was to risk undermining the all-important suspension of disbelief. Needless to say, this did not stop film composers from scoring biblical epics with nineteenth-century symphonic language—and still doesn't—but audiences were accustomed to this convention. An electric guitar in the Wild West was a decided risk, but Morricone got away with it. And the reason he got away with it offers one more argument for the notion that a film composer's principal craft lies in the skillful use of signs.

In 1948, a former rodeo rider named Stan Jones penned a song whose full title was "Ghost Riders in the Sky: A Cowboy Legend." The minor mode melody recalled "When Johnny Comes Marching Home" and the lyric took the ancient northern European myth of the Wild Hunt and placed it on the high plains of Wyoming. The effect of both was haunting, and the song became a hit for a number of pop and country-western artists, among them Vaughn Monroe, Frankie Laine, and Johnny Cash, beginning in 1949 and continuing through the 1950s. In almost every case, the song's most identifiable element was its twangy, *hell-bent-for-leather* electric guitar, and with that certification, the sound of amplified six-strings became the sound of cowboy music. Then, in 1958, the great Dimitri Tiomkin composed the Main Title theme for the long-running TV western, *Rawhide*, complete with whoops and whistles, and again, in a minor key. One of *Rawhide*'s stars was a then unknown young actor named Clint Eastwood.

Ennio Morricone was almost undoubtedly aware of this legacy when he sat down to score *The Good, the Bad and the Ugly* in 1966. American pop culture, then and now, plays well in Europe. An *American* film composer, however, would not have taken the chance. The American western score was still firmly indebted to Aaron Copland. It took the "outsider" perspective of a composer an ocean and a continent away to trust that the world cinema audience would know how to read the signs.

While we're calibrated to Dorian mode, old things made new and new things made old, there's a segue well worth making, and that is to Ernest Gold's Oscar-winning score from *Exodus*, Otto Preminger's 1960 dramatization of the birth of the state of Israel. Here is a reduction of the eight-bar "A" section of the Main Title theme:

Figure 3.4. Ernest Gold, *Exodus* theme (excerpt)

Ernest Gold

This is as good an example as I know of how a single theme—in truth, a single phrase—can win a score the Oscar. (It still happens: consider *Brokeback Mountain* and *The Social Network*, neither of which was a symphonic score like *Exodus*, but both of which had indelible themes). What Gold (who received three more Oscar nominations in subsequent years and then dropped out of sight) did here is pretty ingenious. The opening four-note statement (beginning with the pickup) is Dorian. The C major chord makes it so (a C minor chord might have been more authentic, but not as potent). Gold is trying to evoke not the Israel of 1948, but an eternal Israel, as much one of biblical myth as biblical history. One that stands firm against all foes and bends only to the will of God. What's more, Gold's theme was adapted to song, sold a forest's worth of piano-vocal sheet music (people still gathered around the piano in 1960), and made a hit record by squeaky-clean pop balladeer, Pat Boone, with these lyrics to the opening two-bar phrase:

This land is mine

God gave this land to me

In the language of the time, that pretty much defined "epic." And the fact that the theme is still being used on hip-hop tracks to convey this quality is evidence of its durability, even if today's film composers would never be permitted to make such a grand musical statement. Once he's gotten our attention with that perfect leapfrog of a P4 followed by a P5, then dropping a step to fill in the leap, Gold leaves the confines of Dorian mode (at least in terms of harmony) and does something that anyone who listens to or plays rock music will recognize. He shifts into natural minor mode, lowering the sixth degree, and climbs back to the tonic G minor by whole steps via E-flat and F major chords. It's *Stairway to Heaven* and *All Along the Watchtower* and hundreds of indigenous folk songs from around the world. What it *isn't* is very Jewish, but this is a movie score, and movie scores rarely keep kosher!

The element of surprise in the *Exodus* theme—the unexpected thing—arrives in the second phrase, when the melody leaps a minor seventh and lands on a v chord (D minor) that is then briefly tonicized by treating it to the same stepwise return (VI–VII–I) from B-flat to C major, but landing on a triumphant D *major*, which then serves as a dominant and takes us not to G minor, but fleetingly to a key center of G major. To students of Renaissance polyphony *and* the Beatles, who know their "Picardy thirds," none of this will seem that unusual, but in nominally symphonic music of the time, it was a boldly modal statement that prefigured *Gladiator* and *Game of Thrones*.

I mentioned that some theorists believe *meaning* in music comes from surprise. Of course, in film scoring, we can't simply drop meaning in anywhere. The musical gesture has to occur in proper relationship with a cinematic gesture: a cut, a change in camera angle, an off-screen sound effect or a look crossing a character's face, and if it occurs as little as two frames too early or late, it can confuse rather than clarify meaning. Today's composers have to be far more subtle with such gestures. Big shifts in tone can draw too much attention and diminish audience immersion to mere observance. But we can understand the *subtle* only if we know the *sweeping*, and here is one of the grandest examples of surprise in the symphonic repertoire, from the final movement of Saint-Saëns's Organ Symphony No. 3:

Figure 3.5. Saint-Saëns, Symphony No. 3, main theme, bars 1–2

The grand staff labeled "Piano 2" represents the organ part, heard initially in the strings at 8va with soft organ accompaniment. The arpeggios in grand staff 1 are two pianos. So far, no harmonic surprises. In fact, aside from the magically eerie sound of the high-register violins at a dynamic of *p* and the twinkling of the dual pianos (also 8va), both of which are sonic signatures of Saint-Saëns, the writing is almost archaically simple: Triadic harmonies, a hymnlike chord progression performed in a stately, measured fashion—deeply moving, but completely diatonic and functional.

Figure 3.6. Saint-Saëns, Symphony No. 3, main theme, bars 3–4

Here, in the second 9/4 measure (note: like the first one, it's a complete phrase in a single measure), the middle cadence D minor–A major–D minor is our first hint of the unexpected, but it's nothing that Bach hadn't done two centuries before. Still, there's a strong sense of mystery in the orchestration, a sense that a curtain is being drawn back on something . . .

Figure 3.7. Saint-Saëns, Symphony No. 3, main theme, bars 5–6

And it is. Hearing a tutti orchestra suddenly drop a semitone in block chord fashion to the completely unexpected E major harmony is almost dizzying, like an airplane suddenly dropping in altitude. It throws everything off in a single gesture, because an E major chord has no functional role in a straight C major chord progression. Yet Saint-Saëns *makes* it function by using the E chord as a pivot to A major, then repeating the Dm–A–Dm cadence to bring us to a vi–I–V–I finish. At this point, the pipe organ enters full throttle. Talk about goose pimples.

This is a straightforward example of what theorist and Yale professor Richard Cohn calls "triadic post-tonality."[1] It's also an instance of the

1   See Richard Cohn, *Audacious Euphony: Chromatic Harmony and the Triad's Second Nature* (New York: Oxford University Press, 2012).

ancient-modern paradox, where chord settings that might have sounded quite normal in the late Middle Ages or Renaissance have a striking quality in the context of modern music. We'll encounter something similar in the analysis of Danny Elfman's *Alice in Wonderland* "Main Title" in chapter 8.

Director George Miller of *Mad Max* fame used Saint-Saëns's chordal melody brilliantly as an anthem for the orphaned animals in his underrated *Babe: A Pig in the City*. Saint-Saëns, a contemporary of Debussy and a forerunner of Ravel, has a lot to say to film composers. His "Aquarium" from *The Carnival of the Animals* has been used repeatedly as a style model in films, most notably in Terrence Malick's 1974 masterpiece *Days of Heaven*, where it served as the Main Title and its harmonic language was brilliantly interpolated into the score by composer Ennio Morricone (in the cue entitled "The Harvest").

Spellbound

Miklós Rózsa (1907–1995) was introduced to film music by Arthur Honegger in 1934, when he was still writing concert music in his native Hungary. Like most first-generation film composers, he was consummately trained in the European tradition and initially saw the cinema only as a supplementary source of income. He arrived in Hollywood with Alexander Korda in 1939, and a year later received his first Academy Award nomination for *The Thief of Baghdad* (a model for Disney's animated feature hit *Aladdin*). By 1945, when Rózsa stepped in for an unavailable Bernard Herrmann to score Alfred Hitchcock's *Spellbound*, he was an established presence in the early film music community.

Rózsa's *Spellbound* score is notable for a number of things: It is the first example of a Hollywood studio film in which the score was used to portray a psychologically altered state. It was composed fifteen years before *Psycho*, and its musical vocabulary was still very much of the late romantic—early modernist period of Gustav Mahler. It introduced to the American cinema, however, not only some new harmonic language, but a strange proto-electronic instrument called the *theremin*, which from that moment on became a *signifier* of both great dramatic—and later, comedic—power. *Spellbound* was the score that drew a young Jerry Goldsmith into the profession. It was the first and last time Rózsa worked with Hitchcock, who disliked the score and returned immediately afterward to the more astringent style of Bernard Herrmann.[2] But it won Rózsa his first Oscar (which is in keeping with the notion that it's "the familiar unfamiliar," or *ostranenie,* that gets the attention of even musically untutored listeners—especially in the film business). Most important for the present discussion, it created a musical *sign*. We'll look at it in the next example.

---

2   There may be a "theremin curse" in film music. The first and last time Howard Shore worked with Tim Burton was on a score that featured a theremin, *Ed Wood*. After that, Burton returned immediately to his own Herrmannesque partner, Danny Elfman.

Figure 3.8. Miklós Rózsa, *Spellbound* "Dementia" theme (excerpt)

The reduction from Rózsa's lush orchestration is only a bare-bones approximation, but it highlights the most prominent elements of the "Dementia" theme—those that remained signifiers of the uncanny for the following twenty years or so, after which their use quickly became parodistic. The "melody," if it can be described as such, opens with an "A" motif that is a three-note chromatic descent from G5, dropping a tritone to D-flat.

Because of the theremin's design and the way it is played, every pitch change comes with a portamento effect, so I haven't included glissando markings in the reduction. Even if you have never heard Rózsa's score, the iconic signature of this motif will be evident from the dozens of campy sci-fi movies that have imitated it, and the hundreds of comedies and cartoons that have had fun with it. But it wasn't either campy or cartoonish in its first outing, and we can still learn important things about the creation of musical signposts from (1) Rózsa's deliberate choice of an "alien" timbre to convey an altered reality;[3] (2) the *isomorphic* use of melodic shape and direction to convey a "descent into madness; and (3) the affective nature of this kind of raw chromaticism.

---

3 Rózsa used the theremin to similar effect in another score from the same year (1945), *The Lost Weekend*.

Spellbound may be the first "psychological thriller," and the prototypical example of Hollywood Freudianism. It's also one of the first mainstream films to use amnesia as a plot point. The protagonist, Dr. Anthony Edwardes (Gregory Peck) is a psychoanalyst who has lost his memory and fears he may have committed murder. Treating him (and, inevitably, falling for him) is another shrink, Dr. Constance Petersen (Ingrid Bergman), and his analysis includes a surrealistic dream sequence designed by Salvador Dalí. It is a film of many "firsts," and it's when a composer is facing a new dramatic problem that he or she must take the boldest steps. There was nothing in the late romantic—or even the early modernist—repertoire to guide Rózsa in portrayal of a psychotic state induced by a guilt complex, although the harmonic language was there for the taking courtesy of Schoenberg, Webern, and others of what was known as the Second Viennese School.

The theremin (doubled with violins) floats over a bed of dark brass clusters and harps arpeggiating a G diminished seventh chord. There are nods to atonality in such gestures as the sudden augmented chord (beat 4 of measure 3) and to the noir-ish jazz of the war years in the pizzicato bass line that mimics the theremin. None of these things are gratuitous: they all serve a dramatic purpose, and despite the clichés, the effect is still disturbing. It's interesting to note that even though Miklós Rózsa and Bernard Herrmann were as different as could be, Herrmann utilized a similar (albeit far more eccentric) palette six years later in his score for the sci-fi classic *The Day the Earth Stood Still*.

Staying with the genre of psychological thrillers (possibly Hollywood's richest vein), we'll look next at Jerry Goldsmith's now iconic Main Title theme for *Basic Instinct*. The breaking down of musical signs sometimes requires an ice pick.

Figure 3.9. *Basic Instinct*, excerpt from Main Title

In his score for the 1992 *Basic Instinct*, Goldsmith—at the summit of one of the longest and most productive scoring careers on record—did what every film composer *should* hope to do when creating music for a big-budget Hollywood genre film: he simultaneously honored the tradition initiated by Rózsa and Herrmann *and* broke new ground. He accomplished this by picking up on something that was implicit in the vocabulary as far back as *Psycho* (1960), but until *Basic Instinct* never fully displayed: big-screen murder can make for perversely beautiful music.

The opening of *Basic Instinct* shocked audiences in 1992 with its conflation of kinky sex and bloody murder, and still shocks today. It's a death by ice pick to the jugular (and a few other veins, as well) in the lap of Northern California luxury, blood saturating the silk sheets and spattering the surrounding objets d'art. Directed by Dutch filmmaker Paul Verhoeven—also at the peak of his powers—the entire movie has a kind of gunmetal blue sheen, and its two leads, Michael Douglas and Sharon Stone, never look anything less than smashing. Like his composer, Verhoeven knew that he was treading on sacred cinematic ground in a mise-en-scene rich with Freudian symbols and film noir references: it's impossible to see the luster of Sharon Stone's platinum blond hair and not think of Kim Novak in *Vertigo*. To sum it up without spoilers, it's a classic noir setup: an erotically charged cat-and-mouse game between Stone's Catherine Tramell and Douglas's Nick Curran, one a sexy crime novelist suspected of murder, the other a San Francisco detective (*Vertigo* again) who knows he's capable of it. Like Kim Novak's Madeleine, Catherine is a creator of stories that have a way of ensnaring "innocent" men, and we know from first encounter that Nick will have to follow her into the trap.

The quintet of artists responsible for *Basic Instinct*'s fidelity to the genre—Verhoeven, bad-boy screenwriter Joe Eszterhas, Douglas and Stone, and Jerry Goldsmith—all knew exactly what they were doing, and though the movie they made is no *Vertigo*, it was and remains a great cinematic guilty pleasure, a blast of uncut cocaine to the right-brain. This is, after all, the film in which Sharon Stone casually exposed her vulva and made a hundred million jaws drop. That naughtiness, perversity, glamour—and guilt—are all reflected in Goldsmith's score, and most pointedly, in his theme.

The first notable thing in the Main Title music—and the first musical sign—reveals itself in the second bar, even before the entry of the theme. In the *Vertigo* chapter of this book, I digressed for a paragraph (Figure 1.7) to highlight Herrmann's use of minor harmonies with root movement by thirds around a common tone (respectively, the third and fifth of the two chords) and referred to it as the "Herrmann effect." As inventive as Herrmann was, he didn't originate the use of so-called *mediant* harmonies. They can be found in Wagner, and in the work of the Russian "nationalists" and French impressionists. But Herrmann, as mentioned, put this harmonic device in bold relief, unsoftened by extended passages of chromatic voice-leading. He made it a museme, which can still be heard today in any sci-fi film, and especially in the work of Danny Elfman. The *Basic Instinct* cue opens with a hypnotic, sixteenth-note "looplike" figure in muted violas, harp (and what sounds like a marimba or kalimba synthesizer patch) that quickly establishes that the harmonic basis of the piece will be the metrically regular shift from D minor to F-sharp minor. The nominal key center would seem to be D minor, but that's the thing about nonfunctional harmonies: you never can tell. The important thing to note as you play the viola figure on a keyboard is that the common tone of A-natural serves as a fulcrum for this otherwise floaty and unanchored chord change. The change requires that two pitches, D and F, shift by a semitone, D dropping to C-sharp and F ascending to F-sharp, with the A common to both.

This may not seem like as big a deal as I'm making of it, until it's realized that a huge chunk of the spectrum of contemporary film score harmony is based on modal exchange and chromatic voice leading around common tones. Except in period films or the most conventional scores, this has largely displaced traditional harmony. As with most changes worth making in the craft, there are good dramatic and aesthetic reasons for this. Filmmakers like ambiguity and suspense. Plots and character arcs are often not resolved until late in the final act, if they are resolved at all, and modern filmmakers don't want the music to telegraph resolution before it has occurred. In the sort of "extended tonality" pioneered by Herrmann in *Vertigo* and *Psycho* and utilized by Bernstein in *To Kill a Mockingbird*, the composer can suspend resolution indefinitely.

When Goldsmith introduces his "melody," which is really a haunting one-bar motive for two voices, it's first played by the clarinets, then taken up by the flutes. It's a snaky, subversive little fragment of a tune, entirely chromatic, and except for the octave displacement of the final two notes, all contained within the compass of a M2. Two voices, a M3 apart, descending and ascending in parallel. The composer of *Patton* and *Chinatown*, both harmonically sophisticated scores, shows us that when it comes to sex and the human brain, "basic instinct" can be summed up in a single measure.

But what a difference that octave displacement makes. Without it, Goldsmith's musical honey trap might sound far less forbidding. The serialists understood the power of pitch displacement and inversion, and this wasn't lost on Jerry Goldsmith. After dropping the octave, the second ingenious thing he does is to leave the phrase unfinished. Since the harmony shifts to an F-sharp minor chord, the lower voice of the melody ought to ascend from E to F-natural to F-sharp, but it stops at F, leaving the violins (measure 4) to supply the missing pitch.

Each one of these devices: the two voices in parallel, the chromatic descent and dizzying drop of an octave, and the unfinished line, is driven by story. Without taking analysis to extremes, I think it's fair to say that the two voices moving in tangolike lockstep are Nick and Catherine, and that drop is their vertiginous attraction. If you've seen the movie and know how it ends, even the unfinished phrase makes sense. The melody speaks to the characters, while the mediant harmony speaks to the genre.

Before you object that this is far too literal a reading of what semioticians call "the text," let me be clear: I'm not saying that Jerry Goldsmith worked all this out in advance, or even that he realized it in hindsight. That's the beauty and mystery of the creative process. Whether your medium is paint, pixels, words, or notes, if you are an artist, they tend to take the shape of your subject. Consider an example from the score that is probably *Instinct*'s most obvious influence: the string "stabs" from the famous shower scene in *Psycho.* They've been described by critics as everything from the screeching of Norman Bates's stuffed birds to the sound of Norman's hysterical mother echoing in his aberrant psyche, but it seems clear enough that Herrmann intended them as a musical isomorph of the thrusts of a knife into flesh and muscle, coupled with the internal screams of the victim (the scene is played without production sound). Goldsmith was an extraordinarily acute "scene reader." If his music is not as well known or frequently performed as that of such composers as John Williams and John Barry, it may be in part because he wrote from "inside the movie," his pencil moving across the page like the needle on a seismograph, sensitive to every small tremor. Over fifty years of consistently exemplary work, Goldsmith earned only one Oscar—for a horror film, *The Omen.* But he is remembered by his peers as "a film composer's film composer." Chapter 12 is devoted to a single cue from his landmark score for *Patton.*

We've drawn a line directly from *Spellbound* to *Vertigo* and *Psycho* to *Basic Instinct.* Let's see if we can go one step further and extend that line to 2014 and a score that, on the surface, bears little resemblance to the others.

Figure 3.10. Mica Levi, *Under the Skin*, "Andrew Void" (excerpt)

British composer Mica Levi, who goes by the stage name Micachu, was barely twenty-seven when she received the call to create the music for Jonathan Glazer's eerily beautiful *Under the Skin*, her first film scoring assignment. Young, but hardly a novice. She'd been writing and performing music from the age of four and had attended London's prestigious Guildhall School of Music and Drama. Levi is a good example of the sort of hybrid talent that, with increasing frequency, is crossing over from the "new music" world into cinema and is equally comfortable performing avant-garde pop, DJ'ing, or fulfilling a commission from the London Philharmonic Orchestra. In Glazer, who had directed two little seen but highly influential films, *Sexy Beast* and *Birth*—the latter of which arguably launched the international career of Alexandre Desplat—she found a director who was willing to give full rein to her musical experimentation.

Under the Skin stars Scarlett Johansson as "Isserley," an extraterrestrial being dispatched to earth to harvest human beings for consumption on her home planet. At least, this is the plot overview of the Michael Faber novel on which Glazer loosely based his film. Neither the Johansson character's name nor her extraterrestrial backstory are ever addressed in the movie, which renders it, depending on your point of view, either wonderfully immersive or impossibly obscure. But however one feels about the film's inscrutability, there is no denying its visual power or the deeply disturbing atmosphere that it conjures as Isserley drives the stark, rain-swept motorways of the Scottish Highlands looking for male hitchhikers to seduce and process into dinner for her alien overlords. Glazer must have thought long and hard about the music.

A note needs to be inserted here about the challenge of transcribing and doing traditional analysis on what have become known as *hybrid scores*. This category, which now accounts for the vast majority of film, television, and game scores, utilizes both conventional orchestral performance and very sophisticated use of electronics—not only digital instrument libraries and synthesizers, but everything from "found sound" to highly processed acoustic instruments and atmospheres that often render the line between music and sound design very, very gray. The two composers probably most responsible for the shift to hybrid scoring that began to occur in the early nineties are Hans Zimmer and Thomas Newman, and we'll face the challenge of representing their work soon enough. But the style has now moved beyond what they envisioned thirty years ago to become what amounts to a wholly new way of conceiving the role of music in film. Such directors as Glazer now expect the score to be a fully integrated element of the film's soundscape, and this means far less of the traditional symphonic statement and far more that doesn't lend itself to conventional notation. If you're only reading the score, you're often seeing less than half of the composer's intention.

At the same time, the twin phenomena of *new music* and *classical crossover* have now fully invaded the turf once held exclusively by a core group of film and television composers in Hollywood and their counterparts in Europe. A movie's "temp score" (the music assembled by the editors to accompany test screenings of the picture) is now as likely to include Arvo Pärt, Sigur Rós, or Kronos Quartet as John Williams, and the great conservatories of Europe that once solely produced composers who sought orchestral commissions are increasingly looking toward the "applied music" they once disdained. Although there are certainly those who lament the passing of big anthemic scores, such as *Back to the Future* and *Star Wars*, the crossfertilization of film music with experimental, electronic, and avant-garde forms has injected new artistry into the craft and kept it from becoming an anachronism. Mica Levi is one among this new strain.

The reduction of Levi's "theme" for *Under the Skin* shown in Figure 3.10

is, at best, a thumbnail. The central three-note motif, with its rapid slur from A-natural to B flat and theremin-like glissando to a high E flat, is heard with both natural and heavily processed strings (I have it in the violins because of the register, but Levi has said she did much of the score with viola), as well as human voice and other effects that have been cleverly subjected to digital signal processing (DSP). The effect, much like some of new music's *spectral composition*, is to bring out the overtone content in such a way that a single line becomes an otherworldly chorus of sounds. The arrangement is austere and haunting, like the images in the film. The cue opens with a rich bed of looped "industrial" textures, then adding a deliberately "lo-fi" percussion part on the quarter-notes and eventually bringing in celli playing *sul ponticello* (bowed near the bridge, where the timbre is steeliest and coldest) with an agitated tremolo. The sound is more Trent Reznor than Erich Korngold.

Here we have a genuine trip into the "uncanny valley,"[4] which is exactly where Glazer wants us to be. His protagonist *looks* human, but she's not. She speaks in Scarlett Johannsson's dulcet tones, but there is something *foreign*, almost rehearsed, about her words. She seduces her hitchhikers, but not in any way that puts them at ease, and when we witness what happens when she lures them back to her lair, we understand fully the reason for our discomfort. It is these seduction-murder scenes that are scored with Levi's "uncanny" theme.

But in spite of all the edginess and new technique evident in Mica Levi's score, it's also plainly evident that she is aware of and playing upon the semiology of psycho-killer music, from *Spellbound* to *Psycho* and *Basic Instinct*. She has overlaid her new map on an old map like a palimpsest, thereby tapping into our sense of the *familiar-unfamiliar*. If it were not for our recognition of certain gestures and musemes—the shrill glissando up a tritone, *ponticello* bowing, tremolo strings and the ominous bass entry in bar 7—we wouldn't react as we do, and reviewers would not have described the score as brilliant.

Speaking of musemes and scores described as brilliant, let's turn next to the main theme, "Hand Covers Bruise," from Trent Reznor and Atticus Ross's Oscar-winning score for David Fincher's *The Social Network*. This is a score that, quite frankly, many in the film music trade dismissed as "fashion," but a closer look may reveal its genius.

---

4 http://en.wikipedia.org/wiki/Uncanny_valley. In 1970, robotics researcher Masahiro Mori theorized that people experience a deep revulsion as robots begin to look "just human enough" to fool us for a second. We are fine with R2D2 and C3PO, but add prosthetic hands, facial expressions, and most important, *skin*, and we begin to react as if we are seeing a corpse, or a "pod person" sent to replace us. This shows up on a line graph as a dip, or "valley," which then levels off again as the automaton becomes fully human. Some experts believe that negative audience reaction to the animated characters in Robert Zemeckis's film adaptation of *The Polar Express* was due to this effect.

Figure 3.11. *The Social Network,* **Main Title,
"Hand Covers Bruise" (excerpt)**

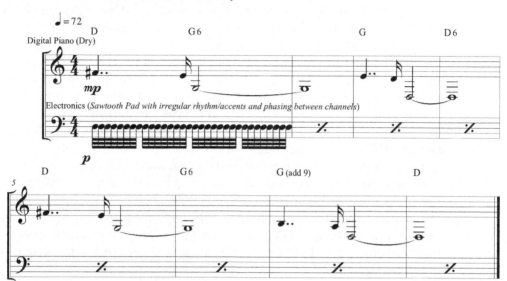

If your senior composition instructor or a trusted mentor told you that all you had to do to win an Academy Award was write these eight bars of completely naked, unorchestrated music, you would probably think he was nuts. And he might be, if he failed to mention that the eight bars were written for a very high-profile, hot-button film about the founding of Facebook, directed by David Fincher and featuring a definitive performance by Jesse Eisenberg as an antisocial computer prodigy who "can't find two friends to rub together." It certainly didn't hurt that the lead composer was a rock star whose work with Nine Inch Nails many in the cinema community had found compelling. But I'm inclined to think that the score would have been recognized even if the only name in the credits was Atticus Ross.

Why?

First of all, audacity inspires admiration. Musical audacity can be characterized by vaulting ambition and virtuosity, as in Elliot Goldenthal's *Alien 3* score, or boldness of concept, as in Hans Zimmer's *Inception* (see page 74). But in these stripped-down, deconstructed, and deeply ironic times, it's the audacity of simplicity that is more likely to draw positive attention (see, for example, Nicholas Britell's score for the 2016 Best Picture winner *Moonlight*). At the time of this book's writing, midway through the second decade of the twenty-first century, audiences tend to find complexity suspect. Musical "spaces" create openings through which our mind can wander and even impose our own design. All the more so if those spaces are demarcated by the sort of agitated but strangely familiar drone texture that underlies the piano melody in this cue: it's "the Gentle Hum of Anxiety," as Reznor/Ross label it in another cue. Old-school film composers are apt to describe this kind of thing as "wallpaper," but is it wallpaper if it weaves a spell, or is it something closer to the hypnotic effect of a Middle Eastern mosaic?

The piano melody itself, performed utterly without expression (and without reverberation) using a stock digital piano patch, has a surprising tenderness, and a pathos that no one who has ever sat alone in a college dormitory on a Saturday night will fail to sense. It's accentuated by both the tentative, geek-boy quality lent by the double-dotted quarter-notes—seemingly waiting until the very last moment to move to the next note—and the long drops: first a major sixth, then an octave. I remarked in the discussion of the *Basic Instinct* motif that without the octave displacement of the last two eighth-notes, it might have been far less striking. Something similar is going on here. Those drops are surprising, and as has already been said, musical semioticians contend that *meaning* results, in part, from surprise. Harmonically, the theme could not be simpler. The I–VI–VI–I chord changes I've written into the reduction are only *implied* by the overtones created when certain keys are held down. There is no accompaniment other than the edgy drone, to which low strings are added later in the track, and that drone is a straight D.

Again, let's be clear: Trent Reznor is neither Jerry Goldsmith nor Jonny Greenwood, and would probably be the first to say so. It wouldn't surprise me, given his nature as an artist, if his reaction to being awarded an Oscar for *The Social Network* were a huge case of survivor's guilt, or a case of the "imposter syndrome." We're not going to hear him writing anything like *The Matrix* in years to come. But he did create a piece of music that lodged itself in the brains of his audience, and from that, we can all learn.

The Power of Brass

To wrap this chapter up, we'll examine two pieces whose compositional signature is defined by aggressive brass, but are in all other respects completely different, the signature thematic elements from the James Bond series, and Hans Zimmer's mighty and monolithic homage to Edith Piaf's "Non, je ne regrette rien" in *Inception*.

The story of how the über-iconic Bond theme came to be is part drama, part farce, and a lot that we'll probably never know. Eon Productions, in the persons of the legendary "Cubby" Broccoli and Harry Saltzman, approached a well-regarded British tunesmith by the name of Monty Norman (born Monty Noserovitch in working-class Stepney) to pen a theme for the very first entry in the Bond franchise, *Dr. No* (1962). Norman was no piker. He'd fronted British big bands as a singer for the likes of Ted Heath and Stanley Black, written hits for fifties pop idols, such as Tommy Steele and Cliff Richard, and had authored a successful West End musical (*Expresso Bongo*, later a 1959 film with Laurence Harvey). He was a logical choice for the Bond filmmakers: then, as now, producers often turned to pop songwriters for movie music, and then, as now, the results often require "doctoring."

According to what now stands as the official record, Norman delivered to

Broccoli and Saltzman about 90 percent of what have since become the definitive Bond signatures: the big, brassy E minor 6/9 chord stabs that open almost every popular band arrangement of the theme, the rising and falling B/C/C-sharp/C string line (harmonized here as Em–C–Em6–C), the Gatling gun/surf guitar that inevitably accompanies Bond's dead aim in the opening titles, and the vampy four-bar swing melody that mixes so perfectly with Bond's dry martinis. The British courts have ruled in Monty Norman's favor over ardent protests from John Barry, composer of the underscore for eleven Bond films, beginning with *Dr. No*, as well as cowriter of some of the franchise's biggest hit songs, including *Goldfinger*.

According to Barry's testimony, he was handed a lead sheet with Monty Norman's thematic ideas roughly laid out, and asked by the producers to arrange, rewrite as necessary, and produce the recording, which he did for the flat fee of £250. (The guitarist on that famous session was paid £6.) Barry was a seasoned big band arranger and first-rate trumpet player who had studied jazz arrangement with another iconic figure, Bill Russo, and done charts for the same Ted Heath Band that Monty Norman had fronted. He was also a staff orchestrator for EMI and had done songwriting and scoring for films featuring another fifties pop star, Adam Faith, including the immortal *Beat Girl* (1960). He contends that he cowrote the Bond theme, and he certainly had the chops to do it. But we will never know. John Barry is dead and Monty Norman is eighty-seven.

Two things are clear beyond any doubt: the identifying signature of the Bond series music is as much a "sound" as it is a "theme." The second thing is this: whoever *did* compose the lines of music excerpted in Figure 3.12 can lay claim, now and in the hereafter, to having created one of the most widely recognized musical signifiers in cinematic history. Strike up the band anywhere from Tulsa to Taipei and listeners will take the same message from the music: sex and danger (inseparably bound), savoir faire, pluck, wit, and a certain reckless daring—all of which Western culture has largely drilled out of the corps or relegated to parody, but which we secretly (men and women alike) long for (witness the continued worldwide popularity of the Bond franchise). How did Monty Noserovitch and John B. Prendergast achieve this?

They had a couple of things working for them. Musical tropes and style signatures associated with a well-defined epoch have staying power. Think of the Gay Nineties or the Roaring Twenties, or even the Renaissance. In the case of Bond, that epoch is the early, pre-Woodstock sixties of cool jazz and cold war, John F. Kennedy and Marilyn Monroe, cigarettes and vodka, and the last licks of the Beat Era.

Figure 3.12. Excerpt from opening of the James Bond theme

Figure 3.13. Excerpt from opening of the James Bond theme (continued)

The first of these period signifiers is visible on the very first downbeat. The key signature is E minor, and reading the opening harmony as an embellished E minor chord, we have—as "melody"—a strongly accented F-sharp to E motif in the brass. This prominent use of the second scale degree as an embellishment of a tonic minor chord is an unmistakable signpost to the late jazz era and the distinctively moody drama of the decade of 1952 to 1962 that gave us *A Streetcar Named Desire* (composer: Alex North), *On the Waterfront* and *West Side Story* (composer: Leonard Bernstein), *Rebel Without a Cause* and *East of Eden* (composer: Leonard Rosenman), *Walk on the Wild Side* (composer: Elmer Bernstein), and such singer-songwriters as Gene Pitney (*Town Without Pity*). The image that goes to the amygdalae and hippocampi (both part of the brain's limbic system) is a dark, rain-slicked street, a man lighting a cigarette below as a woman observes from a lighted window above, some bad business between them, and a heartache that must be hidden.

When you deliver this sonority with the kind of muscle used in the *Bond* theme—*fortissimo* with a "rooftop" accent and punctuated by trap kit and lots of reverb, it makes a statement that is at once deadly serious and thrillingly fun.

The most identifiable expression in the Bond lexicon, however, is probably the phrase taken up by the violins in measures 3–4. This is the element without which the *Bond* theme would not be the *Bond* theme. As in the opening brass statement, a characteristic jazz dissonance, the sixth (C-sharp over E minor) is used to lend both mystery and urgency. That feels like a serious statement. The arrangemental element that tells us we don't need to take it all *completely* seriously are the trombone punches on the offbeats, which lend the passage a kind of swagger.

Enter the Duane Eddy meets Dick Dale guitar, played on a hollow-body Clifford Essex Paragon Deluxe and purportedly miked through a Vox AC15 amplifier. That slightly "exotic" feel is no accident. One of the things that cinched Monty Norman's copyright claim was his insistence that he'd gotten the idea for the lick from a vocal melody he'd previously written for a film set in India. And the "surf guitar" had long had an Asian connection. Dick Dale, the original surf punk, knew the *oud* before he knew the guitar, and his signature song, "Misirlou," proudly wears its Middle Eastern ancestry. The twangy, rapid-fire picking used in the Bond theme guitar part resembles performance technique on many non-Western instruments: not only the *oud*, but the *zither* and hammered instruments, such as the *santoor* and *cimbalom*. Bear in mind that the Bond films were the first truly *international* film franchise, and that their backdrop was the cold war—the paradigmatic Occident v. Orient confrontation. Using the Main Title music to relay signals corresponding with a western audience's presuppositions about "the sinister East" would not have been a bad move, and in the 2012 edition of the series, *Skyfall*, composer Thomas Newman takes things considerably further by incorporating elements of authentic Middle Eastern *taksim*. One other thing is for certain about the original: in the setting of Barry's arrangement and the trademark Main Title visuals, Monty Norman's guitar becomes not just a piece of exotic ornamentation, but the musical signifier of an automatic weapon.

Inception

Closing this chapter with the musical séance for Edith Piaf, hidden in plain sight in Hans Zimmer's Möbius strip of a score for *Inception,* is entirely fitting. The doomsday two-note brass motif that was born from the ultra-stretched 12/8 rhythm of the original 1960 Piaf recording of "Non, je ne regrette rien" became an Internet museme overnight. And this, it appears, was just as intended by Mr. Zimmer.

"I had to go and extract these two notes out of a recording. We got the original master out of the French national archives, and then found some crazy scientist who would actually go and take that one cell out of the musical DNA," he says.

The song, which is Edith Piaf's most anthemic (it was adopted by the French Foreign Legion), had been written into Christopher Nolan's script as a kind of "Easter egg," or if you prefer, a MacGuffin.[5] "Non, je ne regrette rien" has the kind of loping "dotted" rhythm, characteristic of mid-century French *chanson*, that can feel simultaneously like a march and a waltz. It's a *stand-up-and-feel-your-chest-swell* song that is, at the same time, intensely personal and poignant. It was used, in all its scratchy vinyl glory, as an audible warning to Dom Cobb (Leonardo DiCaprio) and his crew of oneironauts. The dream was ending: time to get out. "You realize," Zimmer explains, "that the elements we extracted from the Piaf song are the

---

5 A "MacGuffin" in films and narrative fiction is a plot device—often an object, person, or place, but just as easily a song—that served as an "unexplained driving force" for the protagonist, and may have meaning only to him/her. The term is folk Scottish in origin, but was made popular by director Alfred Hitchcock.

way you get from one dream level to the next." Those elements, lifted from the song's introductory vamp, were interpolated throughout the score, most markedly in the cue titled "Half-Remembered Dream."

The appeal that the lyric must have had for the director is fairly obvious: it's a song about what we've left behind, and just as important, how to move past it. *With my memories, I light the fire . . . I don't need them anymore.* It embodies a uniquely French sort of romantic existentialism: fatalistic, but leaving room for that one last chance at love. Despite all the pain, all the loss and disappointment . . . *Today, it begins with you.* That longing for another chance is what drives Dom Cobb, who has left behind something he fears he can never recapture. His sole motivation—notwithstanding all the plot mechanics that pull him in other directions—is to get back to the wife and child he has lost. So, in terms of musical signs, he is also (and sometimes quite literally) *driven* by the song and by the score's ingenious allusions to it.

When film music fans think of *Inception*, they inevitably think of monstro-brass: trombones the size of an oil tanker. And indeed, the sonic fingerprint of the work, a hyperdense layering of live orchestral performances, electronics, Johnny Marrs's guitar, and elements from the massive Zimmer sample library, is heavy on metal.

The cue I've thumb-nailed (see Figure 3.14) includes that brass signature, used in a dramatically very meaningful way, but it is also one of the shortest and most ephemerally delicate pieces in the score. I alluded earlier to the difficulty of making conventional reductions of contemporary hybrid scores, and that difficulty increases exponentially with a Hans Zimmer score, which may comprise hundreds and hundreds of tracks. It's impossible to depict in a reduction even a fragment of what we're actually hearing. What I've attempted instead is a kind of bare bones "schematic" of "Half-Remembered Dream," highly condensed in both content and bar count.

Figure 3.14 Hans Zimmer, *Inception*,
"Half-Remembered Dream" (excerpt/fragment)

Since Hans Zimmer maintains that, for him, *Inception* was a meditation on time and love more than an investigation of the nature of dreams, I trust he'll forgive my elliptical and compressed approach to his music. What I wish for students and other readers to take away from this snapshot is a sense of Zimmer's architecture, as well as his unwavering fidelity to concept. Christopher Nolan's *Inception* is a masterwork of cinematic architecture as much as it is a masterwork of cinematic imagination, and it's no accident that he has found his match in a composer for whom the *conceptual* element of composing music is paramount.

Notice first that the "Non, je ne regrette rien" rhythm is present from bar one. This is not literally—aurally—what happens in the cue, but I've inserted it on the percussion stave to show that it's the "skeleton" behind everything else. I can't say for certain that Hans and his team beat time in 12/8 meter, but that's the time signature of the Piaf original, and furthermore, Zimmer had this to say:

"Just for the game of it," Mr. Zimmer said, "all the music in the score is subdivisions and multiplications of the tempo of the Edith Piaf track. So I could slip into half-time; I could slip into a third of a time. Anything could go anywhere. At any moment I could drop into a different level of time."[6]

The recording serves up a deep well of ambient sound, and as this is an aural transcription, some note values and chord spellings may be off. Some of the chord tones shown may in fact be overtones brought out by recording technique or by the formant of the instruments (whether acoustic or electronic). What *is* entirely faithful to the cue's construction is that the fateful brass figure that signals immersion in a wholly new level of dreaming is "bracketed" on either side, first by piano, then by high strings, a P5 apart but playing the same exquisitely simple and deeply affecting sequence.

For some composers, the power of music to convey not just emotional truth but *meaning* may be secondary to more aesthetic/structural considerations. But Hans Zimmer has always been a spinner of wild ideas and philosophies whose medium of communication just happens to be notes. It does not seem at all out of character that the book he read to prepare for *Inception* was Douglas Hofstadter's *Gödel, Escher, Bach*: "a metaphorical fugue on minds and machines in the spirit of Lewis Carroll."

Let's return for a moment to the lonely road of this chapter's opening, to the hands of our protagonist gripping the wheel, and the waving figure seen through his windshield. The single most important thing for an aspiring film composer to know is that *anything* he or she writes—even if it's nothing more than a drone or a pulse—will have meaning to an audience. While the visual elements of film supply *information*, it's often left to the audio track—dialogue, sound effects, and music—to provide *meaning*. Whatever we erect between the bar lines will be a sign, and given the ambiguity of a visual such as the one described, music may be the *only* clear signpost on this deserted stretch of highway. This is what fascinates and frightens filmmakers about music: its capacity to alter completely the interpretation of a scene by its percipients. This is also why they react so strongly and viscerally to codal incompetence; that is, music that sends the wrong signal. (*"No! No! I hate it! Get rid of that sound, whatever it is!"*)

In the hands of a skillful composer, this capacity for *significance* is a powerful tool, and one whose use must stem from the fullest understanding of the story.

---

6 Dave Itzkoff, *New York Times*, July 28, 2010, https://artsbeat.blogs.nytimes.com/2010/07/28/hans-zimmer-extracts-the-secrets-of-the-inception-score/.

FOUR PERFUME

THE SCENT OF MURDER

V.O. of Narrator: By the age of five, Jean-Baptiste still could not talk,
but he had been born with a talent that made him unique among mankind . . .
Increasingly, he became aware that his phenomenal sense of smell
was a gift that had been given to him and him alone . . .

Photograph by Michael Roud

Tykwer, Heil, and Klimek

The narrator is describing the protagonist of *Perfume: The Story of a Murderer*, German director Tom Tykwer's 2006 adaptation of Patrick Süskind's best-selling novel. He is Jean-Baptiste Grenouille, born beneath a fishmonger's stall in the teeming and profoundly smelly Paris of 1738. Although Jean-Baptiste has no body scent of his own, he possesses the uncanny ability to sniff out and identify any odor produced by God or man. He is, in other words, a freak of nature, and this presents a unique challenge to composer and filmmaker alike, since the entire story is seen through his eyes, or rather, smelled through his nose. Jean-Baptiste lives for one thing alone: to "capture," and in some manner, to possess, everything he smells. This lust for scent, and not some intrinsic evil, is what leads him to the act of murder. In truth, he is a perfect innocent.

In the unusual case of *Perfume*, composer and filmmaker are, in part, one and the same, as credit for the score is divided equally among Tykwer and the two writing partners with whom he electrified global cinema in 1998's *Run, Lola, Run*: Johnny Klimek and Reinhold Heil. All were participants in the heady postreunification culture of 1990s Berlin. Heil had been keyboardist and cowriter for the Nina Hagen Band, a touchstone of early eighties theatrical punk, and had produced the 1983 Europop hit "99 Luftballons." Klimek was an Australian expat whose Berlin-based band, the Other Ones, had charted two new-wave hits in 1987. Tykwer's biography leaves fewer clues about his musical background, but the integral role played by music in all of his cinematic efforts leaves no doubt about where his heart lies. He has said on more than one occasion that he believes the process of score composition begins with the writing of the script, and when Klimek, Heil, and Tykwer joined forces for his 1997 film *Winter Sleepers*, they inaugurated a methodology of combined music and story development that has remained their modus operandi all the way through their most recent collaboration on 2012's *Cloud Atlas*.

However considerable the musical talents and instincts this trio brought to their partnership, the fact was that none of them had ever authored a fully orchestral film score, much less the sort of "period score" that an elaborate costume drama like *Perfume* seems to beg for. That something as delicate and sophisticated as the score we're about to explore emerged from their third effort has a touch of the supernatural about it. It also argues for an aesthetic of film music that we see indicated again and again in the success of such composers as Danny Elfman, Clint Mansell, Gustavo Santaolalla, and Trent Reznor: an effective film score is at least 50 percent *conceptual art*. The author needs to know, often before a single note is written, how the musical story goes—or at least, the *kind* of story it will be. In some manner, an *image* of the score—what psychologists and metaphysicians called an *imago*—must preexist the thing itself. No amount of musical technique, melodic invention, or theoretical training will produce a great score if the concept is weak (not to say these things don't help immeasurably in actually getting through it!). If this hasn't been demonstrated already by our investigations of *Vertigo* and *To Kill a Mockingbird*, and glances at scores like *The Good, the Bad and the Ugly*, it will be demonstrated by *Perfume*. Because not only did Klimek, Heil, and Tykwer dive headfirst into the symphonic world occupied by such forces as Simon Rattle and the Berlin Philharmonic, who performed the score, they set for themselves the task of creating music that would evoke—or more precisely, *capture*—the realm of *scent*, the subtlest and most ancient of our senses.

There were precedents for this kind of "synesthetic music."[1] Claude Debussy and such symbolists as Alexander Scriabin come to mind, but these were composers of high art and vaulting ambition who'd been taught from childhood how to use the orchestral palette. If you have the intellectual muscle, however (which our trio clearly did) to *imagine* how a Debussy or Scriabin might have chosen his musical colors, then the rest—bit by bit and note by note—can be learned. Film score composers are, by nature, hungry learners. They have to be. The assignment demands it. And then there is the mysterious effect that comes into play when multiple creative minds merge. The iconic example is John Lennon and Paul McCartney, whose work together was far greater than the sum of its parts. *Perfume* brought three minds into play toward a single goal, and as always in this craft, important support came from their B team, including orchestrator Gene Pritzker and Jonathan Levi Shanes, to whom we owe the engraved score from which the reductions used here were made.

Taken as a seamless whole, the *Perfume* score seems "scented" of Frederick Delius and Camille Saint-Saëns (a composer whose work we touched on in the last chapter, and whose impact on film music is underappreciated), and this only shows that its authors were aware of their stylistic predecessors. In other respects, however, it represents a very new approach. Most of the music was conceived *and even recorded* before a single frame of film had been shot, much less edited, and then treated as raw material for processing in ways that are more associated with electronica than "symphonica." There are moments in the score that sound as if the orchestral waveform had been broken down spectrally and then built back up again with the addition of purely digital and/or electronic elements. This technique of "scoring the script" (or even the *treatment*) as series of "suites" or tone paintings, and then tailoring them to the finished film, is becoming increasingly popular even with such mainstream composers as Hans Zimmer. It's both a marked departure from the traditional process of underscoring "locked picture" and a concession to the reality that in the digital era, the picture never "locks." What is surprising is that it yields a score that feels so entirely organic to the movie.

---

1 Synesthesia is a neurological phenomenon in which stimulation of one sensory or cognitive pathway leads to automatic, involuntary experiences in a second sensory or cognitive pathway; e.g., "seeing sounds" or "tasting colors." In the case of *Perfume*, it is hearing scent. The word means "union of the senses." Alexander Scriabin considered himself a synesthete.

In brief, the story is this: Jean-Baptiste, after a near-brush with death beneath the fishmonger's stand, is raised in an orphanage and indentured to a brutal tanner as an adolescent. His remarkably resilient constitution allows him to survive the tannery, and finally, as a young man of nineteen or twenty, he is cut loose to wander in the streets of Paris, where a seemingly infinite variety of new scents are available to his hungry nose. Fittingly, the first major theme to be introduced accompanies this scene, and the cue is entitled "Streets of Paris." Here is a distillation of the first eight bars of the cue.

**Figure 4.1. *Perfume: The Story of a Murderer,*
"Streets of Paris," bars 11–18 ⓐ 14:40**

The "Streets of Paris" theme enters fully on a harp glissando (these play a major role throughout the score in gesturing "the release of scent") at 14:40 into the film, with the melody at *forte* in the violins over a stately I–VI–III–V chord progression. In a manner somewhat reminiscent of Morricone's Main Title music for *The Mission*, a two-bar phrase is repeated three times, then varied by a single M2 drop from E to D on the final beats of the last two measures, bringing us in timeless fashion to the dominant chord. The reduction in Figure 4.1 shows the straightforward counterpoint in the lower strings. Nothing musically revolutionary here, and that's fine: when stating a theme for the first time, it's usually best to state it plainly. Still, there is something going on . . .

What makes the entrance of the melody in bar 11 so satisfying and conveys the sense that a whole new world has opened to Jean-Baptiste is that *twice* in the preceding ten bars, the two-note motive (G to F-sharp) around which the melody is written is foreshadowed in a very different harmonic and emotional context. Here is what happens in bars 7–10:

Figure 4.2. *Perfume: The Story of a Murderer*, "Streets of Paris," bars 7–10 @ 14:24

I have octave-doubled the motive in the right hand of the piano part just to bring attention to the fact that it's the principal voice—as it should be since it's preparing the way for the theme. Contrary to appearances, the F-sharp is not functioning as any sort of conventional leading tone. The thematic melody enters on a C major chord, and the broken chord in the left hand of the piano in the preceding bar 10 is clearly the V of C major. Nothing about this thematic setup is conventional except perhaps for the big harp glissando that occurs over its final two bars (not shown here).

For clarity, the reduction in Figure 4.2 also eliminates the artificial harmonics that in the concert score are sounding the written pitches in each section of the strings. These create an effect that is far more ethereal and far less discordant than it appears on the page. Remember the concept: music as scent. The dramatic reason for both the dissonance and the string harmonics is that Jean-Baptiste is being overwhelmed to the point of dizziness by all the new odors (both good and bad, but he makes no distinction—it's all perfume to him). Like the proverbial kid in a candy shop, he is trying to grab them all at once. The harmonies indicated by the broken chords are the same as in the full thematic statement that follows: C–Am–Em–G. But the strings are in a very different place. I'm not sure it's useful to attempt any sort of harmonic analysis: the string writing here is clearly for effect and not function. And because *Perfume*, like Hans Zimmer's *Inception*, is a score assembled from many layers of both orchestral and electronic tracks in which a range of parameters—pitch, phase, timbre, etc.—have been altered through digital signal processing (DSP), a reduction such as the one in Figure 4.2 can only approximate what we hear. The point here is to illustrate how the composers have chosen to introduce their first important theme.

As Jean-Baptiste staggers through the crowded streets, we hear the narrator say, "The goal was to possess everything the world had to offer in the way of odors . . . the only condition being that they were new ones." Here the scene opens up into a kaleidoscopic montage of scent sources: oysters being opened, wigs being powdered, exotic fabrics, flowers, wine, pastries and rotten teeth. The theme now morphs into its third statement, this one animated by the winds as shown in Figure 4.3. Here we see the strongest effort thus far to make music an olfactory experience. The melody now shifts to the horns (with oboe), thus clearing the higher register for the woodwinds to portray the scents borne on the warm breeze. The reduction in Figure 4.3 shows only these instruments, but both melody and harmony are amply supported throughout the orchestration. The passage is repeated in the original concert score, measures 29–36. Notice that the flute and oboe parts are voiced so as support an A minor 7 to E minor 7 shift in harmony from bars 29–30 to 31–32. The line is written mostly in thirds, but switches to fourths or even M2s to maintain the chord.

**Figure 4.3. *Perfume: The Story of a Murderer*,
"Streets of Paris," bars 29–30 ⓐ 15:37**

This orderly pitch distribution in multiple lines of parallel harmony is a feature of the score and part of its diaphanous quality. We'll see it most memorably used in the "Distilling Roses" cue (Figure 4.7) that accompanies Jean-Baptiste's mastery of the art of perfumery and the "Perfume Distilled" cue that closes the film after his final apotheosis into a spirit of scent. What's notable here isn't the ornamental use of high woodwind runs to "animate" a melody. We see that in the romantic repertoire and hear it in any John Williams score, especially when someone or something is in flight. But in *Perfume*, this device is used to convey a purely subjective, internal experience, and it works.

Figure 4.4. Perfume: The Story of a Murderer, "Streets of Paris," bars 31–32

This simple but effective use of a musical *isomorph* to portray the way scent is carried on the wind offers a valuable hint to composers faced with illustrating sensory experiences like "a sudden chill," "a wave of heat," "a gentle touch," "a burning wound," or such ephemeral emotional states as panic, longing, reverie, or the sting of desire. We can look for a physical analog or metaphor for the feeling, and then search for the musical expression that best represents that physical state, action or form. Examples might be:

- blood *runs cold*
- *gripped* by panic
- *waves* of longing
- *throbbing* with anticipation
- *racked* with pain
- *shrill* with anger
- *fluttering* with anticipation

Care has to be taken not to fall into cliché or mimicry. A too-precise illustration will come across to sophisticated filmgoers as hackneyed or overly literal—and that's only if it makes it past the filmmakers, who are likely to describe it as "on the nose" or "over the top." The first half a century of cinema taught us to recognize the signs; now they can be given with considerable subtlety. But subtle does not mean invisible, nor does it require the kind of musical flatlining we sometimes hear in bad TV drama. If you're the sort of composer who keeps sketchbooks, it's not a bad idea to catalog some of the most common sensations, states of mind, moods, and feelings and sketch out musical shapes, gestures, clusters, and figures that come to mind when you think of them.

The next major cue in the film introduces the first murder victim, and both the scene and its music are justly admired for their combination of sensuality and menace. The title is "Pélissier/The Girl with the Plums" (in some scores, these cues are split). Drawn down a side street by a new and exotic fragrance, Jean-Baptiste finds himself staring longingly into the shop window of the celebrated perfumer Pélissier, who is at that very moment testing a drop of his latest creation, called Amor and Psyche, on the wrists of two ladies of Parisian society. Jean-Baptiste has discovered something wondrous: a synthesis of scents.

The combination of wonderment, childlike curiosity, and the birth of a new sensibility in Jean-Baptiste as he gazes from the street into the diamond light of the perfumer's and observes the enraptured women is captured beautifully by a bit of musical exotica that is reminiscent of the (deleted) opening bars of *To Kill a Mockingbird* in its use of Asian modality (the mode is clearly minor based on A, but with the fourth scale degree omitted). A reduced excerpt is shown in Figure 4.4, "Pélissier."

Figure 4.5. *Perfume: The Story of a Murderer,* M08/09, "Pélissier," bars 43–46

Following this, bowed *crotales* and *tam-tam* signal the entrance of a new mood and a new fragrance even more compelling than Amor and Psyche. Jean-Baptiste turns his nose from the window as Plum Girl passes, invisible but for the scent she leaves behind. A soprano emerges from the mysterious sound bed (nothing sounds as mysterious as bowed percussion) as if capturing the new scent in a single voice and in the Italian phrase *nel semplice segreto che si libera una carezza* (in the simple secret that frees a caress), sung to the pitches that will evolve into the next important theme. It begins with a stark, four-note phrase: B-flat(4)–F(5)–B-flat(4)–E(4), the second leap's lowered fifth telling us we're entering darker territory. The phrase is repeated, and then on the words *si libera* and our first good look at the girl with the plums, the consequent phrase relieves the tension by resolving the dim5 to a P4 (E-flat). Up to this point, the editor has revealed only small pieces of the Plum Girl, but now we see that the bouquet that has intoxicated Jean-Baptiste arises from her virginal décolletage. It's in the skin. In a rallentando, the soprano climbs in fourths from B-flat to E-flat to A-flat on *"una carezza,"* and is then left absolutely alone for a full bar. At 19:06, she is joined by choir, strings, harp, horn solo, and clarinets (as well as electronics) for the full statement of the theme (see Figure 4.6).

Figure 4.6. *Perfume: The Story of a Murderer*, M10,
"The Girl with the Plums," bars 78–89, @ 19:06
(bar numbers 31–40 in split score)

Figure 4.6B. *Perfume: The Story of a Murderer,* M10, "The Girl with the Plums," bars 90–93 @ 19:06

The melody introduced by the soprano soloist is now octave-doubled in the first violins and given added luster by the choir. Now we hear what that flatted fifth meant in terms of harmony, and it is exciting and *instantly* memorable. A chord change from G-flat major7 to C7 is a very exotic animal. With reference to the preceding paragraph, it isn't *unprecedented*. Remember, the trio's referents for this score are such composers as Debussy,

A Note About Originality

A curious thing happens when film music is discussed with academic music theorists. As often as not, they take the position that it has offered the world absolutely nothing that hasn't been done better before—usually somewhere between 1850 and 1930. For each example of bold invention a film music professional can cite, the classical scholar can name a half a dozen forerunners from the concert music world. Bernard Herrmann's diminished harmonies? Thank Richard Wagner. His signature use of harmonies based on root movement in thirds? Wagner again, as well as Rimsky-Korsakov, Arthur Honegger, and others. Jerry Goldsmith's experiments in bitonality and virtuosic use of orchestral percussion? Bartók and Stravinsky. John Williams's masterful command of symphonic color? Richard Strauss. As with many broad generalizations made by educated people, there's an element of truth. Of course, there are antecedents, and no serious film composer who sets out to write an orchestral score ignores them. The master composers of what is known as the common practice period wrote for a musically literate audience of wealthy, propertied Europeans who were often familiar with the artist's body of work and had allowed it time to "steep" in their mind. Film composers write for filmgoers, and must communicate more or less instantly. It's this imperative to telegraph immediately to the brain (and heart)—usually cited as shortcoming of film music—that has engendered its distinctive vocabulary. The best film composers have extracted techniques often used only incidentally in concert works and put them front and center. This is very much the case with *Perfume.*

Ravel, Saint-Saëns, and Delius. But it's pretty striking to hear those chords in block fashion, over the image of a beautiful plum vendor being *stalked* by a savant through the backstreets of eighteenth-century Paris. If the scene itself were not so exotic and deliciously twisted, we might almost feel this harmony to be too rich, but remember: we're in Jean-Baptiste's head, and his head is delirious with scent.

The high strings seem to "swim" toward the leaps (I've tried to indicate this with glissando lines in Figure 4.5, though they aren't written as glissandos in the concert score). The supporting string section "breathes" the chords in a way that's as organic as it is purely musical. Look at the continual crescendo-decrescendo in all the sections, like the human breast rising and falling. The harp simply and delicately keeps things in motion. And when the harmony drops a minor third to E-flat, and then falls to D-flat7, we know Jean-Baptiste is "in love"—as much as his odd psychology will allow him to be.

Even the most striking chromatic chord changes usually involve a common tone. If they don't, the chords are known in neo-Riemannian theory as *hexatonic poles*[2] (e.g., a change from C minor to E major). This is the most radically disturbing chord change that can be made in the context of triadic harmony, and because film scoring demands subtlety so as not to pull the viewer out of the film, we won't hear it much. Far more useful to the film composer are chord changes based on chromatic inflection, mode mixing, or even bitonal relationships. The G-flat major7 to C7 progression that underlies the "A" phrase of the melody in "Girl with the Plums" requires three small moves from the root position G-flat maj7 chord, each of only a semitone: G-flat rises to G-natural while D-flat falls to C (this is another example of what I called "valving" in the chapter on *Mockingbird*—opening and closing like a bellows or an accordion, and this goes with the "breathing" implied by the cue). The F-natural that provides the major seventh in the first chord resolves down to E, as would be expected. The common tone is B-flat.

When the harmony is added, the stark, spectral sound of the a capella phrase retains its haunting quality but takes on elegance. We can almost imagine that Jean-Baptiste and the Plum Girl are Amor (Eros) and Psyche from the Greek myth. This elegance would evaporate without the common tone, and is enhanced by the M7 (F) embellishment of the G-flat chord and the M3 (E) of the C7 chord. The overall effect of the melody, harmony, choir, and orchestration is rapturous. So here is a question: if this kind of chromatic harmony has such a powerful effect, and if there is precedent for it in the work of romantic and impressionist composers, why don't we hear more of it in film music?

Part of the answer may be that most film composers simply don't listen to enough orchestral music that *isn't film music* (this is a far bigger problem

---

2   According to music theorist Richard Cohn, hexatonic poles are two triads, one major and one minor, derived from the same pitch set, a hexachord with the intervals 1–m3–M3–P5–m6–M7, but having no pitches in common. Simply put, a major triad and a minor triad that are a major third apart.

now than it used to be). But I think the better and truer answer comes from the things that ought always to affect the composer's choices most: *story values and drama*. Not many composers are offered scenes like this one: *In the streets of pre-Revolutionary Paris, a heartbreakingly sensual girl passes in the night, carrying a reed basket of ripe, golden plums, exuding the scent of girl-becoming-woman, and is pursued into the darkness of the poorer quarters by a strangely gifted man-creature who has no idea that she will be his first murder victim.*

So, it goes without saying that a composer couldn't write this cue for a contemporary romantic comedy, and that if he or she did, it would never work. Still, there's a lot we can learn from this cue that is applicable to many scoring situations. Notice how the main "heart-leaping" motif (B-flat–F–B-flat) remains the same in bars 86–87 of the reduction over the descending cello line (E–E-flat–D-flat) and progression to an E-flat7 harmony. Only one note changes. Likewise, in measures 90–92 of the reduction, the shape of the melody changes from musical leaps to musical "sighs": C-flat to B-flat to E-flat to A-flat, accompanied by chords, A-flat minor to B major7 (enharmonically notated here as C–flat major7) to D-flat7 that elegantly bring us back to the dominant of G-flat and the next statement of the theme.

It is at just about the thirty-two-and-a-half-minute mark that we first hear the melodic strand that will become the score's most haunting—and most musically enigmatic theme. Some days have passed in film time since the night Jean-Baptiste followed the scent of the Plum Girl, and then, out of panic and ignorance far more than malice, killed her. Fleeing the scene of the crime—after trying in vain to "scoop" the sublime scent from her corpse—he is collared by the brutal tanner and returned to his work in the hellish tannery.

In a new story thread, we meet the down-on-his-luck perfumer Baldini (Dustin Hoffman), whose best days seem to be behind him and who spends the day in an empty shop, dreaming of the day he'll create a scent to vanquish his rival, Pélissier, whose Amor and Psyche has claimed the heart of Parisian women. Baldini's last loyal assistant has brought him a sample of the celebrated perfume to test, and once he's alone, Baldini retires to his lab to analyze its ingredients—a process more art than science. He is able to identify a few of the oils and essences that form its *head chord* (the first impression) and *heart chord* (the "theme" of the perfume), but those in the critical *bass chord* (the lingering trail) elude him. He's lost his touch. It's important for us to know these terms of art, both for understanding the story and for decoding the score, because they relate the craft of perfumery directly to music. And the music we hear as the old master tries to break down the chords is the perfectly symmetrical double helix of the score's musical DNA: mirrored eighth-notes running up and down a B-flat minor chord with an added ninth, or in this case, since the introductory cue is in 3/8, dotted quarter-notes instead of eighths.

From such simple but elegant ideas are great themes born. Earlier in this book, I mentioned the powerful effect that the second degree of a natural minor scale has when heard directly over the root in a tonic minor triad, or directly before or after the root in an arpeggio. This effect has been used to great purpose in countless works, but never so successfully as in film music. The (flatted) sixth degree of a natural minor scale, used the same way, has a similar but less astringent effect, and is even more widely used in films with a dark or somber undertone (think: John Carpenter's *Halloween* theme as an iconic example). A case could be made that the Aeolian second and sixth, the Lydian fourth, and now, thanks to Thomas Newman and the rebirth of modality in film music, the flat seventh, are the most important pitches in the film composer's palette. But that would mean taking them out of context, and as Baldini learns in this scene, context is everything when analyzing *chords*. We find our place in music by reference to what's around it. A pitch, isolated from all others, has no more meaning than an essence isolated in a perfume. The possibilities for blending essences and pitches haven't yet—and may never—be exhausted. And so each time a film composer finds a new way to assemble the puzzle, it is well worth a look.

The basic cell, which for identification purposes we'll call the "Essence" theme, is D-flat(5)–F–B-flat–C–D-flat(6)–C–B-flat–F, landing back on a B-flat minor chord. It looks like this when harmonized an m6 and P5 *below* the melody, as it typically is in the film. (Note: harmonizing "from below" in a more or less parallel manner was a characteristic of Renaissance forms, such as organum; it was also characteristic of early Beatles harmonies!)

Figure 4.7.

Now watch what happens.

What Baldini needs to recover his greatness is a godsend. A muse. A miracle. And he gets it one day, when a filthy and famished, but very determined Jean-Baptiste barges into his shop and declares, in his halting language, "I can make Amor and Psyche for you, Master. But I can make something even better." He goes immediately to work, pulling down essences from the dusty shelves and riffing like a great jazz player. In a matter of minutes, Jean-Baptiste presents a finished *new* scent to a stunned but still dubious Baldini. Alone in his shop after Jean-Baptiste has returned to the tannery, the old *parfumier* samples the improvised creation and is transported to an earthly paradise. *Now* he believes. Having demonstrated his uncanny olfactory skills to Baldini's satisfaction, Jean-Baptiste is finally freed from his enslavement to the tanner and taken on as assistant, and the two begin to work together on a new scent. First, however, Baldini must school his new protégé in the art of the three chords. Each chord contains four essences, or "notes," composing a finished scale of twelve tones, just as in music. But an ancient legend, Baldini explains, tells us that the *ultimate scent*—one that would enrapture the entire world—contains a mysterious thirteenth essence.

We know from this moment that Jean-Baptiste will set out to find the thirteenth essence, and we have a strong suspicion as to where he may look for it. "The soul of beings is in their scent," he says, repeating his teacher's lesson. "Teach me everything you know, and I'll make you the best perfume in the world."

At 49:48, more or less the beginning of the "second act," the "Essence" theme unfolds like a peacock's tail feathers in a remarkable cue entitled "Distilling Roses." This is in many ways also the signature "fragrance" of the score. Figure 4.8 provides the full score for measures 1–12. As the cue enters, Jean-Baptiste and Baldini are ferrying a boatload of vibrant red roses across the Seine to the laboratory for distillation. As the roses tumble through the river door into the lab's receiving chamber, Baldini says, "Imagine, Jean-Baptiste . . . ten thousand roses to produce one single ounce of essential oil! Now, take care not to damage them. *We must let them go to their deaths with their scent intact!*"

Inspiration is a difficult thing to pin down. As much as we—like Jean-Baptiste—might like to capture and bottle it, it's far too ephemeral. All we can say is that a couple of things seem to be true of inspiration: (1) It almost never comes from nowhere, like the proverbial stroke of lightning, nor does it arise from a passive state. Your chances of finding it are far better if you're operating at a very high level of function, like a runner with his "runner's high." (2) Inspiration is very often a "lock and key" affair. When you suddenly locate the key, the story reference, the *conceit*, or the stylistic model, the door swings open to genius. This cue, more than any in the film, opens that lock.

The first thing we see is the "Essence" theme, now rendered in three-part harmony. Notice the voice exchange that allows each part to retain the same shape. We can say that the "parent scale" in "Distilling Roses" is a B-flat melodic minor, but the seventh degree is altered freely. Look at the arpeggio in bar 2 of the celesta as if each vertical stack of eighth-notes was an individual chord. This isn't the way it was written, of course. It's in no ordinary sense a "chord progression," but organizing it this way helps us to understand its beauty. Each vertical spells B-flat minor except for those on the "and" of beats 2 and 3. These are dominant chords. But there is also another way to look at it.

Figure 4.8. *Perfume: The Story of a Murderer,* "Distilling Roses," bars 1–4 @ 49:48

Taking the perfumer's metaphor of the "three chords" a step further, suppose we read each of the three parts as a *broken chord*. The top line (a first inversion B-flat minor chord with an added ninth) is the "head chord." It forms the first impression. The middle line is the "heart chord." It's a B-flat minor triad in second inversion. But what then is the "bass chord?" The scent that lingers, as Baldini explains, "even for days." It's a broken B-flat mM7 chord, sometimes called a "Bartók chord," but known more famously in film music as the jarring, stabbing harmony that opens Bernard Herrmann's *Psycho* score (see Figure 1.8). Not just the chord "type," mind you, but this very pitch group.

Coincidence? Perhaps. But considering that the secret ingredient of the perfume that will be Jean-Baptiste's masterpiece is the essence of murdered virgins, maybe not.

Figure 4.8B. *Perfume: The Story of a Murderer,* "Distilling Roses," bars 5–8 ⓐ 49:48

Bar 6 introduces an elegantly cascading line for the violins and violas (boxed in red) that seems to blossom out of the celesta. Here we really are looking at something that Delius might have conceived. If we look once again at vertical structure, from violas up, we see these harmonies: B-flat minor/A-flat/F/B-flat minor, and then: E-flat/A-flat/F minor/C minor. The cadence on the last two quarter-notes in measure 10 seems to be D-flat M7 to C minor, but spellings can be ambiguous.

Figure 4.8C. *Perfume: The Story of a Murderer,*
"Distilling Roses Harmony," bars 8–10

And here is the conclusion of the thematic statement.

Figure 4.8D. *Perfume: The Story of a Murderer,*
"Distilling Roses," bars 9–12

There is always a risk that analyzing a piece of music will steal its
mystery. In the case of "Distilling Roses," the mystery lies not only in its

structure and vocabulary, but in its synthesis with story and character, and the "alchemy" that results. Horrible things are going to happen—are, in fact, *implicit* in the cue—but for the moment, all is beauty. The music paints a picture of desire, and what is more desirable than the "essence" of something? The scene ends, in fact, with a single drop of essence of rose falling from Baldini's alembic into the waiting glass vial. It's as if he had distilled the *elixir vitae*.

Once this conceptual choice had been made, what musical references and stylistic guideposts did Klimek, Heil, and Tykwer have available to them? As always, composers can and should consider (1) period and place; (2) the social milieu of the principal characters; (3) the genre of the story; and (4) any specific literary or musical references made in the script. (This applies, of course, to the entire score, not only to a single cue.) The novel on which the film is based tells us that Jean-Baptiste Grenouille was born in 1738, which makes the period of the story the late 1750s and early 1760s. This is the period of Couperin, Rameau, Telemann, and Scarlatti—high baroque. And there's no doubt that the social class of the major characters (excluding Jean-Baptiste) would have made them part of this world. And yet the music in the film sounds both more ancient and more strikingly modern. "Neo-Renaissance" might be a convenient handle. Complete with some nonfunctional harmonies, and electronics . . .

There is, in fact, one quite recent "classical" composer—and even a specific composition—that may have given our intrepid trio a hint or two. He is the Estonian "holy minimalist" Arvo Pärt, a one-time serialist who emerged in 1976 from a self-imposed four-year period of silence with an austere but deeply affecting new approach to composition he called *tintinnabuli* ("little bells") after the overtone characteristics and intermingling voices of church bells. During his isolation, he had abandoned modernism and devoted himself to studying the medieval and Renaissance polyphony of the Notre Dame organum school, and such composers as Guillaume de Machaut, Jacob Obrecht, and Josquin des Prez. His international breakthrough accompanied the release in 1984 on the German label ECM of the CD *Tabula Rasa*, a cultural event that a European artist like Tom Tykwer could not have been unaware of. Beginning in the early 1990s, Pärt's contemplative style became increasingly popular with serious filmmakers. Its influence can be felt particularly in the work of such composers as Thomas Newman, and more recently, in that of Danny Bensi and Saunder Jurriaans.

The very first piece to have a public performance after Pärt's monastic retreat was a two-page (15-bar) piano composition titled *Für Alina*, in honor of the young girl he'd written it for—a piece so simultaneously simple and confounding that it might have been the musical equivalent of a Zen koan. Pärt's *tintinnabulum* is a two-voiced approach: one voice triadic and the other "melodic," and in *Für Alina*, the counterpoint is strictly note against note. A child could play it, but a child might not understand it. Here is an excerpt, showing measures 5–7. In Pärt's score, as in plainchant, there is no time signature and no note stems: duration is left to the performer. There is, however, a perfectly symmetrical, "pyramidal" structure, wherein the number of "quarter-notes" increases with each measure, beginning with just two and increasing to seven before returning to its starting point. The use of time signatures in Figure 4.7 highlights this structure. The music emerges from and returns to silence.

Figure 4.9. Arvo Part, *Für Alina* (excerpt)

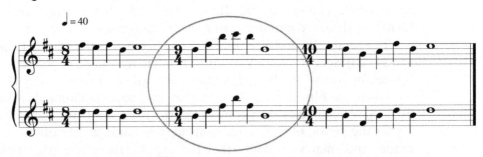

The resemblance between the shape and intervallic relationships in the middle bar of the *Für Alina* excerpt and "Essence" motif in *Perfume* could also, of course, be entirely coincidental. It's not as if this kind of line has a claim to being sui generis. But in a way, I hope that the kinship was deliberate. As discussed earlier in this chapter, nothing but good things can come of film composers being aware of what is "out there." And in the realm of music, things have a marvelous way of "getting into the air."

Whatever the influences that brought "Distilling Roses" into being, it remains one of the most singular pieces of film music created so far in the new century.

Not long after the "Distilling Roses" scene, Jean-Baptiste leaves Paris for the Provençal village of Grasse, the mecca of eighteenth-century perfumers' art. His purpose is to learn the mysterious technique of enfleurage, whereby subtle scents can be extracted by animal fat rather than through distillation. Baldini has suggested that this method may provide a more effective way to "capture" scent, as Jean-Baptiste passionately wishes to do. He doesn't know, of course, that the scent Jean-Baptiste most wants to capture is the one he first sniffed from the Plum Girl: the scent of virginal flesh.

It is in Grasse that the major dramatic events of the story occur, and where Grenouille earns notoriety, near-execution, and ultimately, a kind of deification. In a nutshell, he does indeed manage to use enfleurage to capture and bottle the sublime scent he's after, and in the process, distill the legendary thirteenth essence that Baldini told him would transport those who breathed its bouquet to an earthly paradise. That essence is in some manner the *innocence* of the girls he murders: the virgin daughters of the leading citizens of Grasse. He is apprehended within minutes of having completed the final chord of his new scent, and condemned to a grisly public execution for his many crimes—the worst of which seems to be his utter alienation from humanity. And yet, when Jean-Baptiste, wearing the perfume he has perfected, steps up to the gallows to meet his death before a crowd of thousands, he is suddenly perceived as an angelic presence, even a messiah figure. The executioner falls to his knees in obeisance, followed by all those in the crowd, who then proceed to engage in an orgy of love in his honor. In fact, *Perfume* may be able to claim the most epic orgy scene in cinema.

Alas for Jean-Baptiste, adulation and fame are not enough. The only genuine redemption would come from being fully human, and from being able to love and be loved as such. And so, he returns to Paris and the spot of his misbegotten birth, where in the film's most overtly allegorical scene, he pours the sacred elixir over his head and is literally devoured by the fervent love of the outcasts and rabble of prerevolutionary Paris. Here is the voice-over narration that introduces the film's final cue:

On the 25th of June, 1766, at around eleven o'clock at night, Grenouille entered the city of Paris through the Port d'Orleans, and like a sleepwalker, his olfactory memories drew him back to the place where he was born . . .

Figure 4.10. *Perfume: The Story of a Murderer,* "The Sacrifice" (excerpt) @ 2:14:33

As the ragged people, sated with their Eucharistic meal, wander away from the site of the feast—where nothing remains of Jean-Baptiste but the empty amphora—*Perfume* closes with the ethereal theme that opened it, performed by a chorus led by sopranos and altos, and accompanied only by percussion effect and low strings. It is a theme every bit as haunting and evocative as the others, and leads us into the extended reprise of "Distilling Roses" (titled "Perfume Distilled") that plays over the closing credits.

FIVE CARMEN IN HELL

DAVID NEWMAN'S *THE WAR OF THE ROSES*

David Newman

How does a composer ride the knife-edge between humor and horror in the darkest of comedies? How can a score possibly "keep it light" in a film that has a husband and wife trying—sometimes quite literally—to tear each other to pieces, and which concludes with a double *mariticide* on a crystal chandelier?

An attempt to answer those questions is the subject of this chapter. It's not an easy question, and *The War of the Roses* isn't an easy film, but if composer David Newman had to answer with a single bar of music, it might look like this:

Figure 5.1. *War of the Roses* motif

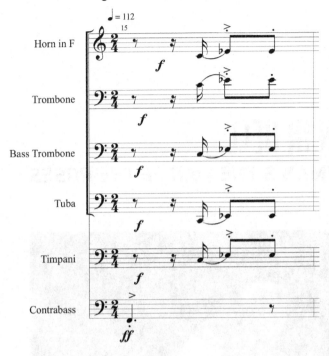

It almost seems to say, *"So there!"* if not something more unprintable. In no score we've examined so far has the meaning and importance of musical *gesture* come into such bold relief. In chapter 3, a gesture was defined as "a succinct and widely understood expression of meaning, attitude or sentiment," and that definition seems to apply to gestures of both the physical and musical kind. What we see in Figure 5.1, an extract of brass and percussion lines (with an added pedal note in the basses) from bar 15 of the Main Titles (1M1), is a bravura gesture that's also (1) a leitmotif; (2) an "intertextual reference;" and (3) a musical punch line. That's a lot to achieve in two beats. But Newman's no ordinary film composer, and *Roses* is no ordinary movie.

Here is the same gesture, this time subordinated to the chromatic melody that will become the Main Title theme. It's written in bars 10–14 of 1M1 as a solo for *bandoneon*, the traditional instrument of Argentine *tango*. Now the instrument itself carries gestural and semiotic power because of its association with the dance and its aggressive, take-no-prisoners attitude. If you play through this excerpt on your keyboard, you may begin to feel the tingle of the *familiar-unfamiliar*. We'll discover why shortly.

Figure 5.2. *War of the Roses*, Main Title bandoneon

The film was released through 20th Century Fox (which is itself a kind of "intertextual reference," given the Newman family connection—more on that later) in 1989, and carried a potent creative lineage, going both backward and forward in time. It was produced by Arnon Milchan (*Birdman, 12 Years a Slave, Gone Girl, Fight Club, Brazil, L.A. Confidential, JFK*, etc., etc.) and

James L. Brooks (*All in the Family, Terms of Endearment, Broadcast News*). Brooks would later go on to produce the longest-running animated television series in history: *The Simpsons*. (*Roses* features a small but critical role played by the future voice of Homer Simpson, Dan Castellaneta). The director was veteran comedic actor Danny DeVito, who also costars, and had done two previous hit films, *Romancing the Stone* and *Jewel of the Nile*, with his leads, Michael Douglas and Kathleen Turner. All participants—including composer—were at the top of their form. If this wasn't enough creative weight, the Main Title sequence was created by Saul Bass, the legendary title artist responsible for *Psycho, Vertigo, North by Northwest, The Man with the Golden Arm*, and toward the end of his life, Martin Scorsese's *GoodFellas*. (The title sequence of AMC's *Mad Men* is an homage to Bass.) On top of this, the film was based on a successful novel, whose title referenced the bloody internecine fight for the throne of England between the Houses of Lancaster and York during the years 1455–87, same history that inspired *Game of Thrones*.

Not only had the two stars of *The War of the Roses* worked with DeVito before, so had David Newman—and on a particularly devilish dark comedy called *Throw Momma from the Train*. This was the project that affirmed their creative affinities, and also allowed the emergence of an aspect of Newman's musical personality that hasn't often been given expression over his long history of composing in Hollywood. That is to say, the mischievous, impish, and even perverse personality that owes more to Prokofiev's *Lieutenant Kijé* than to *How the West Was Won*. There are few rules and no tried-and-true formulas for success, but one thing has proven itself axiomatic:

To express your most authentic voice as a film composer, you've got to hook up with a director whose style and temperament encourage it.

To put it another way:

If you want to write like Nino Rota, you need a Federico Fellini (or at least a filmmaker who thinks like one).

This is easier said than done, of course. Composers have to pay the rent, too. But finding the right partner is critical. When the right match is made, extraordinary things like *War of the Roses* happen.

Very briefly, Oliver (Michael Douglas) and Barbara (Kathleen Turner) Rose have what seems to be the ideal marriage. Until they don't. As DeVito, who plays Oliver's divorce lawyer, Gavin D'Amato, says in the preface, addressing a prospective client (Castellaneta), "They met great. But the way I saw it, the poor bastards never had a chance." They are, in fact, entirely incompatible, but oblivious to this, they acquire an enormous and opulent house, expensive cars and habits, and two somewhat misbegotten children.

Oliver is a successful lawyer, Yankee-bred, Yale-educated, handsome, but an unsupportive husband who doesn't consider Barbara his intellectual match. Consequently, *he* can sometimes be a jerk. Barbara is a can-do American spitfire, a former high school gymnastics champ and heartland sweetheart who's all bristling physical energy and natural hauteur. But she's resentful of Oliver's pedigree, and consequently, *she* can sometimes be a bitch. Despite warning signs, they create a dream house that will become both a prison and a nightmarish playground of tit-for-tat malice.

Now let's look at the full statement of David Newman's theme and see what it tells us about this star-crossed marriage. It occurs first in bars 27–32 and the reduction in Figure 5.3 will show the essential parts: flutes, oboes, bassoons, horns, piano, and strings.

Figure 5.3. Excerpt from *War of the Roses*, 1M1, Main Title, bars 27–29

Look at the clash in the circled parts. The instruments that have the gesture stick stubbornly with its E-flat, implying a tonal center of C minor. The celli, bassoon, and piano have E-naturals, and broken F major and *C major* chords. The melody is chromatic. So, does this piece have any sort of textbook "key"? I challenge you to find it! There is, however, another kind of key: the key to the score's "conceit." Look at the first two-bar phrase in Figure 5.3. It might sound more natural as a descent over a straight C minor harmony, rendering the E-flats consonant. But that's not what Newman does, because that would reveal the "key" and rob the piece of the circuslike surreality created by those clashing minor and major thirds.

Figure 5.3B. Excerpt from *War of the Roses*, Main Title, bars 30–31

So, how is the harmony *functioning*, if indeed it is functional at all? What Roman numerals would be assigned in a traditional analysis? I'm inclined to hear this as "disguised" or "obscured" tonality (we'll see whether Figure 5.4 may bears me out!).

Here's what the cue might look like if the melody were presented in the context of C minor and retained the Latin rhythmic propulsion of the two-beat gesture.

Figure 5.4.

The first four measures are the *War of the Roses* chromatic melody very simply harmonized in an unadorned C minor, with meter and tempo altered to provide a little more of the traditional *pasa doble* feel traditionally associated with Spanish music. The melody line is enclosed in an oval. But what are the next five measures? You may well already have picked up intimations of it. They're a reduction of the famous Habanera from Georges Bizet's *Carmen*, sung by the title character, a bold, free-spirited Gypsy who gets the best of her pining lover, José, but is ultimately done in by him—and by fate. Here's the first stanza:

L'amour est un oiseau rebelle (Love's a very rebellious bird)
Que nul ne peut apprivoiser, (A bird that no one can ever tame)
Et c'est bien in vain qu'on l'appelle (You can call her, but quite in vain)
S'il lui convient de refuser. (If it suits her not to come)

You can call her, but quite in vain . . . if it suits her not to come. As we move through the score and through the story, it will be clear, I think, how well this lyric describes Barbara Rose, and what the method to David Newman's musical madness was. The war of Oliver and Barbara Rose is like a toxic tango (or a bullfight!) from which neither party will emerge ungored. Other than Wagner's *Tristan und Isolde* (which we saw Bernard Herrmann infuse into his *Vertigo* score), there are few stronger operatic signifiers for love and death than *Carmen*. Its use here is every bit as clever as the use of Piaf's "Non, je ne regrette rien" in *Inception*, and because the Habanera is now heard as almost cartoonishly melodramatic, it also helps enormously in keeping the film in the realm of comedy.

Now the concept is in place, and as was said in the last chapter, that is a sine qua non of great film scoring. Let's revisit the Main Title near its climax. Here, at bar 58 of the concert score, the trumpet takes an elegiac solo over harmony based on a root movement of a tritone! (F-sharp major to C major.) The most perverse variant yet.

Figure 5.5. *War of the Roses*, Main Title, bars 58–61

That harp glissando you see leading up from the last measure will take us to the final statement of the theme, shown in Figure 5.6. What's interesting about this trumpet passage is its poignancy. It's been said that nothing is sadder than the death of love, and if so, this passage is a kind of twisted elegy. And as we go deeper in the score, it will be clear that another of Newman's accomplishments is to evoke pathos and even tenderness amid all the Sturm und Drang, the comedy and the horror.

Figure 5.6. *War of the Roses*, **Main Title, bars 62–65**

David Newman's orchestrations never suffer from a lack of motion. Look at the horn line. At *fortissimo*, that's a part that may cause even the best players to crack. It's also (in the best way) a sort of musical madness. This entire passage, in fact—which comes very near the close of the opening titles—feels right on the verge of losing control. The chromatic *War of the Roses* theme is there, along with its supporting "Carmen" motif, but there's also a lot more (and this is only half the orchestration). I have doubled the horn line in the upper stave of the piano part in order to draw attention to it, but everything else is as it appears in the concert score. Note that each time we've seen the melody, it's been harmonized differently, but always in a way that subverts the underlying tonality.

All three film-scoring Newmans—David, brother Thomas, and cousin Randy—are fond of using what are conventionally thought of as dominant seventh chords in a way that defies functional harmony. The Brothers Newman, in particular, seem inclined to use them to obscure key center. The four measures excerpted and reduced in Figure 5.6 can hardly be characterized as nontonal, nor do they sound quite like what's commonly called *extended tonality*. But neither is this piece of music diatonic. Something else is going on. In the blues or gospel music, a string of (flat) seventh chords is not at all unusual, but in the context of orchestral film music, it's much rarer. Remember that the harmonic vocabulary of most film music derives from the second half of the nineteenth century. Adventurous things were going on during that period, but even Wagner, who could hold off resolution almost indefinitely, relied upon the V–I axis for closure—even if the dominant chord seemed to have been prolonged for half the piece! The section quoted in Figure 5.6 is, of course, incomplete, but take my word for it: there is no resolution. In the sense of being both tonal and "keyless" at the same time, it is somewhat reminiscent of the Main Titles from *To Kill a Mockingbird*, except that there, the Lydian augmented fourth masqueraded as a leading tone. Nothing here *even pretends* to be a leading tone.

In fact, as we saw in Figure 5.3, there are times when the Main Title theme seems to occupy two different keys at once (is that F7 a tonic or a subdominant?). This ambiguity isn't true throughout. There are dramatic and comedic situations that call for traditional harmony, and Newman delivers it. But it is a signature of *The War of the Roses*, and it's worth a brief digression to investigate another place, at the heart of the twentieth-century "art music," where we *do* hear this kind of mischief—for example, a Russian work that premiered in 1918.

Figure 5.7. Igor Stravinsky, *L'Histoire du soldat* (excerpt)

This is a reduction of an excerpted section from part 1 of Igor Stravinsky's theatrical work, *L'Histoire du soldat* (A Soldier's Tale). It was written for what was essentially a "pit band" of clarinet, bassoon, cornet (or trumpet), percussion, violin, and double bass, and it is one of the clearest examples of *bitonality* in the modern classical repertoire. Notice that although the piece has no key signature, almost everything in the trumpet, violin, and the upper staff of the piano is diatonic to the key of A major. Yet the bass parts (piano lower and double bass) ignore this "key signature" entirely and march to G major. The effect isn't a brutal dissonance so much as a whimsical off-centeredness. There are a number of similarities between the style and satirical theatricality of *L'Histoire* and David Newman's Main Title: tempo, march feel, and the mutability of melody. But the most useful lesson for film composers is to see the effect that the "occlusion" of tonality has on such things as mood, character, attitude, and so forth. We are thrown off balance in a dramatically useful way by hearing music that *seems tonal* but isn't.

It needs to be stated—and probably restated repeatedly—that stylistic references do not amount to appropriation. Music, like literature, is a form that depends in part on reference to convey meaning, and any literate composer will be able to put this to good use. The bi- and polytonality employed by such composers as Stravinsky and Milhaud in the early modernist period (*L'Histoire* was first performed in 1918), before the gray wall of midcentury atonality banished whimsy along with most melody, has become a hugely important part of film music language—especially when it comes to the Brothers Newman.

Two more important themes are introduced in the Main Title, and before we move on, a quick thumbnail. The first one I'll call the "Christmas" theme, as it appears to reference the carol we know as "The First Noel." This theme is associated with "the good times" in the Roses' marriage—the sweetness before it all turned sour.

Figure 5.8. *War of the Roses,* Main Title, "Christmas" theme," bars 17–22

Notice that even here, in the most conventionally diatonic and "classic Hollywood" thematic statement in the score, we see a "Newman twist." The melody is stepwise and the apparent tonality is F major, but the cellos are rapidly trilling between the pitches F–C and G–B-natural, one of those "in-folding" intervals we saw in *To Kill a Mockingbird*. The implied G major chord is borrowed from the "phantom key" of C, just as it was in the last variant of the Main Title theme in Figure 5.6, and the rapid alternation creates a kind of Lydian blur beneath the melody.

The third idea introduced in the Main Title (in alto sax) is rarely heard independently of the "Carmen" theme, and can be thought of as a development that sheds light on Newman's quirky harmonic language. It first appears in measures 46–55 in the concert score for 1M1, and I'll call it as the "Vamp" theme." Here's a four-bar excerpt.

Figure 5.9. *War of the Roses*, Main Title, "Vamp" theme

Now, equipped with the key themes and a sense of the score's vocabulary, we can dive headlong into lunatic heart of the film and observe how David Newman makes use of his material to support the drama and sustain the madcap visual style. As every experienced film composer knows, underscoring is the hardest part of the job. We'll drop in at 50:21, a little before the halfway mark. The scene takes place at night in the Roses' lavishly appointed bedroom, and both Roses are in silk pajamas. Not only has Barbara just informed a shell-shocked Oliver that she wants a divorce, she has also landed (with some provocation) a bare-knuckled punch to his chin and drawn a little blood. As he stalks out of the bedroom, he says, "The next time, I hit back. And you'd better get yourself a damned good lawyer." "The best your money can buy," she retorts, doing her all to retain both composure and bravado. Once alone, however, the reality of what she has done sinks in, and as the camera draws back, revealing her solitude, cue 6M1 enters.

Figure 5.10. *War of the Roses*, 6M1 @ 50:21

A typical theatrical feature film can contain from thirty-five to ninety minutes of music, broken down into forty to one hundred individual "starts" or cues. (These are average stats, of course, and there are exceptions) Many, if not most, of these cues will be under a minute in length, and few of them will be showstoppers. The majority will have to do the tough, workmanlike business of advancing and supporting the story in a musically integrated way. *War of the Roses'* 6M1 is such a cue. Why take the trouble to examine a piece of music that is so incidental and so short? Because it's instructive to see how a pro handles it.

Up to this moment in the film, we have seen Barbara and Oliver Rose as a couple, for better or for worse. This is also the way they've seen themselves. Now, suddenly, having declared her independence, Barbara is alone, and the artful camera pullback—to the bedroom window and beyond—makes this very clear. A camera move is one of the best "ins" for music, and pullbacks and push-ins are especially strong triggers. Although film audiences have long since gotten accustomed to them, interior moving camera shots are, by their nature, a little eerie, because they suggest the presence of another person in the room. Hitchcock used this to great effect. They invite the composer to comment on the predicament the character or characters find themselves in. In 6M1, David Newman's score makes two trenchant comments.

The "Carmen/Tango" gesture is still there in the flutes (with oboes doubling), but no longer with the haughty self-assurance we've heard before. It's less a fiery dance rhythm than a quietly ticking time bomb. The only thing left of dance in this cue is its unlikely triple meter. So, too, is the chromatic descent of the *Roses* theme present in the alto saxophone part, but likewise stripped of its bluster. Against these familiar elements is an ominous and arrhythmic ostinato in the piano and harp: a three-note chromatic figure (E–E-flat–C) whose opening pitch is starkly dissonant with the G minor tonality of the cue. Like the "Sleep" cue from *Vertigo*, 6M1 says a lot with a little, and in a very short time.

By the time we get to 9M2, which enters at 1:24:26, the film has taken a decidedly menacing turn. The possibility of real violence no longer seems at all remote. After briefly moving to a hotel room, Oliver and his lawyer, Gavin D'Amato (DeVito) discover an obscure ruling in state law that allows for couples in the process of divorcing to continue to share the principal residence. Oliver, ever alert for the legal edge, subdivides the palatial house in separate "his" and "hers" sectors, keeping a watchful eye to make sure Barbara does not sell off the couple's prized assets—including a collection of Staffordshire porcelain dogs that are perhaps the only things they ever loved equally. "The gloves are off," Oliver tells Barbara after she has crushed his beloved Morgan roadster to scrap metal beneath the wheels of her truck. The children have fled and the family dog is in hiding. Slowly but surely, the house has become a war zone.

Figure 5.11. *War of the Roses*, 9M2, bars 21–22 @ 1:24:26

In this scene, the Staffordshire dogs become guided missiles (along with a good portion of the family china), and Oliver stalks the darkened house with a tire iron in his hand. He's not yet ready to use it on Barbara—in fact, naively, he still thinks he can win her back—but in the melee that erupts, we can't be sure blood won't be spilled. The visual style of the film grows increasingly surreal, with wild motion control effects, oblique camera angles, and a lurid color scheme. The director is letting us know that we're about to enter Hell. Only two things maintain the "comedy": the almost cartoonish physicality of the action, and David Newman's fidelity to his themes—and especially, the *gesture*.

Figure 5.12. War of the Roses, 9M2, bars 23–24 @ 1:24:26

Looking at the woodwinds in bar 1 of the reduction (bar 21 in the concert score), the very first thing we see is the rhythm and melodic shape of the "Christmas" theme shown in Figure 5.8. There's nothing unusual about a composer interpolating his own themes throughout the film. But here, Newman is quoting the most lyrical of his themes in the scoring of the film's most violent scene so far. We hear it as Oliver is pursuing his terrified but defiant wife up the staircase with a crowbar, and as she cartwheels down (she's a former gymnast, remember?) and lands with a thud. The musical choice allows us to laugh through our horror. It also reminds us that, yes, this is the same couple that once shared many loving Christmases together, and has that history.

"So far it was a pretty normal divorce scenario," says the couple's lawyer. Then, opening a bottle of Scotch he keeps in his office, he pours two shots, one for himself and one for the prospective client whose visit serves as the film's framing device. "But I think you should have a drink for this next part." He hands his client the glass. "There are two dilemmas," he says. "That rattle the human skull: How do you hold on to someone who won't stay? And how do you get rid of someone . . . who won't go?"

Figure 5.13. *War of the Roses*, 10M3, "The Bald Avenger," bars 33–36 @ 1:34:18

Figure 5.13 is a four-bar excerpt from cue 10M3, which enters at 1:34:18. If it had a title, it might be "The Bald Avenger." Despite the comedic flavor of that title (yes, it's Barbara's pet name for Oliver's penis), the scene depicts what nowadays would be called marital rape. It takes place in the Roses' attic, lit in the deep violet that dominates the final act's color scheme. Barbara is hiding out, having gone up to loosen the bolt holding their enormous

crystal chandelier—with intent to drop it on Oliver. Oliver tracks her down, wrestles her to the floor, and becomes aroused. It's important to note that while Barbara's wish is for freedom, Oliver's is for things to be "the way they were." He's the one who's trying to "hold on to someone who won't stay." And so his passion—though hardly consensual—is genuine. Barbara, on the other hand, seeks only to escape, and sees only one way. "I wanna say hello to the Bald Avenger," she purrs.

The four measures excerpted in Figure 5.13 underscore the brief inter-lude between Barbara's tease and her taking a bite out of the Bald Avenger. Once again, we hear the bell-like ascending parallel sixths that characterize the "Christmas" theme, in the key of A-flat major, only now against a very unromantic D-natural pedal. If this is love, it's a very twisted sort. When Barbara's teeth snap shut, all possibility for peace vanishes.

Cue 11M2, which follows and leads us into the film's climactic scene, might be titled "Only You," or perhaps "Last Chance for Romance." At this point, Newman is scoring the movie almost as gothic horror—a choice that entirely suits the quality of the final act. But it is horror within the context of a marriage that still has not seen its bitter end.

Figure 5.14. *War of the Roses*, 11M2, bars 6–11 ⓐ 01:40:17

The house is dark. Oliver sits in the grand foyer beneath the crystal chan-delier, getting quietly drunk on red wine and accompanying his off-key vo-cal rendition of the Platters' "Only You" by running a wetted finger around the rims of his growing collection of semifilled crystal goblets. It's an eerie and unsettling sound that Newman makes even eerier with string harmon-ics. Barbara appears on the second floor landing above, and quotes Dorothy Parker: "What fresh hell is this?" Oliver calmly replies, "Hi."

The clarinet enters with a variation of the "Carmen" gesture, leading into a descending-ascending *whole-tone* line in triple meter that is only recognizable as the "Christmas" theme by its shape. Note how stark and unadorned the lines are, and yet we can still sense what it is and what it means. Once upon a time, there was love here.

"I brought a surprise for you," he says, looking up, and a fleeting look of hope crosses Barbara's haggard face. That hope is conveyed by way of the score's most poignant statement—and the film's cruelest. We pick up with 11M2 at measure 13.

Figure 5.15. *War of the Roses*, 11M2, bars 13–17 @ 01:40:22

The only way a film score's effectiveness can be evaluated—and the only way it can be studied—is as a complete and organic work, laid against the drama that it supports from beginning to end. When we, as composers, see a film for the first time, it's best for us to see it as an audience does, without interruption, but with our ears alert for the music. But when we're analyzing a score, we try to see it as the composer did, and he/she does not conceive the score in scenes, but in an arc from start to finish. David Newman and his director knew where this story was going, and it was not to a good place (not for the Roses). In the thirteen measures of music we're about to see, they wanted to offer Oliver and Barbara one last chance. A choice. After all, that's the way life—and divorce—work. Divorce is ugly, but most of all, heartbreaking. Yes, the movie is wickedly funny, and at this point in the story, a thrill ride. But it would not have the dramatic impact it does if Newman had not chosen to play scenes like this one straight. The "surprise" that Oliver has brought is the couple's most treasured (and valuable) objet d'art, an exquisite Asian figurine of a reclining woman. It is perched on the balcony railing, within Barbara's reach: an offering—the kind of little signal couples send each other. But it's attached to a trip wire, and the wire is in Oliver's hands.

In the violins, the whole-tone line begun six bars earlier by the clarinet is picked up sweetly by the violins, now dramatically harmonized (E-flat minor to C major) and altered so that the diminished fifth (G-flat) is suspended over the C major chord in the fashion of the "Tristan's Anguish" motif in Wagner's Prelude. In fact, it is a pretty Wagnerian moment in the film. *Love and Death*, face to face. Oliver's flashlight beam tracks across the banister, and then harp, celesta, and keyboards reveal the figurine.

Figure 5.16. *War of the Roses*, 11M2, bars 18–22 @ 1:40:59

As Barbara moves across the balcony, Oliver's eyes track her like prey, and over the same descending melodic line and chord change, the first violins begin to ascend chromatically (measure 9 in the reduction; bar 21 in the concert score) and build dynamically. Second violins animate the ascent with sixteenth-note figures that create additional tension. At measure 11 of the reduction (23 in the score), the entire orchestra crescendos as she draws nearer; Oliver grasps the wire and prepares to trip the booby trap. As she reaches it, the brass holds and violins descend to the downbeat of measure 13 (25), when her prize is cruelly snatched away from her. In the flash of a 2/4 bar and a rapid-fire run on harp and celesta, all hope is lost. Only the bizarre denouement remains.

Figure 5.17. *War of the Roses*, 11M2, bars 23–26 @ 1:41:08

We now move twenty-six bars on to the climactic section of the cue, and the film. Figure 5.18 is in four parts and excerpts measures 53–68 of the score. Cue 11M2 deserves a longer look because it's perhaps the most challenging scene in the film, the one that most perilously walks the line between black comedy and horror. We enter after Oliver takes a swing at the china figurine and knocks a shard into Barbara's eye. Instantly remorseful, he rushes up the stairs to her side, dropping the crowbar on the floor. Big mistake. Barbara is not in a forgiving mood. She seizes the crowbar and lands a blow on his cheek.

Figure 5.18A. *War of the Roses*, 11M2, bars 53–56 @ 1:42:30

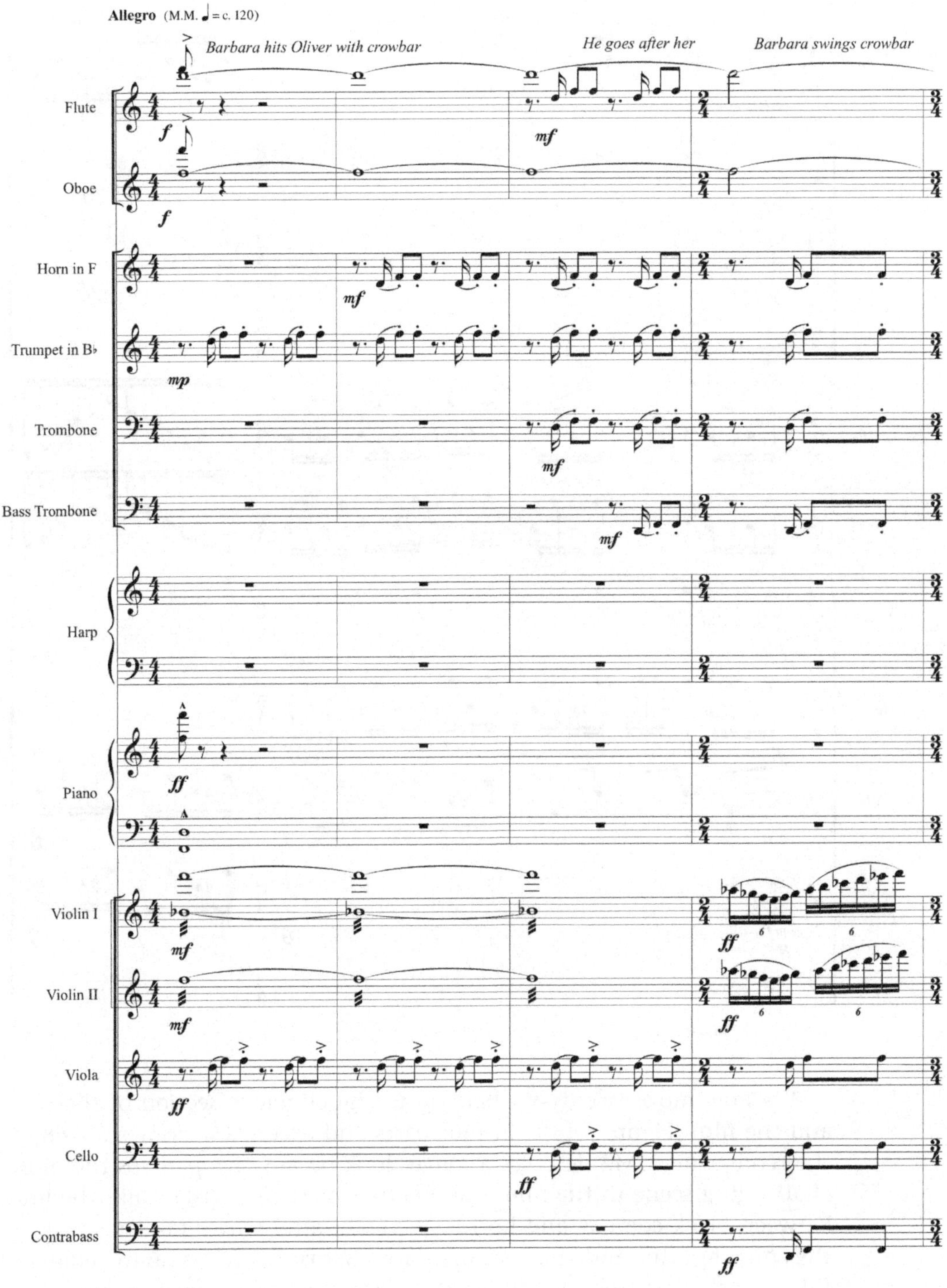

He moves to grab it, she swings again, and losing her balance, Barbara crashes through the wooden banister, teetering two stories above the terrazzo floor. Her sole chance for survival is to leap for the crystal chandelier. And the chandelier's moorings have been loosened—by her.

Figure 5.18B. *War of the Roses*, **11M2, bars 57–60 ⓐ 1:42:36**

The "Carmen" gesture, which has been with us all along, maintaining at least a semblance of comedy, returns in bar 1 (53) as a madcap scherzo. Likewise, the "Christmas" theme returns in its whole-tone guise over a tremolo pedal in bar 6 (58) and again in bar 11 (62) as a tuba solo.

Figure 5.18C. *War of the Roses*, **11M2, bars 61–64** @ 1:42:44

Then a striking new trick in bar 16 (67), based on the iconic leap from the classic 1950s ballad, "Only You," one of the few pieces of licensed music in The War of the Roses.

Figure 5.18D. *War of the Roses,* **bars 65–68** ⓡ **1:42:54**

"Only You" was the kind of slow dance number about which couples of a certain era might have said, "Darling, they're playing our song." I can't say whether it figures into the novel from which the movie was adapted, or if an earlier scene of Barbara and Oliver dancing under the moonlight might have ended up on the cutting-room floor. But it does figure hauntingly—and in a weirdly touching way—into the opening of this scene (Oliver singing), and we know that for Oliver, there will always be "only Barbara." That's a strong enough dramatic springboard for a composer to launch from, and Newman does.

As Oliver watches helplessly—almost admiringly—as his gymnastically inclined wife swings back and forth 30 feet above the stone floor and manages to lever herself into a sitting position on the chandelier, the first and second violins (doubled by woodwinds) leap a M7 in parallel thirds under the direction *"molto espressivo"* and sing out a line reminiscent of "Only You"'s iconic opening phrase. (The song's leap is a less dramatic M6, and its accompanying chords are a second inversion B major to root position G diminished.) Newman's harmonization, as befits the scene, is far more astringent, and it gives the melody a surreal dizziness that the composer describes as "taking them deeper and deeper into their intoxication with destroying each other." As with the "Carmen" and "Christmas" themes, David Newman has taken what are essentially story—or "textual"—references and transmuted them into musical elements he can use to great dramatic effect. This is the composer functioning as a codramatist, and *that* is the name of the game.

Because the score has succeeded in bringing an almost operatic symmetry to the film, a study of it would be incomplete without mentioning its final statement about the Roses. It occurs as they lie dying. The chandelier—carrying both Barbara and Oliver—has broken loose from its anchor and brought them crashing to the floor with an explosion of crystal. They lie side by side, with what we must assume are fractured skulls and multiple internal injuries. Oliver turns his head slowly toward the love of his life—lifts his hand painfully, and rests it on her shoulder. Her eyes flutter open, she turns to look at him, and a deeply felt reprise of the "Christmas" theme invites us to believe that maybe, at least, the Roses will die like the loving couple they once were.

It's not to be. Barbara reaches for her husband, nesting her fingers against his skin, and with her last ounce of strength, flings his hand from her shoulder: a final *fuck you*.

Now that, as they say, is harsh. It is also savagely funny in a fatalistic way that Shakespeare himself might have admired. And what makes it so is what David Newman does with it. Because as she gives the kiss-off, the last cocked Carmen shoulder to the husband she has fought so hard to unload, a single alto flute plays *her motif*. Three notes, and three notes are all that are required. When a composer has created and developed a musical gesture as potent as this one for the full length of a film, he has earned the right to bring down the curtain with it.

Barbara Rose doesn't quite get the last word, however. That might have been too bleak even for fans of the blackest comedy. We return to where the story began, in Gavin D'Amato's law office, and his final words of counsel to his potential client, a man who has come to him to initiate divorce proceedings against his wife.

"So look, here it is. We can begin. Or . . . you can get up, and go home. And try to find some shred of what you once loved about the sweetheart of your youth. It's your life. Take a minute."

D'Amato steps to the office window to finish his cigarette, and in the background, we see his client get up and quietly leave the office. And as a gentle night snow begins to fall against the backdrop of the Capitol dome in Washington, DC, and D'Amato calls his wife to let her know he's on his way home, we hear the final reprise of David Newman's "Christmas" theme, soft as a handbell choir on Christmas Eve.

That is, until the raucous trombones signal the roll of the end credits.

There are composers who may be bigger "stars" than David Newman in the firmament of film music—composers whose work is more likely to show up on YouTube, in video games or on fan sites. But that's fashion, and fashion has its own set of (changeable) rules. By the rules of effective film scoring, and of brilliant musical invention, no living composer could have scored *The War of the Roses* better.

SIX WALTZ FOR A DEAD GIRL

CHRISTOPHER YOUNG'S *JENNIFER 8*

Christopher Young

Like wines of a certain vintage or variety, Bruce Robinson's brooding 1992 thriller *Jennifer 8* has aged well. It had its devotees even at the time of its release, but having cost $20 million to make and earning only $11 million at the US box office, it was considered a failure, and Robinson, an Oscar-nominated screenwriter, swore he'd never direct another studio movie. What he probably didn't realize at the time was that his film, like that metaphorical Bordeaux, held a bouquet that would open up beautifully with the years.

That bouquet is, in large part, due to Christopher Young's haunting score.

Film music thrives on the uncanny, the off-center, the quirky, and the idiosyncratic as much as it does on the epic and the mythical. It's no wonder, then, that so many important composers have worked their way into its center ring by way of outliers, especially genre films that in some way alter or even subvert their genres. The list is long: *Birth, Beetlejuice, The Player, Benny and Joon, Blood Simple, Blade Runner.* It goes on into the past and it will into the future. Partly, this is because films like these—usually directed by highly individualistic artists—push composers into that unexplored territory that demands a new approach to an old story. In other words, the familiar-unfamiliar.

Jennifer 8 takes a well-known genre—the police procedural/serial killer drama—and turns it into a film that, like *The Sixth Sense*, transcends its category.

The other cinematic quality required for the emergence of a new scoring voice and style is visual poetry, and all of the movies listed above have very distinctive *looks*—the kind of looks that embed themselves in our memory and that we sometimes confuse with dreams. *Jennifer 8* has an unforgettable look, although in a far more subdued and naturalistic way than something like *Beetlejuice* or *Blade Runner.* The cinematographer was the great Conrad Hall, painting winter in the rain-soaked Pacific Northwest with the sort of bleak, melancholy beauty we associate more with the romantic poets than with the landscape of most serial killer movies. The writer/director was the man who'd penned the screenplays for both Roland Joffe's *The Killing Fields* and Neil Jordan's *In Dreams,* and he also had his reasons for setting his film in a place where it rains, as one character says, "from October to June." I mention the look of the picture—and the weather—because it seems very likely that both influenced the unusual choices that Young made in selecting his own palette. Rain induces reflection, and this is a reflective score.

Christopher Young cut his teeth on horror. His first feature scoring credit, fresh from UCLA, was *The Dorm That Dripped Blood,* and his early successes are linked to such names as Wes Craven and Clive Barker, the slashing auteurs behind the Nightmare on Elm Street and Hellraiser franchises. The thing about horror, from *Psycho* to *The Sixth Sense* and Alejandro Amenábar's *The Others,* is that its reification of nightmare requires *extended techniques*—whether this means *col legno battuto* or some audacious new use of electronics. Young, who went from jazz drumming to György Ligeti without ever losing the common touch, was a natural for this territory. Stirred to action, like so many others, by the music of Bernard Herrmann, he enrolled in the fledgling film scoring program at UCLA, where his first mentor was David Raksin. Since there are few coincidences in the world of film music, it should be noted that Raksin was the first American film composer to depict a purely subjective state of romantic possession in the context of a big studio genre film, Otto Preminger's *Laura.* In that case, a hard-boiled cop falling for a dead dame. And as in *Jennifer 8*, his musical choice was to distill romance from the macabre.

For many of us who've fallen in love with film music, the first blush of romance was brought on by a Main Title. Depending on when we came of age, it may have been Bernard Herrmann's *Psycho*, Elmer Bernstein's *The Great Escape* or *The Magnificent Seven*, John Williams's *Star Wars*, Danny Elfman's *Edward Scissorhands*, or Alexandre Desplat's *Birth*. A well-crafted piece of Main Title music conveys the dramatic *and* stylistic intent of the film, beckons the audience over the threshold of disbelief, and incidentally, wins Oscars and establishes

Composer's Sidebar:
DAVID RAKSIN'S *LAURA*

Laura is one of Hollywood studio system's great noirs, in the same class as *The Maltese Falcon* or *Double Indemnity*, and good enough to make the National Film Registry at the Library of Congress. But it may be the only one remembered and revered as much for its music as for its caustic dialogue and brooding atmosphere. Its composer, David Raksin, had been a student of Arnold Schoenberg and a protégé of legendary Fox Music head Alfred Newman. Listen to what he does at roughly forty-six minutes into the film, when Detective Mark McPherson (Dana Andrews) finds himself alone with the ghost of the murdered title character.

careers. We need only recall recent examples to see this is true: Dario Marianelli's *Atonement* and Trent Reznor and Atticus Ross's *The Social Network*. In a more music-savvy world, Christopher Young's Main Title music for *Jennifer 8* would have put an Oscar on *his* shelf, too.

When a major Hollywood studio allows its fanfare or logo music to be bumped by original score, it's a good indication that they feel they have something special. In the case of *Jennifer 8*, the studio was Paramount, and over the image of the familiar snow-capped peak, emerging from silence, we hear a solo piano in a reverberant space, open fourths arpeggiated over low pedal tones. A suggestion of mystery, but also of *delicacy*.

Figure 6.1. *Jennifer 8*, 1M1, bars 1–4

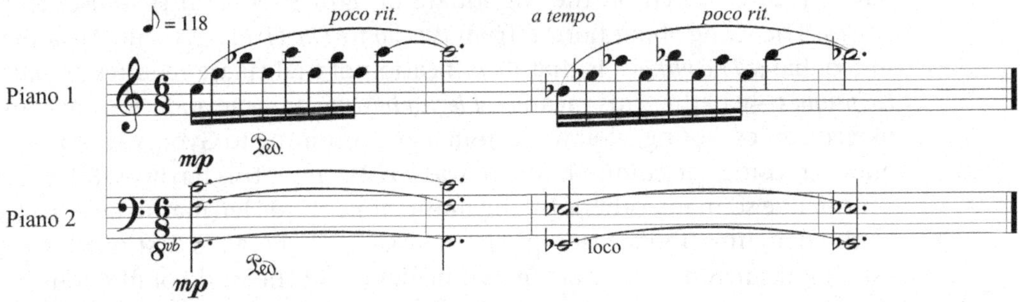

Delicacy? Solo piano? In a film about the hunt for a serial killer who stalks and dismembers pretty young blind women? For more than thirty years, the musical vocabulary for this kind of story had been the one bracingly set by Bernard Herrmann. In fact, in the very same year of *Jennifer 8*'s release, Jerry Goldsmith had demonstrated that the Herrmann tradition was alive and well with his masterful homage in *Basic Instinct*. But after 1992, virtually every moody thriller to hit the screen had a score that referenced *Jennifer 8*. That is how you define a game-changer.

I've mentioned the look of the film. What about its plot? John Berlin (Andy Garcia) is a former Los Angeles cop, burned-out at thirty-seven, a recovering alcoholic psychically bruised by a bitter divorce. He travels north to the woods escape that history and rejoin his former commander, Freddy Ross (Lance Henriksen), who now heads the homicide division of the Eureka, CA Police Department. Ross and his wife, Margie, are not only a professional allies but friends, and John Berlin needs friends. He also needs redemption, and the theme of *redemption*—through love and the baptism of winter rain—is key to both story and score. Here is a reduction of bars 15–18 of the *Jennifer 8* Main Title, cue 1M1. I'll show horns, pianos, and strings.

Figure 6.2. *Jennifer 8*, 1M1, bars 15–18

Because *Jennifer 8* was conceived and composed with piano in mind, its major thematic elements can be neatly expressed on a keyboard, so play along if you're able to. There are two important musical ideas presented in the foregoing four measures, in addition to the prominence of the piano. The first is what I'll call the "sigh" motif, always heard in the high strings. (In chapter 2, we touched on Wagner's notion of a falling semitone as a sigh). The slurs here are almost glissandos. Note that the violins are divisi and that the top line uses harmonics that sound two octaves above the middle line, while second violins hold a high pedal. The other key ingredient is the harmony. If we extract what appear and sound as chord tones from the lower parts and piano, this is how a harmonic blueprint might read:

Figure 6.3. *Jennifer 8*, **Main Title harmonic analysis**

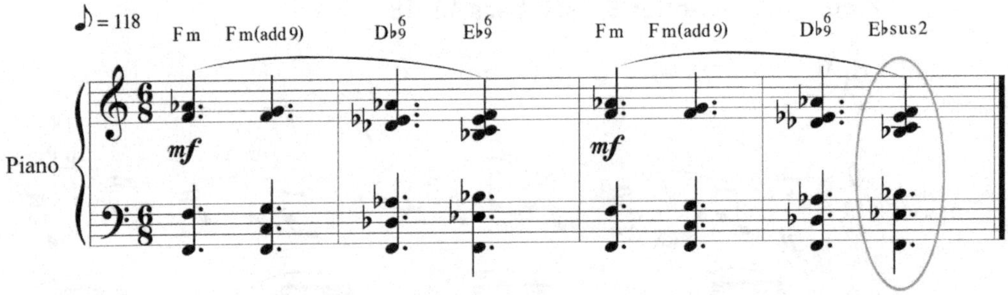

I've circled that last chord because although it sounds to the ear like a sus2 chord, it also prominently features a sixth (C-natural). Two bars earlier in the example, I labeled it a 6–9 chord (without a third). And when the lovely horn line in Figure 6.4, measure 12 (bar 22 in the score) caps it with an A-flat, it becomes something else. This is where conventional harmonic analysis falls apart in film music, particularly when the composer has a fondness for *clustered* pitches. As in David Newman's *War of the Roses* theme, there is no traditional chord function here, so forget about assigning Roman numerals unless you want to force the issue. Harmony results from fluid, moving lines, not from static chords, even when the composer has jazz experience, as Young does.

What we *can* identify here is a modal progression that would be equally familiar to Guido of Arezzo (10th century) and Keith Richards: *flat VI–flat VII–i*. The pillars of this progression are open fifths: F/C dropping to D-flat/A-flat, up a whole step to E-flat/B-flat, and returning to F/C. It's always an evocative progression, somehow both archaic and new, but what makes it especially so here are Young's voicing, embellishments and painstakingly precise dynamics and technique. There are gentle dissonances throughout, swelling in and out under the lyrical piano melody that is the movie's musical signature. And so, we begin, as a visibly agitated John Berlin drives through ancient redwood forests to his destination. The "Jennifer" theme is repeated, with a second ending that returns it to the starting pitch of C. And it will be heard in many variants, keys, and abridgements throughout the film.

Figure 6.4. *Jennifer 8*, 1M1, bars 19–22 with "Jennifer" theme in piano

If Berlin was expecting time to decompress, he won't get it in Eureka, because on arrival, he's immediately summoned by Lt. Ross to the town dump, where two grisly discoveries are made: a homeless derelict with his throat slit from ear to ear, and a severed hand that he'll later determine belonged to a young blind woman. Not far from the hand are found a bloodied bra and a Seeing Eye dog with a bullet through its head.

Before jumping into the body of the score and story, let's return for a moment to the main question. *Why piano?* Why the wistful mood conjured by 6/8 in a minor mode? At a tempo of eighth-note = 118, it could almost be a waltz. We now have a severed hand and a slit throat, and a damaged man carrying "thoughts that lie too deep for tears," a quote from

Wordsworth offered by Helena (Uma Thurman), the blind girl who will become Berlin's witness, his alibi, his lover, and possibly his salvation. This is pretty somber stuff, and it's little wonder that finding the right music did not come easy.

As Chris Young tells the story, he was driving away, despondent, from the meeting at which he'd played his first "Jennifer" theme for the director, on the dub stage at Warner Hollywood. It hadn't gone over well, and he feared—as all newcomers do—that it might cost him the picture. Paramount had already thrown out one score (by Maurice Jarre, no less), and Young had gotten the gig as a result of a happy accident: the music editor had tracked one of his horror cues into an early cut and the director had noticed it. He pulled up to the light at Santa Monica and Wilshire. *Easy come, easy go,* he sighed. And then it came to him.

Take another look at that Wordsworth quote. William Wordsworth was the greatest of the English romantic poets, and the quote is a lift from one of his best-known poems, "Intimations of Immortality." The poem is about how the vision of beauty we have as children grows dark as we age and is eventually lost to us. We can recapture it only if we learn again to see with the "inner eye" of a child. The female lead in *Jennifer 8* is blind, but it's John Berlin who must recover his sight. Now, it's never certain how inspiration comes to a composer, which ideas are openly discussed and which enter through his or her subconscious. But given how creative *synchronicities* work, is it too far-fetched to imagine that in that stray line of poetry, spoken under Helena's breath and barely audible, the writer/director may have revealed the sort of story he really wanted to tell? A romance. In any event, Young kept his job.

The first piece of underscore we'll explore is 3M3, titled "May I See Your Hands?" It enters at just over 24:00 into the film, when Berlin and Lt. Ross meet Helena for the first time at the Shasta Institute for the Blind. Berlin believes that seven blind girls have been murdered (the seventh is the one whose hands were found in the dump). They are tagged "Jennifers" by the investigative team, after a previous, still unidentified corpse. There's reason for Berlin to believe Helena could end up Jennifer #8. So far, however, he's the only one to believe it.

Figure 6.5. *Jennifer 8*, 3M3, "May I See Your Hands?" bars 1–5 @ 24:06

The reduction of 3M3 given here in Figures 6.5 and 6.6 omits a few orchestrational colors, but key ingredients are shown. There are no winds. Young sticks faithfully to his keyboard, percussion, and string-centered palette, denying himself one of the prime conveyors of tension in the thriller genre: brass. Instead, he achieves tension by way of subtle "rubs" in the mirrored vibraphone and piano lines and dynamics that never rise above *mezzo*

piano. This is underscoring in the classic style of his mentor, David Raksin, but dressed in the more austere colors of the 1990s.

Figure 6.6. *Jennifer 8*, 3M3, "May I See Your Hands?" bars 6–10

Take special note of all the "l.v." or "let vibrate" instructions for the chimes, vibes, celesta, and piano. When this is done in a live room, as it was here, it creates a halo of resonance and an impressionistic blur of pitches. Notice also, here and throughout the score, how sensitive Young is to string articulation and dynamics.

Thinking Like a Dramatist

Most film composers receive their training, as Chris Young did, in university music departments, and most such departments have little or no interplay with the school's drama department. That's a shame, because that separation of crafts denies the composer some of the language and "gestural competence" he or she will need to be able to read the scene correctly. When theater and film actors and directors speak of *beats*, they are talking about pauses and turns in dialogue and action that signal a shift in tone or meaning. Composers who are able to recognize these beats score both dramatic and comedic scenes more effectively, as beats are often the places where the music speaks the most clearly.

Every scene has its own "arc," with *beats* that underline moments of tension and release (see sidebar). The composer must identify these beats and decide how to treat them. In this scene, Berlin has two objectives: to learn what he can from Helena about the man who appears to have abducted, and possibly killed, her friend Amber, and to begin the work of gaining her trust. There is abundant tension for Helena: in the presence of two men she can't see, in the winds that buffet the institute above the snow line in the Cascades, and in the isolation she feels. Young plays this deftly, supporting the critical turns in the scene.

In measure six, just as Helena is about to leave to teach a music class (she's a cellist), Berlin asks whether she'll allow him to see her hands. He has found odd striations on the fingertips of the severed hand that he believes are due to reading Braille, and wants to see if this is true of Helena's fingers, too. She is at first unsettled by the request, but agrees, and finds him gentle. Because of the choice Chris Young makes in scoring this brief moment of intimacy, we know that the chemistry of attraction is at work.

When the full violin and viola sections enter in measure 7 as Helena gives John her hands, it is with a cluster chord in which the sweetness of the minor sixth between F and D-flat (and its M3 inversion) are predominant—but not so consonant that the tension is resolved. Far from it. Then, in measure 8, solo piano enters with the steady, pedaled quarter-note chords that are often a cinematic signifier for blossoming romance. But they aren't the triads of a Carpenters ballad! They also are *pitch clusters*, though very gentle ones.

With this cue, the unconventional choice made in the Main Title is fully redeemed, and we know that this very dark, very moody thriller conceals a timeless love story.

But as Berlin's bond with Helena deepens, his relationship with the other cops grows strained. They are jealous of his friendship with Lt. Ross, and suspect that his reasons for reopening an embarrassingly unsolved murder case have more to do with grandstanding than police work. Further, no one believes his theory that the "Jennifer" killer is at large and still in their neck of the woods. Things begin to get ugly when Berlin sneaks into headquarters late at night to comb through the files of the officer originally assigned the "Jennifer" case, John Taylor. Next up is 6M1, "Berlin Searching Files."

Figure 6.7. *Jennifer 8*, 6M1, "Berlin Searching Files," bars 1–5 @ 46:09

This is the kind of cue that any composer working in what used to be known broadly as the suspense genre must learn to write well and often, but for that very reason, it's instructive to look at what a composer who *knows* the genre does with it. These cues aren't showy. They can't be, because they typically occur in dramatic situations that call for restraint. *Why?* Because the protagonist (or whichever character is alone and vulnerable onscreen) is in a potentially hazardous place and is trying not to be seen or heard. The focus is intimate, and the music becomes a second character in the scene: the lookout man, so to speak. The last thing a good composer wants to do is shine a flashlight on the character. In this case, John Berlin, looking for evidence, has broken into the office of the cop we'll much later discover is the killer. Berlin doesn't know this or even suspect it yet—and neither does the audience—*but the composer does*, and he must create just enough tension and menace that, later on, when the killer is revealed, we'll recall this moment and *it will all make sense*. This is key to what we might call the setup. The right music makes the story's development and denouement feel inevitable.

The cue may look simple in a paper reduction, but it's musically very adroit. The essential ingredients are there at the downbeat: the insistent rhythm in the harp and viola, reminiscent of the Herrmann habanera in *Vertigo*, is a staple of suspense. It represents time—the "ticking clock"—and time is always a factor in a tense situation. We are "working against the clock," "pressed for time," or trying to get out before the bomb goes off. Without the time element, a cue like this falls apart. The vibraphone with motor on and the bass harmonics augment the tension and the sense of mystery. Also textbook technique is the use of a more "snaky," slurred, often chromatic statement in the high strings. To reinforce that effect, Young has them in mutes, and marked "*secco*" (dry) and "Wispy."

Two things about this cue are peculiar to this score: the 6/8 time signature, which is consistent with the theme, and the instrumentation, which keeps to Young's brass-free palette and delicate textures. But the most fascinating aspect here is the harmonic language. The constant in the cue are the insistent E-naturals in vibraphone, harp, viola, and basses, to which our ear responds by identifying E as some sort of tonic. When the violins enter in measure 3, however, they execute a chromatic sequence of parallel M3's beginning with B/D-sharp that pull our ear in a very different direction.

Composer's Sidebar: THE SETUP

If we accept that a good film composer must also be a good dramatist, then part of his or her job is to look ahead. Looking ahead is plotting, and plot is critical—especially in a mystery. No good dramatist wants to give the ending away, but the story must be laid out in a way that adds up. This can be done in a linear way, an elliptical way, or with the dreamlike chronology of *Mulholland Drive*, but it has to be done. *The Sixth Sense*, treated briefly in the first chapter of this book, is one of the textbook examples of setup in contemporary commercial cinema. We spend an entire film with a character without realizing he's dead, but when we do, it all makes sense. Music is a critical part of dramatic setup.

Figure 6.8. *Jennifer 8*, 6M1, "Berlin Searching Files," bars 6–10

At first glance, it appears that Young may be using some kind of diminished scale based on E, which wouldn't be at all out of keeping for a scene like this. Then, when the cellos and basses speak in bars 5 and 9, it seems as if the "hidden key" of the piece may have revealed itself as D-flat minor, which would re-label the E's as enharmonic F-flats. But that isn't it, either. More intriguing yet may be an *augmented scale*: a hexatonic (six-tone) scale composed of two interlocking augmented triads with roots a minor third apart. That would fit both Chris Young's jazz background and his affinity for modernism, and an augmented scale based on either E or D-flat would enfold most of the pitches used by the violins. *Most, but not all.* There isn't any single scale that this assortment corresponds to.

Figure 6.9. Augmented scales on E and D-flat

The lines played by the violins in measures 3–4 and 7–8 are purely chromatic, and mimic the shape of the main *Jennifer 8* theme (otherwise, why put them in 6/8?). But, as with *The War of the Roses* and other scores we've seen, this is not a musically "atonal" piece of writing. Rather, it is, caught between tonalities, sometimes drawing our ear toward a tonal center of E and sometimes toward D-flat. I'm inclined to feel that the basic harmonic personality of the cue is "augmented." But whatever it is, it works brilliantly.

The next cue takes us into scarier territory. There's a killer on the loose and a blind girl in danger, and in 6M3, we can see what she can't: that "Someone's Looking In."

Eureka's town garbage dump has now produced a severed head to match the hands, and Berlin's forensics (pre–DNA matches), as well as his convictions, lead him to conclude that both belong to Amber, the dorm mate of Helena's who mysteriously did not return to the institute after Christmas. The institute's director, however (a particularly odious character, along with its creepy Peeping Tom janitor), has turned over to the police a postcard in Braille, purportedly written by Amber from some vacation spot she's decided to remain in with her new boyfriend. Lt. Ross and the other cops are inclined to take the postcard at face value and presume that Amber is alive. But Berlin is convinced that Amber is Jennifer #7, and since Helena was a witness (although, unfortunately for Berlin, not an *eyewitness*) to her abduction, it is only a matter of time before the killer returns. Berlin visits the institute to query Helena on the authenticity of the postcard.

About one minute into the scene, after Helena has given her opinion that the postcard is a fake (Amber couldn't use Braille), the director abruptly cuts to outside Helena's bedroom window, where the wind is howling and someone is watching.

Figure 6.10. *Jennifer 8, 6M3, "Someone's Looking In,"* @ 49:30

The *gran casa* (bass drum) quarter-notes in bar 1 hit the cut to outside the window. The piano and string clusters enter slyly ("sneaking in") as the camera begins to move with the point of view of the observer, and the timpani rolls like distant thunder. The high pedal harmonics in the first violins drop from C-natural to B-natural as the voyeur crouches down outside the window, and then linger way up above the staff as we cut back inside and Berlin makes an awkward and painful exit (it's still too early for them to embrace), leaving Helena alone, feeling his absence keenly, and very vulnerable.

Figure 6.11. *Jennifer 8*, 6M3, "Someone's Looking In," bars 6–9

The lovely, ultraspare piano solo passage that begins in measure 5 scores Berlin out the door and continues as the camera remains on Helena, her feelings beginning to stir. And our feelings are stirred, as well, both by the tenderness and the acutely dangerous situation she is in. Both hands are in the treble clef. The left is a steady pedal on an open A-flat/E-flat fifth. The right hand strikes another open fifth—E-natural and B-natural—and lets them ring. The two open fifths against one another sound hollow, lonely, almost bitonal, as if they were meant to suggest opposing A-flat minor and E major chords (a "mediant" relationship). The passage has the reflective feel of minor mode, but depending on how we interpret Young's chord spelling, that B-natural in both the piano part and the high pedal of the violin could mean something different.

Chord spellings and enharmonic ambiguity are issues that academically inclined music scholars love to hash over, but it's not always possible to affirm a composer's intent based on what name he gives to a note, particularly in film music where tonality is so fluid. It's really not of great importance what we call it as long as we know it works. Even the great Debussy was notorious for calling notes whatever suited him and thereby (possibly deliberately) obscuring chord identity. The fact is that this cue masterfully moves from tension to tenderness without ever letting us to feel secure, and accomplishes another deft bit of story setup: by its end, we know that Berlin and Helena will be lovers.

We now advance nearly forty-five minutes into the film, and a world of changes have occurred. It's still only the top of the final "act" (it's a long movie, nearly 2.5 hours), and the plot is at its densest. John Berlin has taken Helena under his wing and into his bed, and this has complicated things: cops aren't supposed to sleep with witnesses, and Helena remains the only witness to the abduction of the last murder victim. Furthermore, Berlin has not only lost his friend and partner, Freddy Ross, but stands accused of shooting him in the course of a failed Christmas Eve attempt to capture the killer at the Shasta Institute. An FBI investigator (John Malkovich) has been called in for the interrogation, and his suspicion is that Berlin fabricated the entire serial killer story, and drew his partner into a phony raid so that he could kill him "with malice aforethought." *His motive?* It may even be that Berlin himself is the "Jennifer Killer." For the moment, he remains a free man, but if things don't go well, he'll be arrested for first-degree murder. While he undergoes the third degree at the hands of the FBI man, Helena waits anxiously at his house. It's the middle of winter, and the light is a cold blue. There's a sound on the porch, and a shadow on the windowpane that only we can see. "John?" she calls. "Is that you?" Cue 11M2 is called "Someone's at the Door."

Figure 6.12. *Jennifer 8*, 11M2, "Someone's at the Door," bars 1–4 @ 1:35:04

Once again, the element of time is conveyed by the lightest of ostinatos, now in the violas. Around this, the violins weave a serpentine line in parallel thirds, with no fixed tonality other than that suggested by the ostinato and pedal tones in the low strings. At bar 5, the violins begin to climb as Helena approaches the door, and dissonance enters. The tension is briefly "relieved" in bar 7 by what we hear as a D-flat augmented chord.

Figure 6.13. *Jennifer 8*, 11M2, "Someone's at the Door," bars 5–9

That moment of relief doesn't last once Helena realizes there's no one there. But the texture remains very delicate, dynamics barely exceeding *mezzo piano*. *Eerie*, not ominous. *Mysterious and reserved*, as Young and orchestrator Pete Anthony describe it. We get all the *ominous* we need from the howling wind as she steps onto the front porch. Bear in mind, our point-of-view character is a blind girl. She's heard something at the door, and hoped it was John. Now there is only the wind.

Figure 6.14. *Jennifer 8*, **11M2, "Someone's at the Door," bars 10–13**

At bar 11, as Helena backs inside and locks the door, there is the slightest of accelerandos, and a very effective reprise of the "sigh" motif we saw in the

Main Title—those falling minor seconds that feel so much like the breathlessness of animal fear. The motif is stated in violin harmonics, echoed by the celesta, and accompanied by chromatically descending minor chords (B minor/B-flat minor–A minor), flavored with dissonance.

Figure 6.15. *Jennifer 8*, 11M2, "Someone's at the Door," bars 14–16

The cue continues for a few measures after the reduction shown here, as Helena, having made her way upstairs, gropes through the inky darkness, one hand extended in front of her, until at last it comes terrifyingly to rest on a man's face. The killer, wearing a balaclava and speaking in a harsh whisper, doesn't reveal himself, but Helena most certainly recognizes his voice. It's John, all right, though not the John she'd hoped for. We'll all soon learn that the "Jennifer Killer" is Sgt. John Taylor, the cop originally assigned the case, but he hasn't come to murder Helena, only to terrorize her and to plant a gun as evidence against her lover. Murdering her would only serve to give John Berlin, who is at the police station undergoing interrogation, an airtight alibi.

Before continuing on, it may serve us well to take note of the extraordinary restraint shown in the foregoing cue and, indeed, throughout the score, and to observe how that restraint serves paradoxically to *heighten* the suspense. This may be just one more corollary of the "less is more" rule in film scoring: express only what *complements* the drama. It generally isn't necessary or desirable to *amplify* it. Doing too much can take you across the line into melodrama. In the pulp horror of the late 1980s and early '90s, we saw a great many such scenes scored with ominous analog synth drones, unholy voice patches, and big "rise and hit" stings. That approach would have killed a scene like this one. As gruesome as are the events depicted in *Jennifer 8*, and as "masculine" as police procedurals are, this is a film with a feminine soul, and Chris Young never violates it.

I mentioned a few paragraphs back the name of Pete Anthony, *Jennifer 8*'s orchestrator. Anthony has been for many years one of Hollywood's top session conductors and orchestrators, in addition to being a composer himself. There's evidence of his input all over this score, particularly in its painstakingly precise dynamics and articulations. Go back and look at the sheer number and placement of "hairpins" in this and other similar cues: these are what allow the score to breathe like a living thing. The placement of slurs, tenuto markings, and the use of natural harmonics. It's all part of the package. Among many other things, having a great orchestrator on your score can be a bit like strapping an exquisitely sensitive compressor into your mix. The orchestrator will "ride" the score's peaks and valleys, bringing out more when more is necessary, and holding it back when this serves the story better.

Now it's time to move to the climax.

Berlin's grilling by the FBI in the matter of Freddy Ross's murder is unrelenting, but news of the assault on Helena slips into the interrogation room. The presumption on the part of the FBI agent is that Helena has fabricated the assault to provide Berlin with an alibi. It does, however, introduce an element of doubt, which buys Berlin a bit more time to pursue his leads. Furthermore, in the course of the interrogation, the FBI man has revealed a small but critical piece of evidence that draws Berlin from Eureka down to Oakland, and to the house that may have been the killer's childhood home.

It's night, and the house is empty. Berlin finds a wheelchair at the bottom of the stairs, and an eerie lithograph of Christ holding a lantern on the landing. He makes his way up to the second floor, where his flashlight slowly pans across a woman's vanity. We enter 11M3 at 1:50:10 in a reduction for strings only (keyboard/perc parts omitted).

Figure 6.16A. *Jennifer 8*, 11M3, "Berlin Strikes Out," bars 16–20 @ 1:50:10

In this cue, which begins very, very quietly with violins only, we see something that has become exceedingly rare in contemporary film scoring: *counterpoint*. First violins creep in on a high F above the staff. Seconds follow a beat later with a high D-flat falling to a C-natural, establishing a temporary key center of B-flat minor, although the line performed by the first violins is chromatic. Every thriller of this type includes at least one scene in which the principal investigator—whether it be a seasoned P.I. or a college girl looking for her missing roommate—searches a private residence for evidence of a crime, usually by flashlight or sometimes candlelight, almost always in darkness. The investigator is clearly *not supposed to be there*, and is therefore in jeopardy. Furthermore, there's every possibility that the killer, or someone connected with the killer, could at any moment emerge from the shadows and deliver the jump scare. The classic of this type are the searches of the Norman Bates house conducted by Detective Arbogast and Marian Crane's sister in *Psycho*, and in fact, 11M3 is the cue that owes the most to Bernard Herrmann.

Figure 6.16B. *Jennifer 8*, 11M3, "Berlin Strikes Out," bars 21–25

© Sony/ATV

In bar 7 (22), first violins leap by a major seventh, creating additional tension, and execute a similar sequence, while the falling figure in the seconds drops a minor third and is now joined by rest of the strings, rhythmically in line with the second violins but in contrary motion, rising rather than falling—and with the same *poco crescendo/poco decrescendo* "breathing" we've seen throughout the score. The temporary key center has now moved up a semitone with the first violins to F-sharp minor. There is an uncomfortable, voyeuristic intimacy to scenes like this. Our hopes may be with the investigator, but we can't help feeling a little queasy about what he's doing. This is another reason why such scenes must be played delicately, and the simple counterpoint scheme Young has employed here gives the cue a kind of step-by-step subtlety that suits the scene perfectly. Likewise, the astringent chromaticism of both the principal and counterpoint lines reinforces our discomfort. There is, in a sense, a "key," but it's nothing we can hold onto for safety.

Rummaging through a closet in what is clearly a woman's bedroom, Berlin finds a hatbox full of old photographs. As the strings conclude their passacaglia-like descent and hold on a dissonant harmony with A's in the bass, topped by E-natural, G-sharp, E-flat, and B-flat, the first violins rise from B-flat to B-natural, sweetening the harmony to an E major 7 chord with a sus4 as Berlin finds the photographs that may hold the answer he seeks.

6.17. *Jennifer 8*, 11M3, "Berlin Strikes Out," bars 26–28

All of these subtle changes in action are "hit" by the composer through the use of tied notes, meter changes, and most importantly, chromatic inflections in the harmony that allow him to increase and decrease dramatic tension while keeping the cue musical.

The evidence that Berlin finds in Oakland confirms that John Taylor is the killer, but Berlin doesn't get far with it. He's apprehended at the scene by Taylor himself and hauled back to face a first-degree murder charge. Only after Margie Ross makes his bail is he free to drive frantically to the institute and face Taylor before he tries to kill again.

Cue 14M1 enters at 1:58:25, just after John Berlin has been released from custody.

Figure 6.18. *Jennifer 8*, 14M1, "Big Drive to the Institute," bars 17–20 @ 1:59:06

We're back in 6/8, and we return—for the last time—to Chris Young's piano theme. It enters accompanied by furiously arpeggiating violins and violas, along with robust horns, timpani, and tubular bells. This kind of cue demonstrates that the composer has the training, technique, and imagination to develop his thematic material for full orchestral treatment in an action film context.

Figure 6.19. *Jennifer 8*, 14M1, "Big Drive to the Institute," bars 21–24

It's only a matter of time before Taylor comes after Helena. Rushing to the Ross home, Berlin discovers that Margie has taken Helena back to the institute. He arms himself and heads after them. The excerpt shown in Figures

6.18–20 encompass a twelve-measure section beginning at 1:59:06. (Bars 1–12 are actual bars 17–28.) An analysis follows this final four-measure section, which diminuendos in bar 11 for a flashback/memory sequence.

Figure 6.20. *Jennifer 8*, 14M1, "Big Drive to the Institute," bars 25–28

The most remarkable thing about 14M1 may be how well Young's lyrical piano theme and its underlying harmony work in what is fundamentally an action cue. We don't generally think of wistful, somewhat melancholy themes lending themselves to pulse-pounding suspense. Yet in this case, it returns like an old friend just when we need it most. In analyzing the cue, we can see a few reasons why this may be so.

First of all, Young has established the melody, its mood, and its meter with great consistency, so it's not a surprise to hear it here. And as he has said, "Once I was in the 6/8 groove, I felt I needed to find a way to make it work throughout." Second, the melody is now closely associated not only with Berlin's love for Helena, but with his redemption *through* it. His final act of redemption will be to save her from becoming Jennifer #8, so his mad rush through the snowy mountains wouldn't be complete without it. A lesser composer might have gone with loops, pads, and stabs and put the theme aside until resolution of the story. But that would have been a mistake. It isn't a melody of resolution, but one of longing, and the ache of being two apart instead of two together.

Musically, there are a number of factors at work. Putting the horns on the back half of the measure with the chimes, and setting them up with the aggressive timpani, piano, and cello figures (accents on every beat!) creates an atmosphere of both tense drama and heroism. Moreover, neither the first horns nor the chimes are playing "chord" tones, as such—at least not if we take the chords to be G minor and Cm7/E-flat, which is what they seem to be. They pivot from A-natural to F, playing respectively a ninth and a suspended fourth (or, if we spell the second chord as some kind of E-flat, another ninth). This creates unresolved appoggiaturas that are a key ingredient in the scene's suspense (once again, we see the potent effect that occurs when the second degree of a minor scale is sounded directly over the root of its tonic triad). The scale-wise arpeggios in the upper strings are probably the cue's most distinguishing element—and also one we haven't heard before now. They are sixteenth-notes with measured tremolo, and they create an icy, cascading sheen that reflects the snow rushing into Berlin's windshield as he races to his love. The harmonic language used here again demonstrates Young's affinity for both the dense harmonies of jazz and his ability to *hear* how these sonorities will affect the score.

Finally, the melody itself. It's broken into halves separated by two measures containing an imitative cello figure, an effective way to create musical suspense *and* to keep it from sounding like a 1960s French romance. If Young had chosen to state the melody unbroken, this very tense scene would have become too much about the theme and not enough about Berlin's determination. Film scoring is all about choices, and more often about the choice of what *not to do* than what *to do*. Here, it's critical that we hear the theme, but far more critical that we find the scene gripping. Since melody tends to relieve rather than create tension, it has to be used sparingly in a case like this.

My reduction ends well before the actual cue, but in bar 11/27, you'll see where the composer heads next. There's a fifteen-second segment of the scene in which we hear the "voices in Berlin's head," a device that filmmakers can use to create empathy, or simply to remind the audience of key plot points. It's important to support the "interiority" of these moments, and Young does so by reducing the arpeggiated figures to second violins only (marked *"punta d'arco"* for a lighter touch), introducing a new tension figure in first violins and viola, and pulling the entire ensemble down by two dynamics and indicating "less energy." The real fireworks are still ahead.

In almost every talented young composer's career, there is—at some point—a *Jennifer 8*. A chance to step up to drama. Drama remains the holy grail because drama is perceived as having *weight*, and weight makes reputations. Chris Young was very nearly typecast out of the major leagues by his early association (and success) with horror, and particularly the Hellraiser films. He was handed a once-in-a-lifetime break when a young music editor (with a pair of good ears) named Dan Garde temped a cue from *The Fly II* into a preview cut of the film and won over director Bruce Robinson, who then went to bat for a guy who'd never scored a big studio drama before.

Had Young not been able to come back from that first unsuccessful trial on the Warner Hollywood stage and deliver one of the most haunting and memorable themes of the late twentieth century, things might have gone very differently. But he did, and Christopher Young has gone on to become not only one of the industry's most respected composers, but a mentor and cheerleader to hundreds who now walk the path that he has walked. As he said once to a class of my students, "If you ever think of quitting . . . call me first."

(This chapter is dedicated to the memory of Dan Carlin Sr., supervising music editor for Jennifer 8, and the originator of the craft of music editing for motion pictures.)

SEVEN FEED YOUR HEAD

DON DAVIS'S *THE MATRIX*

Don Davis

Certain films have the capacity—in concept, in script, in visual realization—to alter the way we see the world. Even to alter the way we see
ourselves. Everyone who loves cinema has had the experience of leaving a theater with a slightly different walk, talk and attitude, feeling
they've carried a bit of the character away with them. Bogart or Bacall in
The Big Sleep. Belmondo or Seberg in *Breathless*. McQueen or McGraw in *The
Getaway*. Gosling or Mulligan in *Drive*. Sometimes we take away not just the
character, but his or her worldview. *Forget it, Jake. It's Chinatown.*

Only a scant few projects that make it into production have the potential to change the way we perceive reality itself, and of that small number, most fail to deliver once they hit the screen. It's not really surprising that of the few that do pull it off, a high percentage fall into the category of speculative sci-fi. After all, that's the genre of fiction and film that aims to mess with our mind. To make us think outside the box. Occasionally, masterworks of this type, such as Peter Weir's *The Truman Show* or David Lynch's *Mulholland Drive*, even ask us to entertain the possibility that *we're in the box*.

When a film of this genre does succeed at that most daunting task of altering perception, it's very often the music that takes us to "the other side." *The Day the Earth Stood Still, Planet of the Apes, Blade Runner, Inception.* But in no film of the last fifty years has music complemented concept as thoroughly as in *The Matrix,* directed by the Wachowskis and scored by Don Davis. As deftly as the music for *Perfume* evoked the world of scent, Davis's score captures a virtual world rendered in binary code that has fooled *almost* everyone living in it. Talk about suspension of disbelief. And the remarkable thing is that he does it with an orchestra.

In this chapter, we go down the rabbit hole and explore perhaps the only seminal score in recent cinema history that no composer has attempted to imitate.

The Matrix was released by Warner Bros. in 1999, a millennial gesture if there ever was one. It cost roughly $63 million to make and to date has earned more than $456 million in worldwide box office receipts. It has spawned two sequels, innumerable games and comics, and a web subculture unlike anything seen since. Its creators were two siblings from Chicago, Larry (now Lana) and Andy (now Lilly) Wachowski, avid videogamers, part-time Marvel Comics writers, precocious, ambitious, a little bent, and well above standard intelligence. Right from concept, *The Matrix* was in a commercially risky class by itself, although it certainly owed debts to such films as *Total Recall* and *Blade Runner* (both based on short stories by the legendary Philip K. Dick, whose Valis trilogy was a literary inspiration). When filmmakers require that each member of their principal cast and crew read *and be able to explain* French poststructuralist philosopher Jean Baudrillard's *Simulacra and Simulation,* you know something unusual is up.

The philosophical, mythical, and literary lineage of *The Matrix* is deep, long, and decidedly *alternative*. From Plato's *Allegory of the Cave* to the Vedic/Hindu concept of *maya*; from the *Gnostic dualism* that posits an illusory world ruled by a malign force to the postmodern musings of such scholars as Baudrillard, the cyberpunk of William Gibson, and above all these, the aforementioned Philip K. Dick, whose driving theme was the existence of an alien intelligence controlling our destiny for better or for worse.

In a nutshell, the story—which everyone reading this book surely knows—is about a young man (Thomas Anderson, a.k.a. Neo) who, over the course of the film, wakes up to see the world as it really is. Neo is a hacker in the early Internet era who keeps finding enciphered "Easter eggs" that suggest a universal conspiracy revolving around something called *The Matrix* and an enigmatic figure named Morpheus. When, through the intercession of another hacker named Trinity, he is able to track down Morpheus, he's told bluntly that the world he knows is a counterfeit—a digital simulacrum of the preapocalyptic planet that existed before the sentient machines we'd built turned their human creators into power cells. Morpheus offers Neo an irrevocable choice between two alternatives: the *red pill* or the *blue pill*. The blue pill will allow him to slip comfortably back into the world of digital illusion projected by the malevolent A.I. demiurge. The red pill, on the other hand, will open his eyes to a reality that may not be as pretty or as pleasing, but has the virtue of being authentic. Neo chooses the red pill.

We'll hit on key plot points as we move through the score, but for a moment, put yourself in Davis's place. Imagine that you are the assigned composer, seeing and hearing all this for the first time. You know sci-fi, and you know that such men of talent as Bernard Herrmann and Jerry Goldsmith have scored it definitively. You can, to some degree, "go to school" on their efforts. But in other respects, you are in terra incognita. How do you find the musical expression of a mirror-reality generated by a ceaseless stream of digits?

Don Davis had few models, but he did have some "Easter eggs" of his own to guide him into the rabbit hole. The bits and bytes of binary code that make up a digital stream are in some ways like the short motives or "cells" that are woven into a work of orchestral *minimalism*. And minimalism as a compositional style owes a great deal to the schemes of repetition and recombination that characterize much of non-Western art music, particularly Hindustani raga and Indonesian gamelan forms, which are in many ways a musical codification of some of the very religious and philosophical systems from which *The Matrix* drew its key themes. A practitioner of Hindustani classical music will tell you that a raga is far more than just a "scale" or mode: it is the DNA of an organic chain of meaning that ultimately spells out great and hidden truths. Likewise, the continual rhythmic subdivision and metrical ambiguity of gamelan—especially the interlacing *kotekan* of the Balinese style—are an analog of both ancient concepts of God as number and very modern notions about the *granular* nature of quantum reality at its most fundamental level. Early proponents of Western minimalism, such as Terry Riley, were very much aware of this connection. And in 1986, John Adams's *Short Ride in a Fast Machine* had its debut performance in Pittsburgh and took minimalism an exhilarating sprint closer to the propulsive drive of great film music. Adams's description of his compositional process could well apply to Don Davis's in *The Matrix*: "Rather than set up small engines of motivic materials and let them run free in a kind of random play of counterpoint, I used the fabric of continually repeating cells to forge large architectonic shapes, creating a web of activity that, even within the course of a single movement, was more detailed, more varied, and knew both light and dark, serenity and turbulence."[1]

---

1   "John Adams on Harmonium," https://www.earbox.com/harmonium/.

Davis was, to my knowledge, the first American film composer to evidence a keen interest in Adams's harmonic and rhythmic language. He was also an early admirer of the work of Arvo Pärt, which makes him indeed something of a pacesetter. We'll return to *Short Ride* a bit later, but now, let's take a step-by-step look at how Davis's justly celebrated Main Title music wove the Wachowskis' vision into musical form.

Figure 7.1A. *The Matrix*, 1M1 logo, bars 1–4

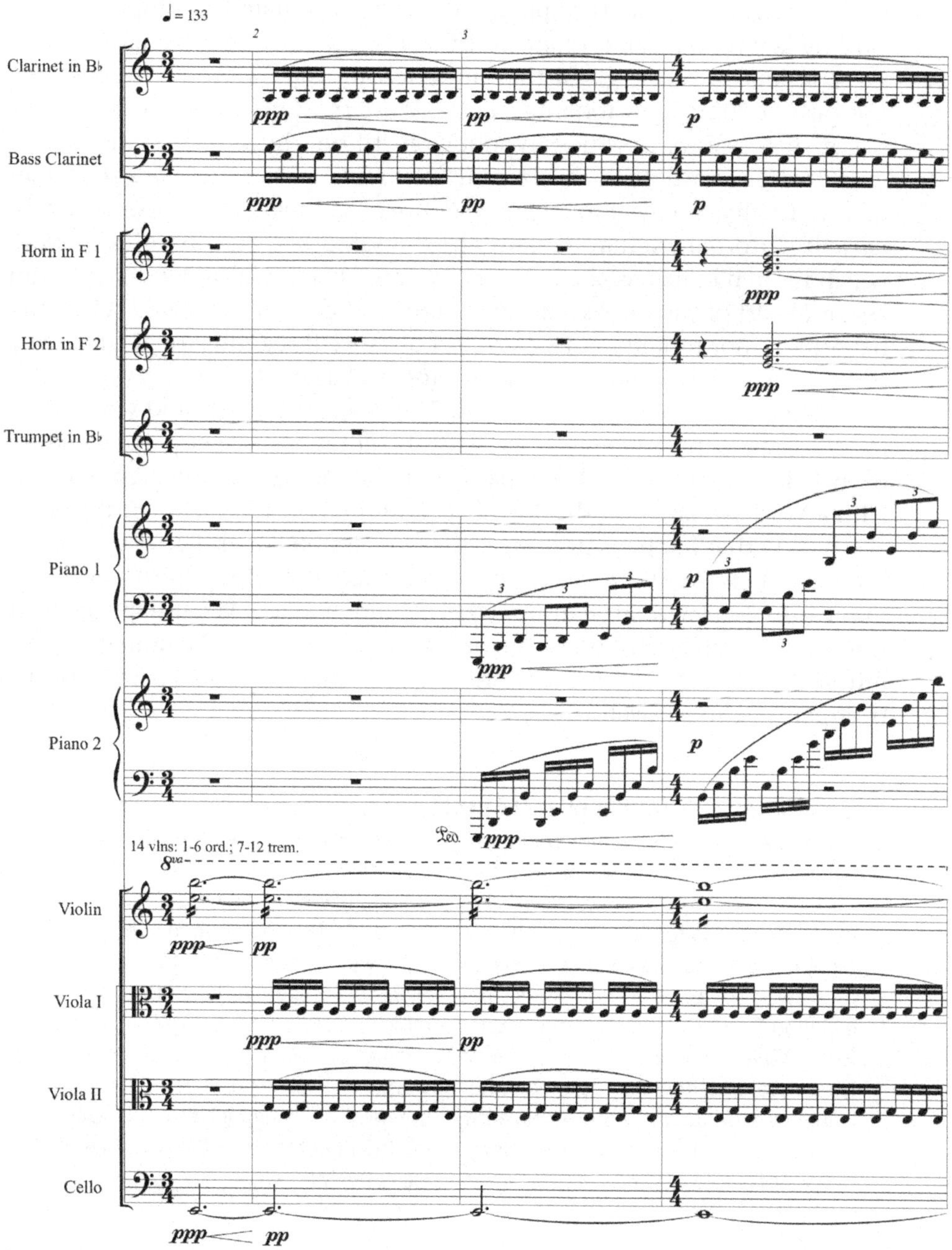

Figure 7.1A shows the initial four measures—the music heard as the Warner Bros. logo appears on the screen. This is a reduction for clarinets, horns, trumpets, piano, and strings. Because *The Matrix* is not a homophonic score, but a musical machine made of many working parts, reductions are tricky. How do you choose what to eliminate when every part is critical? In this case, I omitted percussion, harp, trombones, and other members of the woodwind section, such as bassoons, whose figures either double or mirror those of clarinets and violas. I believe what remains illustrates the essential design.

Utilizing a minimalist approach tends to eliminate the slipperiness regarding key center that is characteristic of so much contemporary film music. That makes sense, given that minimalism as a movement represented not only a "return to tonality" but a Western synthesis of non-Western styles, such as *raga*, in which hypnotic repetition, rhythmic complexity, ornamentation, and other "horizontal" elements matter far more than harmonic density, tonal ambiguity, and other "vertical" elements. A raga or *maqam* performance may remain "in the same key" for its full duration, which is often in excess of two hours, because in a modal system, "key" is an essential part of the work's emotional and aesthetic impact. Cue 1M1 clearly has an E minor tonality at its root . . . but as we'll see, this tonal constancy just gives Davis a baseline to work around and against.

In bar 2 of the reduction in Figure 7.1B, we see clarinets and violas sharing the same contrary motion in sixteenth-notes, the upper part ascending from A(3) to B(3) and the lower part from G(3) to E(3). So, the figure begins with a M2 dissonance on the downbeat and then opens to a P5. And indeed, everything that happens in these initial bars is about E and B. The dual pianos have them in five octaves. The effect, therefore, of the horns' entrance in measure four with an E minor triad is quite marked. What happens next is more striking. Look closely at measure five in horns and trumpets. The E minor chord in the horns begins to diminish just as a C major triad in the trumpets begins to swell.

Composer's Sidebar: MINIMALISM

Minimalism as a musical movement can be seen as a reaction to what were perceived as the excesses and alienating influences of modernism. Its origins are most closely associated with a coterie of New York–based composers that included Terry Riley, La Monte Young, Steve Reich, and Philip Glass, all of whom were to one degree or another influenced by John Cage. In its early days as part of New York's "Downtown Scene" of the early 1960s, it was known as the New York Hypnotic School, and was also labeled "process music" and "phase music." Most sources credit composer Michael Nyman in a 1968 article with the first use of the term *minimal music*. The hypnotic effect of minimalist music makes it an especially apt choice for *The Matrix*, which depicts a world in which human beings have essentially been hypnotized into accepting the counterfeit for the real. The music *is* the Matrix.

Figure 7.1B. *The Matrix*, 1M1 logo, bars 5–8

Another film composer, competent and seasoned, but perhaps a little envious, once said to me, "What's the big deal? He lays a C major triad over an E minor triad and I'm supposed to think that's 'groundbreaking'?" What I wanted to say was, "If it's so easy, why haven't you done it?" Because the fact is that Davis's musical statement—right at the beginning of the film—is every bit as emblematic of *The Matrix*'s content as was David Newman's "Carmen" gesture in *War of the Roses*. He lays them out, in bold counterposition: the two worlds, the red pill and the blue pill, the form and its mirror image. Here's what Richard Cohn, referencing mid-nineteenth-century German theorists, such as Carl Friedrich Weitzmann, has to say about it: "Accordingly, when C major and E minor are juxtaposed, the attraction of C to B (as in 6-5 in E minor) is as strong as that of B to C (as 7-8 in C major). The semitonal relation thus projects an unstable force field that pulls simultaneously in both directions."[2] In other words, says Cohn, they are *reciprocal*.

In the key of E minor, the C major chord is, of course, the natural *VI* chord, with two common tones. Close enough in nature to be switched. Close enough for one to be the dark mirror of the other. We've seen this kind of chordal opposition before in at least two prominent instances: Elmer Bernstein's accordion-like alternation of A minor and F major harmonies (the same relationship) to suggest the dual nature of Boo Radley as boogieman and savior, and Bernard Herrmann's opposition of E-flat minor and D major in *Vertigo*, to illustrate the duplicity of both the Madeleine character, and of romantic passion itself.

Davis makes the opposition/reflection more marked through dynamic contrast: each chord, in turn, enters at *ppp* and swells to *ff* before being enfolded by the streaming continuum of the minimalist "process" around it. The great maverick physicist David Bohm hypothesized that reality consisted, broadly, of two domains: *implicate* and *explicate orders*. In the former, things lie enfolded only in a virtual, or "implicate" form—particles and antiparticles in chaotic dance—in the latter, they *unfold* into the material reality we see. But one reality doesn't simply replace the other: they operate in a continual succession, so you never quite know which reality you currently occupy. This is the way Don Davis's cue feels. It is disorienting, but in a thoroughly captivating way.

In the final four measures of this excerpt, we begin to see another important design element, one that suggests even more strongly the near infinitude of overlapping data streams that would be required to construct a virtual world. Davis uses the subtlest of articulation differences to vary the phrasing of his 2–4 note cells. Notice the placement of slurs for the bass clarinet in bars 10–12. They have the effect of creating "enfolded" two-, three-, and four-note subphrases within and between the beamed units. We'll see this technique fully at play in the next cue to be explored, "Trinity Infinity."

---

2   Richard Cohn, *Audacious Euphony* (Oxford University Press, 2012)

Figure 7.1C. *The Matrix*, 1M1 logo, bars 9–12

The story opens in a grimy warehouse district of Chicago (with Australian locations standing in) as police and agents of the Matrix under the command of Agent Smith stake out a rundown hotel in which Trinity awaits a call from Morpheus. Agent Smith knows what the police don't: that Morpheus, leader of the Resistance, and Trinity, his senior hacker, have identified the young man who may be "the One," a savior-figure who can free mankind from its imprisonment in the illusory reality of the Matrix. His hacker name is Neo (an anagram of both *one* and *eon*, in addition to being a prefix meaning "new"), and later that same evening he'll receive instructions from his computer screen to "follow the White Rabbit." But first, Trinity must escape the police (whom she dispatches easily with a display of the airborne martial arts skills the movie made famous) and the far more dangerous and agile men under Agent Smith.

Figure 7.2A. *The Matrix*, 1M2, "Trinity Infinity," bars 1–6 @ 00:42

Figure 7.2 displays, without reduction, the first six bars of the cue. At this point, all we see is a close-up of a flashing cursor, vintage computer green, in the upper left corner of the monitor screen. And yet, the music invests this meaningless signal with portent. Soon, we know why. Woodwinds drop out momentarily, leaving cellos trembling alone at a whispery dynamic of *pp*. A message scrawls across the monitor screen: "Call trans opt: received. 2-19-98 13:24:18 REC: Log>." It means nothing to us. A phone rings, and a woman answers. "Is everything in place?" she asks. Bass clarinets reenter. Random digits stream across the monitor, in that same backlit emerald green.

In the course of a brief, terse telephone conversation, we will learn that Trinity has a somewhat skeptical partner, Cypher, and that there's more than a little friction between them. We also learn that the phone call has been traced, and that's not good. Within seconds, the cops will arrive, followed by the agents, and Trinity will have to make a run for it in one of the late twentieth century's most gripping opening action sequences.

Before we jump into that action, take another look at the placement of slurs in Figure 7.2. Here, Davis has expanded a few of what I called "subphrases," but what could also be characterized as "musical bytes," from two to four notes up to as many as six (see bass clarinets in bar 3). Moreover, he has connected all of them. Look up and down the page: there isn't a single "gap" that isn't bridged somewhere by a slur. With a few notable exceptions, the motion is stepwise, and the pitch set is limited to the E-natural minor scale. It's the variation in the *ordering* of pitches that makes the passage come alive. As for variations in phrasing, they appear random, but are they? Doubtful. This isn't aleatoric writing, like Newton-Howard's "buzzing bees" in the chapter 1 excerpt from *The Sixth Sense*. I wouldn't go so far as to suggest that Davis has given us a musical cipher of some sort, but it's safe to say that everything he's done is quite deliberate.

Once Trinity has taken care of the Chicago cops, there's a breathless moment for her to take a call from Morpheus himself, who warns her that agents are on their way. Since she is an interloper in this artificial world, she's in great danger. If she dies here, she will also die in the flesh-and-blood body she has left behind. Morpheus tells her she must get to a phone booth "at Wells and Lake" to receive the call that will safely pull her out of the Matrix and return her to her body. Her dash across the rooftops gives both the SFX crew and the composer a chance to do a little showing off.

Figure 7.2B. *The Matrix*, 1M2, "Trinity Infinity," bars 115–118

No action film is complete without a couple of good chases. They raise the heart rate and encourage identification with the protagonist. They're often highly choreographed in a way that lends itself to music (and just as often, cut to some form of temporary music that did not originate with the film's assigned composer).[3] Almost every composer likes writing them, but few do it well. The mistake that's often made is to assume that it's *all* about the pulse—jackhammer eighth- or sixteenth-notes with an ominous drone

---

3   In the case of *The Matrix*, there seems to have been closer collaboration than usual between filmmakers and composer with regard to the rhythm of each action scene. See discussion accompanying Figures 7.3A and 7.3B.

underneath and an occasional "rise and hit," and you're there. But the best chase cues are those that create maximum tension, and tension comes from a different musical parameter.

The pulse is important, but so is what pulls against it. The counter-rhythms, particularly syncopated counterrhythms, are what create the sense of imbalance, and thereby, jeopardy. (If you throw us off, we get edgy) Don Davis was entirely familiar with the way in which his forbears had utilized this rhythmical *push-pull*.[4] But *The Matrix* was a different kind of movie. In some ways, it was the first twenty-first-century film, and required a twenty-first-century score. What we see in the reductions in Figures 7.2A and 7.2B is a score structure derived from orchestral minimalism, but with a cinematic difference. Three elements work with *and* against each other to produce the push-pull effect, but none of them would be effective if they hadn't been gauged so adeptly to picture.

The dominating motive is the syncopated figure in the flutes, heard also in the rest of the woodwinds and the horns. Against this is another, less active syncopated rhythm in the trombones, also heard in percussion and low strings. Underpinning these two wrestling rhythms are the straight sixteenths in pianos and upper strings that have been with us from the start. This isn't just a chase, but a rooftop chase, with both pursuer and pursued possessing not only athletic prowess but the supernatural ability to move in the movie's famous "bullet time," where background action continues at a normal rate while the foreground character seems able to stop time. We'll see how Davis found a musical gesture for "bullet time," but first, a look at the concert work that may have inspired him.

4   One of the finest (and most groundbreaking) examples of this is in the cue entitled "The Chase" from Elmer Bernstein's score for *The Great Escape* (1962). It occurs after Steve McQueen's character steals a Nazi motorcycle. See also Bernard Herrmann's "Rooftop" cue from the opening scene in *Vertigo*.

Figure 7.3A. John Adams, *Short Ride in a Fast Machine*, bars 20–23 (excerpt)

By the time *Short Ride* had its premiere performance in 1986, John Adams had already insured his place in that rarefied sphere of concert composers famous in their own time. Beyond the hypnotic repetition that characterizes most minimalism, *Short Ride* also employs a number of Adams's signature techniques. Among these are harmonic "gating," a form of extended tonality whereby, in Adams's words, the composer "bring(s) in a new key area almost on the sly, stretching the ambiguity out over such a length of time that the listener would hardly notice that a change had taken place,"[5] and "rhythmic dissonance," a technique that alters the perception of time in much the same "sly" way. In the excerpt in Figure 7.3A, the tonal center is clearly grounded in D (major), but the continual use of the second scale degree (E) in the arpeggiation keeps the tonality up in the air, as does the accent pattern in the winds.

5   Brent Heisinger, "American Minimalism in the 1980s," *American Music* 7, no. 4 (Winter 1989), 430–47. Published by the University of Illinois Press.

Figure 7.3B. John Adams, *Short Ride in a Fast Machine*, bars 72–74 (excerpt)

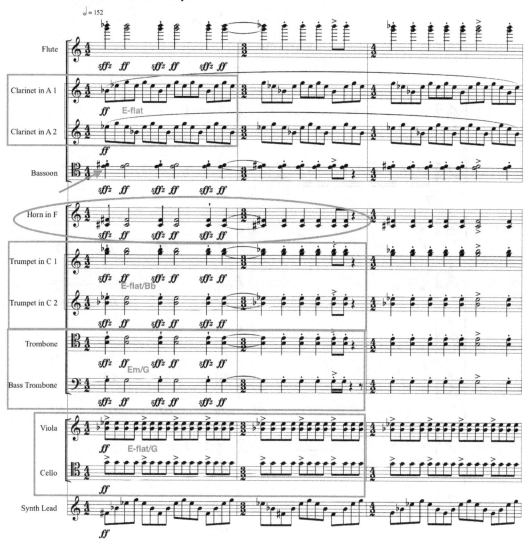

Gating shifts the tonal center not through conventional voice-leading, but by gradual replacement of pitches that define one key center with ones indicating another. You can see this happening in Figure 7.3B, which is well into *Short Ride* at bar 72. The principal tonal center is E-flat major (though almost never spelled in root position). But the brass is beginning to pull us ambiguously away from that center, with the horns pointing up a minor third toward F-sharp major. Likewise, the subversion of metric stability through accent patterns and altered phrasing plays with the way we experience the division of time. Notice also the very decisive dynamic markings for flutes and brass. Both of these observations have direct applicability to *The Matrix*.

Figure 7.4A. *The Matrix*, 1M2, "Trinity Infinity," bars 136–138

A score reduction can't possibly encompass the musical ground that Davis covers in even these short excerpts from "Trinity Infinity," nor can notes on the page convey the furious performance or the sonic assault. Suffice it to say that he's made use of such techniques as *harmonic gating* to produce one of the most thrilling and sophisticated action cues in recent memory. In the foregoing example, which encompasses just three measures of 1M2 (136–138). Trinity is being chased across the rooftops. The relentless ostinatos have moved through three key centers—E minor, F-sharp minor, and now, D minor—providing a kind of substructure over which dramatic shifts in harmony can occur. But now, something extraordinary is going to happen: Trinity is going to defy space and time. What's the musical counterpart of that? (See the highlighted red box.)

Davis sets up Trinity's leap with a *molto crescendo* that fills a 5/4 measure like an Olympic broad jumper's run-up. Horns hold a root position D minor chord while trumpets, starting at a dynamic of just *ppp*, squeeze out a B major chord in first inversion, swelling almost to the level of the horns before dropping, subito, back to *ppp*. D minor and B major share no common tones, and thus operate as harmonic "poles," but they do have the "mediant relationship" that we've often found in cinematic depictions of the fantastical. That isn't harmonically dramatic enough, however, for a leap in "bullet time." In the following measure, the horns reconstitute their voicing into what spells an F major chord, oscillating radically between *fff* and *pp*, like a power transformer during an electrical storm. The first trumpet maintains its high B while its partners shift upward by a tone and semitone respectively, forming an E major chord against the horn section's F major, and occupying the opposite dynamic pole, just as we saw in the opening titles.

The effect is one of supernatural power being *drawn*, or "sucked" from another dimension of reality in order to fuel Trinity's jump. For the length of time she's in the air, the dynamic and harmonic "valving" Davis employs creates a sense of total suspension that allows us to *believe* in "bullet time." Every smart composer looks for keys in the visual and conceptual makeup of a film that may unlock the appropriate melodic, harmonic, and rhythmic language. And it is certainly not unusual for composers to mime dramatic physical actions, such as leaps and dives, with musical gestures that are in some way isomorphic. But in Trinity's first big leap, we hear something new. She makes a safe landing, followed shortly by the pursuing agent.

Figure 7.4B. *The Matrix,* 1M2, "Trinity Infinity," bars 139–143

Because 1M2 is such an important cue, and establishes a template for what's to come, we'll look at one more short excerpt before moving on, this one from bars 157–160 of the original score. The furious ten seconds of score that begins at roughly 05:00 into the film (based on the theatrical version currently available for download) certainly meets John Adams's definition of *rhythmic dissonance.* In fact, without seeing the notes on paper, it's very difficult to separate out the parts from the chaotic whole, and this is precisely what Davis must have intended. The agent in hot pursuit of Trinity has just cleared the urban abyss (he can also leap in "bullet time") and is within shooting range. Her only escape is to make yet another superhuman leap, this time through a narrow window.

In bars 1–2 (corresponding to 156–57 in the original score; see Figure 7.5A), the harmonic tension between horns and trumpets established in Trinity's preceding leap (138–39) is maintained, though now the horns voice a second inversion G major chord, while trumpets have a second inversion E major harmony. In place of the "dynamic counterpoint" used for the leap, they are sandwiched together in a frantic dotted rhythm that suggests Beethoven on anabolic steroids. The same E major/G major "polychord" can be seen traced out in the woodwind quintuplets up on top (D–G–B–E–G–sharp–B). If there is a "key center," the bass instruments would indicate G major, but remarkably, those eternally roiling sixteenth-notes in piano and low woods have stayed with their E minor scale pattern. The Matrix keeps on streaming. This is a polyrhythmic, polytonal cue.

Figure 7.5A. *The Matrix,* **1M2, "Trinity Infinity," bars 156–57**

As Trinity nears the jumping off point for her next laser-guided leap through a tenement window, the percussion section (not shown in the reduction) adds still more tension, and full strings bolster the ominous minor mode thrum of the Matrix motives. When she makes the leap, horns and trumpets reprise the dynamic "mirroring" or *phasing* gesture we now recognize as representing a kind of musical wormhole between worlds, while the strings tremble with the full, stacked E major/G major polychord—and in the same ambiguous spelling that even allows for an E minor sonority to slip in between the cracks, in the same manner we saw in Figure 7.3B. It may be stretching definition to call this a tritonal cue, but it has certainly kept things suspended.

Figure 7.5B. *The Matrix*, 1M2, "Trinity Infinity," bars 158–60

The first act of *The Matrix* could be subtitled "The Illumination of Thomas Anderson," for it's after Neo accepts the red pill from Morpheus that his eyes are opened to the horror that has befallen the human race. Convincing

Neo that his bodily form has been supplanted by a digitized "residual self-image" also makes believers of *us*. The first step in this painful process is a "second birth." At 31:54 into the film, Neo is harnessed to an array of computers that will send him out of the counterfeit world and into "the desert of the real." This regenesis is accompanied by a cue that's an outstanding example of sci-fi scoring.

Figure 7.6A. *The Matrix*, 2M4, "Switched for Life," bars 66–70 @ 00:31:54

At the point we're entering the cue (measure 66 of the *Matrix Live* score), Neo is coming on to the effects of the red pill and becoming aware of some very disturbing changes in the makeup of reality—among them, a super-cooled, mercury-like liquid that sheathes his hand and then his entire arm. His reaction, naturally, is, "This can't be . . . " But it's the job of Morpheus, the CGI team—and Don Davis—to assure us that it *can*. Neo is undergoing "replication" and, quoth Cypher, "Kansas is going bye-bye."

The first thing to take notice of is the time signature: 6/8. A compound meter allows Davis more room to maneuver with rhythm, and he takes full advantage. In bar 68 and elsewhere, we see 4:3 tuplets against straight eighths and sixteenths. The second thing that's evident is the use of fantasy scoring's most reliable convention: the opposition of chords with a "mediant relationship," in this case, C minor and A-flat major. Just as with the emblematic E minor and C major chords of the Main Titles, there's only a semitone's difference between these triads, but in direct opposition and interlocking rhythm—as they are in the horns and trumpets in bars 68–69, it becomes the difference that opens the portal to an altered reality. In the strings, broken C minor chords and block A-flat major chords are placed directly on top of one another, as in the violins and violas. From a C minor reference point, the pitch class "A-flat" (the sixth degree of a natural minor scale) is an ornamental neighbor note and a staple of film music melody. From an A-flat major reference, the pitch class "G" is a chordal embellishment that, when added to the triad, makes it an A-flat major7 chord. In a cascade of sound such as this one, the overall sonority really ought to be A-flat major7, but that's not what we hear. We hear the two chords in distinct opposition because of the way that opposition is highlighted.

Figure 7.6B. *The Matrix*, 2M4, "Switched for Life," bars 71–74

One of the key things that keep the harmonic language of *The Matrix* so bracingly clear and unmuddied is that Davis employs—almost exclusively—triads. The various mash-ups and mirroring techniques used throughout the score work because the identity of the chords is so unambiguous. In music that is principally about linear development (just about anything from the common practice period in Western art music), triads must take on accomplices so as to achieve modulation and other forms of development, and in the impressionist period exemplified by Debussy, chord identities became highly ambiguous. But the humble triad remains a potent kernel of musical meaning—a signifier in itself—and its luster has been restored in recent years,[6] most notably in Arvo Pärt's *tintinnabuli*. Don Davis, as noted earlier, was an early admirer of Pärt. A whole new kind of *nonlinear* development occurs when triads go head to head. In the next four measures of 2M4, Davis underscores Neo's increasing panic over his transformation. The dynamic hasn't been increased, nor has the basic clockwork design of the cue or the density of its elements been altered. Just one thing informs us that the situation has grown more urgent. In measure 72, the trumpets step up one semitone to a B major harmony.

In measure 76, the entire orchestra notches one dynamic up and trumpets move in parallel to a D-major chord, hammering out 4:3 tuplets against the horns' insistent C minor. These chords, like those in the preceding four bars, have no common tones, ensuring maximum clash at the point when Neo's system is showing strain.

Composer's Sidebar:
ARVO PÄRT, HENRYK GÓRECKI AND "HOLY MINIMALISM"

Perhaps in reaction to the fact that "the world of appearances" had become so much about vulgar display, concert composers in the last quarter of the twentieth century began to turn toward a more contemplative style, one whereby the music again became something to be experienced and not merely admired. Film composers—those with their ear to the ground—picked up on this shift. We've already credited the contribution of Estonian composer Arvo Pärt to this revolution. Of nearly equal impact was the release, in 1992, of a new recording of the Third Symphony of Polish composer Henryk Gorecki, subtitled "The Symphony of Sorrowful Songs."

---

6   See also Cohn, *Audacious Euphony*.

Figure 7.6C. *The Matrix,* 2M4, "Switched for Life," bars 75–78

At bar 79, we arrive at the climax of the cue as the crescendo that began in measure 78 brings Neo to the brink of cardiac arrest, just as Apoc, the senior hacker, finds the "target location" for his painful rebirth. The one bar sequence that bassoons have cycled from the start continues, doubled by harp and piano. Trumpets leap once again—this time by M3 to an F-sharp major chord. Notice that the gap between the "two worlds" (horns and trumpets) has steadily opened up: from m6 to M7 to M9, and now, an augmented eleventh. Strings (excluding basses) have doubled their ratio from 4:3 to 8:6, and no two cells are identical.

Figure 7.6D. *The Matrix*, 2M4, "Switched for Life," bars 79–81

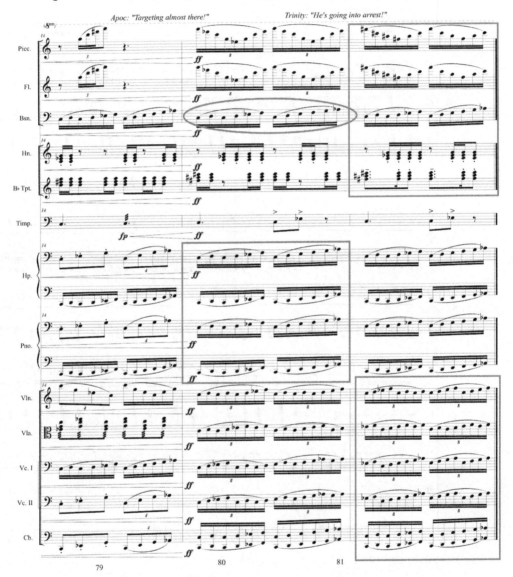

At no point during the foregoing sixteen bars of screen time have any of the characters attending Neo's redelivery moved more than inches from their position. All but Morpheus have remained at their respective stations, and even Morpheus hasn't been allowed much mobility. No one has thrown any punches or broken into a mad dash—no shots have been fired—and yet this is in every sense an *action* scene with an *action* score. The tempo has remained steady and the dynamic hasn't exceeded *ff.* It's the *relative density* of Davis's minimalistic counterpoint, the shifts in register among and between parts, and the correspondingly greater dissonance that have created the great sense of urgency. Don Davis has written a cybernetic fugue—not by mimicking Bach with synthesizers, as in the famous Wendy Carlos recordings—but by representing the digital realm with analog instruments and purely orchestral technique. In many ways, this is the scene upon which the credibility of the concept behind *The Matrix* lies. And it works.

One of the greatest mysteries of the creative process lies in the fact that the "process" part of it is most often not very mysterious at all. It is a brick-by-brick, brushstroke-by-brushstroke, note-by-note enterprise that involves an enormous amount of trial and error. Works of the deepest complexity and loftiest ambition can evolve from the simplest of materials. One reason most artists shy away from delving too deeply into how their works have been constructed may be a justifiable fear that a critic will portray the work as less than what it has become; for example, "Do you mean to tell me that your five-hundred-page novel really began with 'a boy and his dog?'" Great works do begin that simply, the classic examples being the opening motive of Beethoven's Fifth Symphony and, of course, the Bible ("In the Beginning . . ."). Without holding a film score to the standard of either of those, it's fair to say that even a marvel of musical architecture like *The Matrix* begins with bricks and mortar. These are the cells that represent the building blocks of the score. They are, if you like, *diatonic* sets derived from Aeolian mode.

Figure 7.7. The Matrix cells

Borrowing the terminology developed in *set theory*[7] for the study of "posttonal" music, we can also describe these cells as dyad, trichord, tetrachord, pentachord, and hexachord. According to Davis, the first group of

---

7   Set theory is a mathematical approach to the categorization of *musical objects* in the analysis of both tonal and atonal works without reference to a tonic. Its initial formulation is usually credited to Howard Hanson ca. 1960, but it was substantially developed by Allen Forte (1973). See also David Lewin, *Generalized Musical Intervals and Transformations* (Oxford University Press, 2010) and Richard Cohn "Introduction to Neo-Riemannian Theory: A Survey and a Historical Perspective," *Journal of Music Theory* 42, no. 2 (Autumn 1998), 167–80.

cells was *subtractive* and often appeared sequentially; that is, the pitch set would first be heard as the full six-note hexachord (typically in the piano and low woodwind parts) and then sequentially abbreviated until it reached its simplest expression as a dyad. The second group, used more frequently, was *additive* and usually nonsequential. He adds, with some degree of understatement, "I simply stacked them on top of each other, ordering and staggering so as to avoid unisons as much as possible." Needless to say, this is more easily said than done, but the proof that he pulled it off has already been displayed.

Without going deeply into either set theory or its more recent cousins, neo-Riemannian theory and transformational theory, we can say that they share a fundamentally mathematical approach whereby certain "operations" are performed upon pitch groups—such as scales, modes, rows, or other inventions—so as to achieve certain results. These *operations* include our familiar devices of inversion, transposition, retrograde, and reordering of pitches, but are now described without reference to a tonic. In neo-Riemannian theory, for example, Davis's opening chordal gesture of E minor against C major would be described as an "L-transformation" (because a shift of only one semitone, from the "leading tone" of C, is required). As far as I'm aware, Don Davis didn't consciously apply any of these methods to his musical madness, but he clearly did do these two things:

1. He stayed rigorously faithful to his monomodal concept. This decision has the effect of making the Matrix itself a character in the film.
2. His cells function like musical algorithms, further underpinning the omnipresence of the Matrix. They are the musical counterparts of the streaming digits.

We now advance deep into the film's final act and its climactic and now iconic action sequences. If 2M4 was an action cue for a scene in which the violence was metaphysical, then the series that begins with 6M7 (at roughly 1:45:55) consists of action cues that must, in a sense, counterpunch the furious on-screen physical violence in order to keep it real and not simply a CGI-driven martial arts spectacle. Typically, in scenes where a punch registers at 130 db and a knee to the groin rattles the subwoofers, underscoring gets swallowed up by the sound effects and can barely register a pulse. But Davis developed an ingenious rhythmic vocabulary that insured that his brass section would punch just as hard as Agent Smith's fists and his rhythm section kick as powerfully as Neo.

Figure 7.8. *The Matrix*, 6M7, "Dodge This," bars 4–7 @ 1:45:55

There are a number of notable things about 6M7, a cue that scores a rooftop melee between Neo and Trinity, on one side, and a squadron of virtual army troops on the other. They have come into the city to rescue Morpheus, who is being held captive by Agent Smith and his minions, and this fight is the first time we see Neo's newly developed martial arts skills (especially kickboxing) on full display. What is markedly different here is that no trade-off has been made between sound effects and music in the mix. Every punch, kick, groan, and gunshot registers with bruising force on the soundtrack, and yet the music manages to hold its own as a full partner in the scene.

This is largely a consequence of the way Davis has voiced and phrased his brass (trombones are not shown in the Figure 7.8 reduction). The tempo is racing along at 146 bpm, so those clustered sixteenth-note stabs in the horns and trumpets are spit out about as rapidly as they can be—rapidly enough that most of them fall *between* the impact sound of the kicks and punches. Tempo choice is key to any action cue, but here it is critical. If the tempo were any slower, or if the register of the brass parts were lower by even so little as a third, the scheme would not have worked, and most likely the music would have been mixed down so as not to step on the sound effects. Examine most contemporary action cues and you'll find electronics lending the music whatever edge it has, but in 6M7, it's all orchestral. Davis takes an assertively musical approach to scoring action in *The Matrix*, and it pays off by buying him a more prominent place in the mix. Much of the furious action you see in the woodwinds, pianos, and strings is reduced to a texture by the SFX track, which includes such bandwidth-eating elements as a whirring helicopter blade, but it doesn't matter, since it's there to provide a springboard for the brass. This practice will be consistent through all the major fight cues.

We now move into the climactic encounters between Neo and Agent Smith. In these decisive scenes, Davis has not only to compete with a hyperaggressive sound effects track and keep the action moving at breakneck pace, but to convey musically the sense of "bullet time"—a critical story element because it is Neo's mastery of virtual spacetime and gravity in the Matrix that affirms that he is, indeed, "the One." The decisive mano a mano occurs in a deserted subway station, represented as one of the underground stops on the Chicago CTA line. After having successfully held off the army in 6M7, Neo and Trinity are now heading back to the rebel ship, the *Nebuchadnezzar*, by way of one of Apoc's phone booth "patches," when who should turn up again but Agent Smith, mad as hell and loaded for bear. Trinity makes it back to the ship just in time, but Neo is left to face his nemesis on the subway platform. After receiving a thrashing from Smith that shakes him badly, Neo rallies, and in one of the film's most iconic moments, assumes his attack stance.

Figure 7.9A. *The Matrix*, 7M1, "That's Gotta Hurt," bars 140–146 @ 1:56:43

Notice that in measures 1–2 of the Figure 7.9A reduction (bars 140–41), when Neo assumes his stance, Davis reprises the anthemic E minor/C major motif from the Main Titles. Various transpositions and interpolations have been seen throughout the score, but this feels like the most direct recollection of its very first statement, and fittingly so. These are the two worlds in a face-off. Then, on the downbeat of measure 147 (Figure 7.9B) with *sfffz* hits on bass drum, timpani, and anvil, Neo is back in action on a whole new level.

Figure 7.9B. *The Matrix*, 7M1, "That's Gotta Hurt," bars 147–151 @ 1:58:13

It's difficult to overstate the excitement this semiairborne martial arts showdown created at the time of the film's release. Asian cinema audiences had for some years tasted such kinetic fury in the work of such filmmakers as John Woo, but the aerial balletics of *Crouching Tiger, Hidden Dragon* were still a year away when *The Matrix* hit theaters. The Wachowskis' genre innovations may have been derivative, but they deserve credit for both audacity and prescience, not to mention technical and narrative ingenuity. In Neo, they gave us Peter Pan as a kickboxer, and when he rises into the air, it's thrilling.

But as I've suggested, even a fight scene staged as brilliantly as this one might have come off as little more than a clever riff on B-movie convention if not for Davis's approach. His score consistently enables *The Matrix* to have a gravitas it very much wants to have, but couldn't have if the Wachowski's had sought their composer in poorer quarters. The horn section in 7M1 is made even more virile by the substitution of six Wagner tubens, the instrument created for Richard Wagner himself to voice the "Valhalla" motif in *Das Rheingold*. It's a crossbreeding of a French horn with a trombone, with a sound not so much more aggressive as more *focused*. One look at the passage of marcato eighth-notes in measures 147–50 illustrates why Davis desired that focus—but just as important, it is the Wagner tubens in measure 147 that announce Davis's own *Rheingold* gesture.

In the full score, each of the six tubens is assigned its own line, but to conserve space, I've condensed them into a 3-3 split on two lines, with the three trumpets and four trombones similarly condensed. That's a lot of brass, written as tightly as possible, but that's precisely what allows Davis to cut through the Sturm und Drang of the soundtrack and make a truly additive contribution to this memorable scene. Both Wagner tubens and trumpets drive toward a four-note cluster, E–F-sharp–G–A (the tetrachord representing one of Davis's nuclear cells), reached at the end of a 4-bar period composed of two 2-bar phrases. The phrases are defined by those *sfffz* hits in the percussion section (most audibly the anvil), and by the eighth-note rests in brass and strings, but there's some rhythmic trickery in the way these hits/rests are placed. The first one falls exactly where we'd expect it: on the downbeat. But the second falls on the "and of 4," resulting in a powerful turbo-burst of propulsive syncopation. We hear it as a downbeat, but as in John Adams's notion of rhythmic dissonance, it disorients us in the right ways. And what can we say about a cue that has downbows marked in the strings for every single eighth-note at a tempo of 165?

If filmgoers were allowed to remember just one thing about *The Matrix*, it might well be the moment when a stricken Keanu Reeves, out of time, apparently out of tricks, his neck in Hugo Weaving's headlock and a CTA train headed straight for him, responds to Agent Smith's sinister, "Good-bye, Mr. Anderson," with a terse, "My name . . . is Neo."

Figure 7.9C. *The Matrix*, 7M1, "That's Gotta Hurt," bars 204–209 @ 1:58:20

A crescendo as dramatic as they come *(ppp<fff)* sets up the moment when Neo cheats death (not for the last time) and literally springs back into action, flying Smith smack into the subway ceiling and then leaving him on the tracks as he back flips onto the platform just as the train roars by. One of the great delights of *The Matrix* is the way the Wachowskis indulge virtually every grindhouse action cliché in the midst of all the heady and portentous dialogue and concept. But this is not a Chuck Norris movie, and there is never a scene in which Don Davis can get away with "the usual thing."

This portion of 7M1 is one of the score's clearest examples of orchestral minimalism used in counterpoint to violent physicality, and the effect of all the swirling tuplets in the woodwinds, harp, and pianos is to make the utterly fantastical seem plausible. Here we have quintuplets beating against triplets beating against straight eighths, and all of them materializing into another "mediant mirror": C minor opposed to A-flat major. As noted previously, film music scholars, such as Claudia Gorbman and Royal S. Brown, have argued that one of film music's prime functions is to lower the threshold of belief and thus allow audiences to abandon doubt and happily go along for the ride. But it's one thing for a theorist to postulate this and quite another for a composer to figure out how to do it.

In the early days of science-fiction cinema, it might have been enough for the composer to bring out a theremin, which, combined with ominously muted low brass and striking harmony would be enough to draw the audience through the wormhole. The granddaddy of such scores is Bernard Herrmann's inspired madness for the 1951 film *The Day the Earth Stood Still* (remade in 2008 with Keanu Reeves!). Using a battalion of Hammond organs, multiple keyboards, two harps, and *two* theremins, Herrmann created what seemed, in 1951, a believably wondrous, if deeply weird portrayal of an extraterrestrial visit. His fantasy scores set the paradigm for more than three decades.

The Matrix depicts a different kind of alien reality, one that is the conceptual spawn of cybernetics, quantum mechanics, postmodern philosophy and millennial anxiety—but no less marvelous for the passage of a half-century. In his score, and in his use of harmonic and rhythmic oppositions to represent the cognitive dissonance experienced by a man coming to terms with an unthinkable truth, Don Davis has given us a work worthy of Herrmann, and one more faithful to its generating concept than any film score of the last twenty years.

Figure 7.9D. *The Matrix*, 7M1, "That's Gotta Hurt," bars 210–213

EIGHT SUCH A LONG, LONG WAY TO FALL

DANNY ELFMAN'S *ALICE IN WONDERLAND*

Danny Elfman

It seems entirely fitting to follow a chapter about the music of *The Matrix* with an appreciation of Danny Elfman's score for Tim Burton's 2010 version of *Alice in Wonderland*. After all, the Wachowskis used Lewis Carroll's whimsical 1865 fantasy as a virtual playbook for Neo's own adventures in an upside-down reality, beginning with the notion of "going down the rabbit hole," an expression that's now so much a part of our speech that we no longer think about its origins. In fact, *Alice's Adventures in Wonderland* (the full title of the book) is so venerable a touchstone for tales of alternate realities—accessible only to those of an eccentric bent and an ability to adapt to the fantastic—that it seems to have been destined for Burton to direct and Elfman to score.

The critical consensus is that *Alice* is neither Tim Burton's most auteurish film (that would probably be *Edward Scissorhands*) nor Danny Elfman's most emblematic score (many people would say likewise), but it deserves study because it may be their most mature (if that word can be applied to this impish duo) collaboration to date, and because—as mentioned—*Alice in Wonderland* is the film they *had* to make. Burton, a one-time Disney animator, is so purely a visual storyteller that dialogue often seems almost incidental, and *Alice*, with its Walt Disney Pictures imprint and its $200 million budget, gave full rein to his extraordinary gifts of visualization. Elfman, whose best work has always embodied a quality that might be described as "the dark side of Disney," is here given an opportunity (and a budget) to use every compositional muscle he has in service of a full-blown fantasy, and delivers a score that by all rights ought to have won him an Oscar.

Danny Elfman, born in the 1950s and weaned on science fiction and pulp, may be the contemporary film music world's most naturally "symphonic" composer. That assertion may strike some as wrongheaded at best and heretical at worst. Shouldn't that title go to someone like John Williams? Or to Elliot Goldenthal, who studied with Aaron Copland and John Corigliano and writes fully realized symphonic works for both film and concert hall? To back up my opinion, let me explain what I mean by "symphonic."

If we think for a moment about the classical repertoire's most unreserved and uncompromising symphonic statements—the first or final movements of Beethoven's Fifth or Ninth Symphonies, Dvorak's Ninth, Shostakovich No. 10 (feel free to add your own candidates)—we may conclude that what they have in common is a muscular use of motive and an employment of orchestral forces that's almost unitary. That is to say, the orchestra speaks as one, and that the music has a physicality that strives to move its audience out of any sort of polite complacency and overwhelm it with sound. Brass and percussion are key ingredients, as are special colors, such as choir and pipe organ, all of which Elfman uses extensively. Sweeping melody and intricate counterpoint are not as important as insistent rhythm and motive. The composer goes for broke.[1]

In the work of many leading film composers, it's often difficult to hear the music's lineage (aside from other film scores), but Elfman's music is like a spicy gumbo redolent of some of the most enticing flavors of both concert hall and cabaret: Tchaikovsky, Prokofiev, Bartok, Saint-Saëns, Dukas, and Ravel. Add the seasoning of Kurt Weill, Nino Rota, Lou Harrison, Jewish klezmer, Cotton Club jazz, Carl Stalling, and of course, Bernard Herrmann, and out comes a creature a little like *Edward Scissorhands* himself. Exotic, eccentric, slashing, sensitive, just a little bit mad, and perhaps—like Edward— "not finished." And for all these potent influences, Danny Elfman remains

---

1 The most recent example of this—too recent to be included in this book—is Scott Walker's score for Brady Corbett's 2015 film *The Childhood of a Leader.*

very much his own man. If it might once have been easier to point to particular works and artists, such as *Peter and the Wolf, The Sorcerer's Apprentice*, "Minnie the Moocher," or formative sci-fi and fantasy scores as inspirations, Elfman has now so thoroughly absorbed and assimilated these models to his own style that his music can only be described as Elfmanesque. In fact, more often Elfman himself is the one being imitated, and such has been the case ever since he and Tim Burton set off on their journey together with *Pee-wee's Big Adventure* and *Beetlejuice*.

There's a hugely important lesson in his example, for both fledgling film composers and for those who are seeking to refine or reinvent their own compositional voice to present a more defined musical identity to the marketplace. Danny Elfman has said on more than one occasion that the genesis of his passion for film music was sitting in a darkened cinema at age eleven and finding himself spellbound by Bernard Herrmann's Main Title music for *The Day the Earth Stood Still*. The truth of this experience is borne out by our sense that it's "psychically imprinted" on everything he's done since—including his fifteen-year run as an indie rock star and front man for Oingo Boingo, a band he founded with his brother, Richard, in 1972 as the Mystic Knights of the Oingo Boingo.

Three other major influences should be cited in order to fully grasp *l'essence d'Elfman*. One is his enduring fascination with *Día de los Muertos*[2] (The Day of the Dead), a Mexican festival with Aztec roots that now coincides with All Saints' Day on the Roman Catholic calendar. With its masked and ceremonially dressed skeletons and corpses, the Day of the Dead has obvious links to Halloween and pagan precursors going back well into our common African heritage, and had a marked visual impact on a previous Burton/Elfman/Disney collaboration, *The Nightmare Before Christmas*. Another influence is Elfman's early study of Indonesian gamelan, which has flavored the work of composers from Claude Debussy and Benjamin Britten to Thomas Newman and Mychael Danna. Beyond the gamelan's lattice of interlocking motives, there is the haunting and decidedly nonequal tempered sound of its hammered bronze instruments. Finally, Elfman's years on the road in Europe and North Africa as a "Gypsy violinist," busker, and street theater performer while in his twenties can't be overlooked.

Danny Elfman's "inner child" has never been stuffed away in a closet

---

Thought Experiment, Part I

Here is an exercise that is, appropriately, part weird science and part mystical immersion. (Albert Einstein came upon some of his most profound realizations doing what he called "thought experiments.") Find a quiet, softly lit place (a cave or a cloister may be ideal, but your bedroom will do in a pinch) and set aside fifteen to thirty minutes. Free your brain of clutter as best you can, and then try to locate in space, time, and memory your ten- or eleven-year-old self. What experiences—especially, musical experiences—are coloring the imagination of this preadolescent? What's your "Danny Elfman moment"?

---

2 http://en.wikipedia.org/wiki/Day_of_the_Dead.

like a once-beloved teddy bear. Nor has his musical heritage been disguised. If anything, he wears these colors proudly. It may be that the secret behind his misfit's triumph in the late 1980s and early '90s was that he wasn't stealthy enough to cloak his influences as other film composers did. He has always been a bit of a naïf, but it has served him well. His musical identity emerged so fully formed with 1989's *Batman* score that there were some in the academic community (and a few in the Hollywood film music community) who couldn't believe that he'd actually written it. This combination of envy and disdain, largely based on Elfman's lack of conventional musical training, persists today and has probably denied him some of the peer recognition he deserves. But as they say, success is the best revenge, and Elfman is not only successful, he is—along with Hans Zimmer, Thomas Newman, and perhaps John Williams—one of the three or four most widely imitated film composers in the world.

Thought Experiment, Part II
What are your affinities; that is, what things elicit curiosity and fascination? Is there a particular score, pop song, story character, or pageant that provokes a near-obsessive interest? Don't be afraid of the dark. Some of us are drawn to it. On the other hand, if it's the Little Mermaid singing "Part of Your World" that lights up your inner jack -o'-lantern, go with it. These are your musical imprints, and they shouldn't be denied.

Before we plunge into the rabbit hole after nineteen-year-old Alice Kingsleigh, it may be useful to take a brief look at a couple of earlier works that illustrate how Danny Elfman's signature came to be so widely known and imitated. In a number of important ways, *Alice* is a departure from the style that defined him in the 1990s, but it's easier to understand the departure by reference to the original. The following two examples are reductions excerpted from, respectively, the Main Title and End Title themes of *Edward Scissorhands* and *The Nightmare Before Christmas*, both of which are Elfman at his most iconic.

The qualities listeners hear in early Elfman, even if they can't label them, fall under the headings of (1) mode (invariably minor, usually with a raised seventh); (2) harmony (parallel modes, root movement by thirds, diminished chords; and (3) instrumentation (low brass, low woods, choir, celesta and delicate plucked textures, all of which add up to the musical equivalent of bittersweet dark chocolate—a pretty good quality for *cinema fantastique*.

Figure 8.1. *Edward Scissorhands*, 1M1, Main Title, bars 18–33

Edward Scissorhands is a contemporary retelling of a very ancient sort of folktale: the mysterious stranger comes down from the mountain, bringing into the village a wisdom that is almost entirely a product of his innocence and estrangement from society. He is at first sanctified, but ultimately vilified and driven away (if not worse). The fact that Edward, a creature straight out of gothic fiction, finds himself in the most arid and soulless kind of mid-twentieth- century sunbelt housing tract, as opposed to a Mitteleuropean peasant village, adds elements of humor and modern irony, but Elfman's score is there to remind us constantly of the story's timeless provenance. Everything about his theme suggests a wistful cradle song that might have been born in the shtetls. The stepwise, minor mode melody, harmonized in thirds, stands on its own without accompaniment, as all good lullabies do. The leap of a P4 at the end of each of the "A" phrases, followed immediately by a descent to the raised seventh of harmonic minor mode, is also characteristic of Jewish folk song, and the fully diminished (iv) chord under the "B" phrase adds an astringency that's found in almost all of Elfman's early work.

The dominant orchestral colors: double reeds, harp, and celesta, and inevitably, the fairy-tale chorus, keep the score—and the film—anchored in a land of lyrical melancholy that was a rare locus for a commercial film of the time, and still *is* rare, although Burton and Elfman have done a great deal to bring it into pop culture consciousness. Some of the compositional elements—the strictly parallel keyboard and vocal counterpoint, for example—are still a bit naive, but seem completely appropriate for this film and its guileless protagonist. *Edward Scissorhands* remains in many ways the definitive Elfman score.

Figure 8.2A. *The Nightmare Before Christmas*, End Credit (excerpt), transposed from D-flat minor to C minor

The reduction in Figures 8.2A and 8.2B are transcriptions of the "This Is Halloween" section of the End Credit medley. The concert key is D-flat minor, but for ease of study, I've transposed it to C minor. If a single eight-bar section of Danny Elfman's oeuvre had to be chosen as his most emblematic statement, this would be a strong candidate. All the trademark tropes are there: fleeting tastes of everything from "I Am the Walrus" to *Petrushka*. This tasty plum pudding shows just how rich Elfman's palette is. Look first at the rhythm. It's somehow simultaneously a village square march *and* a tango (note the rise on the "and" of beat 4 in low woods). It's also as *pesante* as a Balkan brass band. Then the harmony: we are already in Elf-land by the time we hit the downbeat of measure 2, with the half-diminished seventh chord (the Hal Leonard edition spells it as an Fm6, but the pitches are identical, and I think a diminished harmony is intended), and if there is any doubt, there is the pivot to E minor in bar 3, which sounds as a mediant shift and is the mirror image of the Dm to Cm7-flat5 (half-diminished seventh) signature from the opening titles of *The Day the Earth Stood Still*. Finally, the languorous clarinet line in bars 1–4 (a high bassoon in the score) pulls in an offbeat jazz astringency that could put us in Kurt Weill's Berlin or the Cotton Club.

Figure 8.2B. *The Nightmare Before Christmas,* End Credit (excerpt, continued)

Alice in Wonderland opens with the main theme emerging from an ethereal bed of *sul ponticello* strings, harp harmonics, and glassy synth pads voicing the motivic i–VI–IV chord progression. The progression is picked up by a boys' choir and taken to the dominant C-sharp chord, and then Elfman pulls a characteristic trick.

Instead of resolving the dominant chord back to what has been briefly established as the tonic F-sharp minor, he does something he's been doing since *Scissorhands*: a "mode flip," maintaining C-sharp as the root but dropping into its minor mode.

Strings enter with a gentle but insistent triplet figure and at a brisk tempo of 120 bpm, and the choir introduces us to the melody that will serve the film from beginning to end. It's a melody that could almost have been derived from medieval plainchant.

Figure 8.3A. *Alice in Wonderland*, 1M1, Main Titles, bars 17–20

The reduction in Figure 8.3A is for woodwinds (piccolo and bassoon are omitted), horns (trombones and tuba omitted), celesta, strings, and boys' and adult choirs octave-doubling the melody. The full melody unfolds over sixteen bars, returning to the initial i–VI–IV progression at its close. It is structured as *antiphony*, with the first two four-measure phrases each answered by a vigorous "echo" of triplets in brass and woodwinds, and the final two phrases linked and ending in the refrain "Alice! *Ohhhh* . . . Alice!" This antiphonal structure, like the melody itself, recalls early music, and this resemblance is emphatically underlined by Elfman's choice of harmony.

Figure 8.3B. *Alice in Wonderland*, 1M1, Main Titles, bars 21–24

Take a look at measure 7/23. Things take an unexpected turn—unexpected, at least, in terms of conventional harmony. For the first five bars following the pickup measure, everything is moving along briskly over ostinatos and broken C-sharp minor chords. The tonality appears to be a traditional natural minor. Then, in the sixth bar, the melody steps up to the A-sharp of Dorian mode, harmonized with a IV chord (F-sharp major), and ornamented by a Dorian neighbor note (B-natural). That B-natural might read to the ear like a sus4 over the F-sharp major chord—except that when it falls back to the A-sharp, it is accompanied by a drop (in violas, cellos, and basses) to an E major harmony, creating an augmented fourth with the root of the chord and a wholly surprising Lydian half-cadence. As Blake Neely, a highly regarded American film and television composer (and for some years, the go-to conductor for Hans Zimmer) once told me, "The damn thing gives me chills every time I hear it. It's so simple, but so brilliant." On this kind of unexpected brilliance was Elfman's career built.[3]

If you're reading this book out of sequence, you may want to go back to chapter 4 and review the excerpts from Morricone's *The Good, the Bad and the Ugly* and Ernest Gold's *Exodus* theme. The major IV chord in context of minor mode tonality is a feature of the Dorian mode, and of the mode mixing that's typical of much contemporary jazz and folk, and also of Renaissance music. What makes it sound so striking here is that we typically hear the intervals of the Dorian mode against a drone rather than block chords, and seldom in a symphonic setting. There are exceptions, of course, such as orchestral arrangements of Celtic folk music, but the augmented fourth ornamenting the III chord gives *Alice* an extra kick. The flavor of this score, and the slightly "off" quality that makes it "stick to our neurons" stems to a significant degree from this single bold choice, just as David Newman's clashing thirds and uncertain roots in *War of the Roses* did in that work. And as with Newman's "Carmen" gesture, Elfman has, with one stroke, defined the personality of his score. Now, all he has to do is follow through with it.

Another notable thing about the *Alice* Main Title is its dynamic restraint. Nothing ever rises above the level of *mezzo piano*, so the crescendos and decrescendos in the piece are very subtle. The theme that will dominate the score is displayed for us in full, but in a way that is so understated that hearing it played *ff* and by the entire orchestra will be like hearing it for the first time. This restraint beautifully compliments the "once upon a time" quality of the opening narrative of a fairy tale, and pulls us right in.

Now it's time to follow Alice down the rabbit hole. In Burton and writer Linda Woolverton's telling, she is no longer an alter ego for Lewis Carroll's ten-year-old Alice Liddell, but a young woman of nineteen, facing the prospect of marriage to a thoroughly unattractive member of the English aristocracy. The rabbit hole is her escape from a public answer to his proposal, but we soon learn that she has been down it before. Alice's flight from the scene of her near betrothal is accompanied by a lustier reprise of

---

3   An early example of this is Elfman's minor-mode Main Title music for *Batman* (1989), in which the fifth note of the famous five-note motif is raised a semitone in the motif's second phrase to serve as a leading tone to the key center a whole-step below. Thus, the "tonic" moves restlessly from B minor to A minor to G minor in just the first eight bars without the listener being fully aware of it.

the main *Alice* theme, but her fall into Underland is scored with a piece of classic Elfmania.

Figure 8.4A. Alice in Wonderland, 1M6, "Down the Hole," bars 72–75 @ 12:59

Woodwinds are omitted in this reduction, but the real action is in the strings. As mentioned, our Alice Kingsleigh (Mia Wasikowska), an almost grown-up version of the Alice we all know, has decided she's not quite ready to be a proper British wife, and has fled from her engagement party in pursuit of the White Rabbit. Now, she is falling very fast and very far.

Notice, though, that there are no "falling figures" in the orchestration—
no descending runs or harp glissandos, nothing even remotely isomorphic.
The design of the shots and the extraordinary visual effects provide all the
vertigo that we need. Elfman concentrates instead on the physicality of the
experience and on conveying the alarm we see on Alice's face, employing
heavily accented strings chopping down at their parts in a fashion a bit
reminiscent of "This Is Halloween." His only musical reference to the dizziness of dropping precipitously to what seems the very center of the earth
is in the chromatic string of minor triads (B-flat minor, B minor, A minor,
G-sharp minor) voiced by a Herrmannesque pipe organ and articulated by
the frenetic counterpoint in the strings. The combination of these elements
creates a landscape that is topsy-turvy enough to make us feel the fall.

Figure 8.4B. *Alice in Wonderland*, 1M6, "Down the Hole," bars 76–79 @ 13:04

Speaking of articulation, the command shown in the string writing is evidence of a composer whose comfort with orchestral expression has fully matured. It's still very much the slashing, manic, and slightly menacing Danny Elfman who learned his craft "at the knee" of Bernard Herrmann, but with considerably more refinement of technique than is seen in his early scores. Experienced orchestrators like to say that "if it reads on the page, it'll play on the stage," and all one has to do is scan the string section to know how the composer wants it to sound. Even the way the eighth-notes are beamed in measures 1–4 (72–75) is illustrative of how they should be played. The "tenuto" markings on the first violins, violas, and cellos in measures 5–9 (76–79) weigh against the rooftop accents and strident downbows to ensure *strength* rather than polite staccato.

Once Alice has hit bottom, she begins the familiar journey into Wonderland, or—as clarified in Woolverton's script—Underland, and meets the cast of characters that every child knows, along with a few borrowed from *Through the Looking Glass*. Among them, there is considerable debate about whether she is, indeed, the "right Alice," since she's now a young women and not a towheaded child. A harrowing encounter with the Bandersnatch indicates that she's the girl they're looking for, and that she should be taken immediately to see the Mad Hatter (Johnny Depp) to learn of the reason she has been summoned for a second time to Underland. To summarize: according to the "Oraculum," the prophetic scroll kept in the charge of Absolem, the hookah-smoking caterpillar, Alice is destined to slay the monstrous Jabberwocky (the dragonlike beast under the command of the evil Red Queen) with the invincible Vorpal Sword on Frabjous Day—and that day is coming very soon. Before she can be taken to the Hatter, however, she must rendezvous with the Cheshire Cat, and that brings us to the next cue.

Figure 8.5A. *Alice in Wonderland*, 2M7, "Cheshire Cat," bars 58–61 @ 28:42

If ever there was a character deserving of musical homage, it is Lewis Carroll's Cheshire Cat, with its languorous speaking style and its luminescent grin hanging in the forested twilight long after its body has evaporated. Alice encounters it following her scrape with the Bandersnatch, and Elfman does not give the Cat a theme so much as a sonic identity composed of percussion effects, gamelan samples, two harps, and some very evocative string writing. The heart of the motif is in the top line of violins, sounding two octaves above the staff in harmonics and doubled *normale* by the violas. These are written in the score as *artificial harmonics*, but I've shown them as natural harmonics. The exotic effect of doubling a chromatic line in this register is enhanced by the use of a portamento effect that sounds a little like an otherworldly meow, rendered even spookier by the fact that we hear it before the Cat has actually materialized. This is embellished by a whole tone run on the bass strings of the harp, topped by a chromatic sextuplet run-up as the spirit essence of the animal wreathes around a lost and mystified Alice before appearing on a tree branch. Things get even more interesting four bars later, when the first violins (shown here as I and II) are split and execute a staggered portamento, leaping a m7 from C-sharp to B-natural (over a C-sharp minor harmony established by gamelan bells), before slithering down a whole step and then joining the rest of the strings in a very Elfmanesque C-sharp minor to D minor chromatic cadence.

Figure 8.5B. *Alice in Wonderland,* 2M7, "Cheshire Cat," bars 66–69 @ 29:04

Alice, still convinced that she's dream-walking, proceeds to teatime with the Mad Hatter, who is indeed insane, but has a deep yearning to restore Underland to what it was before the evil Red Queen (Helena Bonham Carter) turned it into a dystopia. Such a restoration requires putting the White Queen (Anne Hathaway) back on the throne, and this in turn demands that Alice fulfill her destiny and slay the Jabberwocky with the Vorpal Sword. In the midst of tea, the Knave of Hearts—the Red Queen's hit man and paramour—arrives in search of Alice, and ultimately, all are hauled before the court. Alice, not yet recognized as the girl she once was, begins to search the palace for the mythical weapon, and runs into a recent acquaintance.

Figure 8.6A. *Alice in Wonderland*, 4M3, "Vorpal Sword," bars 32–36

The cue labeled 4M2/4M3 "Liars/Vorpal Sword" leads Alice to the den of the very same beast who terrorized her and left three bloody gouges on her arm only a few scenes earlier. The Bandersnatch is a fearsome creature, but not without a soft spot for a young woman with the right touch. When Alice wins it over, it licks her wounds clean and allows her to take from its collar the key that will open the trunk containing the Vorpal Sword. The passage shown in Figure 8.6A (measures 32–35) showcases a lovely reconfiguration of the *Alice* theme's five-note cell, stated first as a flute solo, and then in slight variation, on solo violin (36–38). Notice again the "mode mixing" of (i) and (IV) chords, and the substitution of (VI) for (i) on the repeat. It lends a timeless, mythical feel.

Figure 8.6B. *Alice in Wonderland*, 4M3, "Vorpal Sword," bars 37–39

As Alice opens the jewel-encrusted trunk and removes the sword that will earn her place in Underland history, Elfman gives us the sort of moment that Golden Era composers, such as Alfred Newman and Dimitri Tiomkin, were known for, a cue conveying both "sword and sorcery" mystique and a powerful sense of destiny lying in wait.

Figure 8.7A. *Alice in Wonderland*, 4M3, "Vorpal Sword," bars 43–46 @ 1:03:30

"Sword and sorcery" and "destiny lying in wait." Those are two very potent descriptors, and both of them tap into that great reservoir of myth that psychologist Carl Jung called "the collective unconscious." Imagine that *you* are given this direction by a filmmaker. What are the musical signifiers for such abstractions as sorcery and destiny? The scene must inform us that this is indeed the "right Alice," and that she has accepted her fate as slayer of the Jabberwocky and savior of the realm.

Figure 8.7B. *Alice in Wonderland*, 4M3, "Vorpal Sword," bars 47–50

Elfman handles this assignment masterfully. Let's take it step by step and examine how he does it, beginning with Figure 8.7A, bars 1–2 (43–44 in the concert score). These are the key dramatic beats: (1) the "clock is ticking." Alice has only a very limited time to retrieve the Vorpal Sword before she is found out; (2) the Bandersnatch, who guards over the sword, has been temporarily pacified, but he's the Red Queen's beast, and could easily turn on Alice; (3) from the instant she picks up the sword, Alice must realize that it has been waiting for *her*, and the Bandersnatch must recognize this, too.

We begin with chromatically ascending tremolo strings at a dynamic of *mp* over a steady pulse in the basses as Alice unlocks the trunk. By the time we're two beats into the second bar, we recognize the score's central chordal statement: i–VI–IV (in this case, E minor–C–A). E minor and C share two common tones and—as we saw in *The Matrix*—a special affinity; that is, they contrast, but in the way a brother and sister contrast. An A major chord shares just one common tone (E), and the chromatic inflection from C-natural to C-sharp is much more striking. In measure 45, woodwinds join all strings in cascading eighth-note figures that outline and develop the i–VI harmony, but rather than landing once again on the IV chord, Elfman substitutes a sharp vi chord, C-sharp minor, which is related to the nominal E minor tonality only by way of another modal exchange (it's unlikely that Elfman considered this; like most film composers, he's mostly interested in key centers as a place to start from). Six horns enter in unison, leaping a P5 from C-sharp to G-sharp, but at a restrained dynamic of *mf*, and we might mistake this for the classic "hunting call" so common in epic films, except that in the following two bars (5–6/47–48), we see what the composer is hunting. It's the *Alice* theme, heard as we haven't heard it before—not with children's choir or plaintive reeds, but with the full majesty of a horn section supported by the swelling of the i–VI chord gesture in the new "tonal center" of C-sharp minor.

A triumphant A major chord sounds as Alice holds the sword aloft and feels its power run through her, and Elfman's final surprise is a bold A major to F-sharp major shift as the Bandersnatch humbly takes a step back, as if saying, "Your Majesty . . . " Notice how elegantly that final chord is voiced and articulated. The single common tone, C-sharp, is emphasized throughout the voicing. Motion is mostly limited to minor or major seconds, making the chord change strong but smooth. Finally, the grace notes in the lower strings and tremolo in high first violins add a regal flavor. This is our girl: the "right Alice."

Alice escapes the Red Queen's clutches by the skin of her teeth and heads for the palace of the White Queen with the Vorpal Sword in hand, riding on the back of her new ally, the Bandersnatch. The Red Queen's fury leads to a declaration of war: the rival sisters and their armies are to meet on the field of battle on Frabjous Day. The Red Queen's "champion" is the Jabberwocky, but who will champion the White Queen?

Figure 8.8A. *Alice in Wonderland*, 5M4, "Alice Under Pressure," bars 13–16 @ 1:19:5

All heads turn toward Alice. After all, it was her image shown slaying the Jabberwocky in Absolem's compendium. But Alice is not quite ready to accept this fearsome duty, and in an echo of her earlier flight from the scene of her engagement, she runs off to seek the solace of tears in a gazebo overlooking an awe-inspiring gorge, where she finds Absolem dangling from a vine in midmetamorphosis from caterpillar to butterfly. "Remember," he says. "The Vorpal Sword knows what it wants. All you have to do is hold on to it." Now, take a look at the horn in bars 13–16 (Figure 8.8A) and the piccolo solo in canonlike imitation (14–16).

The tonal starting point is G-sharp minor, and though the harmony and phrasing are different, the line of the melody in the horn and piccolo solos is identical to the tune introduced in 4M3 (Figure 8.6), bars 32–35, when the Bandersnatch was healing Alice's wounds. And that melody was, in itself, a mutation of the main *Alice* theme. The same pentachord has now generated three quite distinctive melodic statements. That is an impressive economy of expression. Elfman has been doing this since *Batman,* and it is a legacy from Herrmann, learned not so much through scholastic training as through keen intuition. His musicality is similarly natural and intuitive. Notice again the detail and motion in the string parts. These aren't pads. It's real counterpoint.

The most moving section of 5M4 begins with the ascending sweep and crescendo in the strings at bar 16. The antecedent phrase (C-sharp to G-sharp to B-natural ascending, followed by D-sharp to C-sharp descending a m6 lower) is new, and has an epic quality that suits both the grandeur of the setting and the gravity of Alice's decision, but on beat 3 of bar 18, we see that the consequent phrase has the familiar shape of Variation 3, which is associated with the Vorpal Sword. These two phrases together might be identified as the "Destiny" theme, and by the time this scene has concluded, Alice will have embraced that destiny and prepared herself to face the Jabberwocky.

Figure 8.8B. *Alice in Wonderland*, 5M4, "Alice Under Pressure," bars 17–20

Once again, Elfman does interesting things with block chords in the harmonization of this "Destiny" theme. He opens with a string of minor chords: C-sharp minor, G-sharp minor, and F-sharp minor, and then closes with a string of major chords: E, D, and B, keeping the key center constantly shifting, just as he did almost twenty years before with the *Batman* theme.

Following a flashback interlude that serves to remind Alice (and the audience) that this is indeed her *second trip* to Underland, and that what she's experiencing is not an Oz-like dream but a parallel world in some manner projected by her powers of imagination, she dons her suit of armor, and as the White Queen's champion, takes her side at the head of the army as it prepares to march into battle with the Red Queen's forces. The Queen is on horseback, but Alice is mounted on the Bandersnatch.

The excerpt shown in Figure 8.9 is from the cue titled "Alice Decides" (5M6), and enters at 1:23:03 based on the DVD/streaming video timing. Although the climactic battle with the Jabberwocky is yet to come, the scene scored here is arguably the high point of the story—as it always is when a hero or heroine overcomes fear and reluctance and rises to the challenge. There isn't a film composer alive who doesn't relish writing to scenes like this, but it's also the occasion when the composer is most exposed, for if the "hero" theme doesn't equal the epic setting, it can easily fall flat. This reduction includes most of the key parts. Piccolo and bassoons, which are doubling other parts, are not shown, and the percussion, harp, celesta and choir are also eliminated.

The question as to whether or not Elfman's *Alice* theme has the juice to power the scene is answered decisively in the first three measures. The falling m3 gesture that kicks off bar 49 is, of course, the musical spelling of the name: *Al-ice!*

Figure 8.9A. *Alice in Wonderland*, 5M6, "Alice Decides," bars 49–53 @ 1:23:03

Flutes and horns have the melody, so let's look at what's happening in the strings. Notice (1) that the sequence of pitches in the triplet ostinatos for violins is altered on each beat; (2) that the incomplete triplets in violas induce a sense of propulsion; and (3) that the figures in the cellos are interlocked as precisely as Balinese gamelan. When we arrive at the "harmonic surprise" of bar 6/54, the entire ensemble is in motion. The section ends with a crescendo on the VI (G-flat) to IV (E-flat) progression and a repeat of the *"Al-ice!"* gesture.

Figure 8.9B. *Alice in Wonderland*, 5M6, "Alice Decides," bars 54–57

Alice rides off to face the Jabberwocky

The climactic scenes of a fantasy-adventure film rarely allow a composer to be at his or her most expressive. It's invariably the loudest part of the movie, and there's simply too much happening on the sound effects track (in this case, marching armies, clashing spears, and a roaring Jabberwocky) for the music to speak with any degree of subtlety. The composer's principal job is to fueling the engine of action, and in an orchestral score, that duty tends to fall mostly to the brass and percussion sections, as well as the high woodwinds: these—along with electronic sounds—are the only things able to cut through the din, usually by way of jackhammer motives and pile driver hits. During Alice's confrontation with the Jabberwocky, Elfman does a heroic job of stoking the furnace, but not a lot is new, and his efforts to integrate the *Alice* theme during the final standoff can be only partially successful because the melody, with its square *cantus firmus* design, with its evenly spaced quarter-notes, lends itself more to a march than a big, anthemic treatment.

One lesson composers can take from this is that if a melodic theme is going to be used to play straight action, then the bare-bones design of the theme itself—minus any accompaniment—probably needs to incorporate strong rhythmic elements. Obvious examples would be syncopation, dotted rhythms, pickups, and leaps. The textbook examples of this sort of thing are John Williams's *Star Wars* and *Indiana Jones* themes, but there is probably no better study guide than Elmer Bernstein's action scores for such films as *The Great Escape* and *The Magnificent Seven*. In fact, if Elfman had been *less* creative and relied exclusively on his *Al-ice!* motif to drive the battle scene, he might have found a primal power closer to that of Williams's iconic *Jaws* theme. Sometimes, two notes are all you need.

But neither the movie nor the score suffer for their by-the-book endings. It is, after all, heroic fantasy, and we expect the hero to slay the dragon. What has made *Alice in Wonderland* a genuine enchantment and not simply another $200 million CGI spectacle is that two highly unconventional artists, Tim Burton and Danny Elfman, have employed their unique visions in a way that could almost be called classicism, and the result is a film that's genuinely Disneyesque while retaining an unmistakable Burton/Elfman stamp. This is probably Danny Elfman's least "quirky" score, and many of his signature tropes—boldly nonfunctional harmonies, Gypsy melodies, madcap rhythms, and jazzy flourishes—are left aside. This reserve allows the ascendance of another quality that has always been present in Elfman's work, but has sometimes taken a back seat: *wonderment*. That wonderment comes to full flower in the End Titles, a symphonic treatment of the *Alice* theme, excerpted here in nearly its full orchestration (not shown are piccolo, clarinets, tuba, general percussion, and keyboard, as these instruments are, for the most part, doubling). The section shown here spans a full 12-bar statement of the theme.

Figure 8.10A. *Alice in Wonderland*, 7M2, End Titles, bars 37–40

The key is A minor throughout, and the excerpt shown covers bars 37–50 (the pickup quarter-note in the vocals at the end of measure 36 is not shown). Once again, notice the mirrored, interlocking triplet rhythms in the violins, and how they and the rest of the strings propel the melody. Note also the great attention given to placement of accents.

Figure 8.10B. *Alice in Wonderland,* 7M2, End Titles, bars 41–44

The antiphonal structure of melodic *call* and rhythmic *response* first seen in the opening titles is maintained, and underlined by dynamics: the antecedent phrase is at a dynamic of *mp*, and the consequent at *mf* or *f*. Subtle, but effective—particularly when the response section is tutti and includes horns, trumpets, field snare, and timpani hammering out the triplet tattoo. And although it's a small brushstroke, it makes a difference that the woodwind response is in the shape of a wave rather than a loop-like repetition of motive.

Figure 8.10C. *Alice in Wonderland, 7M2, End Titles, bars 45–48*

Figure 8.10D. *Alice in Wonderland*, 7M2, End Titles, bars 49–50

The grandest gesture—and the score's most indelible signature—is the big crescendo in measures 11–13 (47–49) leading to the closing refrain of *"Al-ice!"* As before, it's the mixed-modal use of the IV chord (D major)—here in a role usually played by the V chord—that surprises our ear, along with a progression (D7 to F to D to A minor) that is more typical of the blues than of orchestral music. But then, of course, Elfman has been riffing on the blues, cabaret, and Tin Pan Alley with ninety piece orchestras from the beginning of his remarkable career. *Alice in Wonderland* may be his closest approach to classicism, but it's still in every sense a Danny Elfman score, and one of his very best.

In the world of literature, the quality of a novel often rests on the strength of its protagonist's "voice." Think of almost any book by Charles Dickens, for example, and the meaning should be pretty clear. The narrative voice is, of course, only an aspect of the writer's own voice. There's no reason to think that the strength of a film composer's work should rest any less on his or her voice. Film scoring may be "assignment work," and no two films demand the same music, but the film composer is, in every sense, a storyteller. All good storytellers have a distinctive way of telling a tale.

But how do we, as composers, acquire such a voice? This question takes us back to the concordance of influences listed early in this chapter for Danny Elfman, and the two "thought experiments" offered alongside them. An artistic voice is a whole greater than the sum of its parts, but it is still very much *formed* by those parts. We are what we love. What knits those disparate parts into something greater is a combination of vaulting ambition and a fervent devotion to *a sound*. Not a sound as an isolated thing, but as a synthesis and signature. The Beatles had this from their middle period on, and so, in a different way, does such a band as Radiohead. So did Debussy, and for that matter, Wagner. Of such passion is memorable film music made.

It's also worth mentioning that Elfman, like his soul mate Burton, has managed to survive and thrive at the epicenter of the commercial film business without ever forfeiting his identity as an *artist*. This isn't just a matter of being "odd" or theatrical (although being a little of both can't hurt your career). It results from a way of seeing the world. If Elfman *could* see the world in other ways, his oeuvre might be far more varied—but much, much less interesting.

The piece excerpted in Figure 8.11, which leads into the "What's This?" section of the End Title medley in *Nightmare Before Christmas*, could not—I think—have been written by anyone other than Danny Elfman. Sure, the influences—eastern European folk music, Tchaikovsky, old Disney films, music box dancers, and even vintage jazz—are clear, but the way they are combined is something we only hear in an Elfman score. Nothing else sounds like it. And that is quite a testament.

Figure 8.11. *The Nightmare Before Christmas*, End Titles intro

NINE SURGICAL PRECISION

ALBERTO IGLESIAS'S *LA PIEL QUE HABITO*

Alberto Iglesias

Like *Vertigo*, with which it shares both visual sheen and the themes of obsession and transformation, Pedro Almodóvar's 2011 deeply psychological thriller, *La piel que habito* (The Skin I Live In) was born from French pulp fiction. Its source is *Mygale* by Thierry Jonquet, published in English as *Tarantula*, but one can also cite the French cult horror film *Eyes Without a Face* (Georges Franju) and the expressionism of Fritz Lang as influences. When these potent ingredients are combined with Almodóvar's signature gender-bending, dark humor, fascination with the feminine mystique—*and* a masterful score by Alberto Iglesias, the result is as close to Hitchcock as we get these days.

The creative kinship of Iglesias and Almodóvar dates from 1995's *The Flower of My Secret*. That's not as long a partnership as those enjoyed by Burton and Elfman (1985), Cronenberg and Shore (1981), or Spielberg and Williams (1974), but there is evidence that it's just as durable. There is a course to be taught, and possibly a book to be written, focused solely on the artistic and personal affinities that forge these bonds, because there seems little doubt that they are the core element of the most successful film-scoring careers. They are stronger than many modern marriages— and probably more stable. Undoubtedly, the things that make for a good marriage—trust, a certain shared worldview, and the ability to communicate in a kind of emotional shorthand—are critical in sustaining them, but the factors of attraction that draw a director and composer together in the first place are just as mysterious in art as they are in romance, as are the reasons why some composers never find their "match." With Iglesias and Almodóvar, it doesn't seem to be a case of "like attracts like," as it is with Burton and Elfman. Almodóvar is a bigger-than-life personage, openly emotional, theatrical, and gay. Iglesias is a soft-spoken, private, reflective and deeply modest person: a happily married family man. There is, however, one important quality they share: both are exceptionally meticulous and precise in the construction of their art. Even Almodóvar's "messiest" films, dramatically speaking, are beautifully put together, as are each and every one of Alberto Iglesias's scores. Maybe this precision of technique—a surgical approach to the untidiest of subjects—is the link, and it's a commonality that also described the kinship between Hitchcock and Herrmann. That parallel is very clear in *La piel que habito*, a gorgeous film about a macabre subject.

Before introducing the story, let's take a look at a bit of the opening title cue, titled "El Cigarral" on the soundtrack album (after the name of the villa owned by the protagonist, Dr. Robert Ledgard, a plastic surgeon portrayed by Antonio Banderas).

Figure 9.1A. *La piel que habito,* "Principio—El Cigarral," bars 24–28

In other chapters, I've discussed the enormous importance of gesture in film music, and particularly in the Main Titles that announce the movie's dramatic "bid." Think for a moment about *Vertigo, War of the Roses, The Matrix* . . . all open with bold gestures. Now look at the placement of accents over the triplets in the divisi *a 3* cellos. Tap out that rhythm. Then look at the pointedly expressed chordal gesture in the violas. Harmonically, it couldn't be simpler. It even has a key signature (G minor), something we rarely see on contemporary American film scores.[1] Rhythmically, it couldn't be cleaner. Every note is a precisely articulated staccato. Formally, it recalls the baroque, perhaps Vivaldi. All of this is entirely fitting, because as we'll see, Dr. Robert Ledgard is a very fastidious man. Every detail of decor in his home speaks of a creature of refined tastes and exquisite control, right down to the elegantly mounted video display in his bedroom, through which he watches his captive experimental subject, the lovely Vera Cruz (Elena Anaya).

---

1 American film composers have largely adopted the posttonal convention of "C-scores," notated chromatically even when the cue clearly has a tonal center. This not only allows for free-floating tonality, but usually proves more efficient on the scoring stage, where composer, conductor, orchestrator, and engineer must all be in sync and all notes are given with reference to concert pitch.

Figure 9.1B. *La piel que habito*, "Principio—La Cigarral," bars 29–34

And yet, despite the sleekness of the arrangement, there's a quality of epic tragedy, conveyed not simply by the minor key, but by the decisive, fatalistic way in which the cadences fall. Bars 32–34 are a basic i–iv–i cadence, but the clipped, accented quarter-notes and the tripling of the fifth in the final chord deny us resolution and suggest an emotional wintriness that may conceal something darker behind its beauty. Things get even more intriguing in the following passage for piano and bass.

Figure 9.1C. *La piel que habito*, "Principio—La Cigarral," bars 40–49

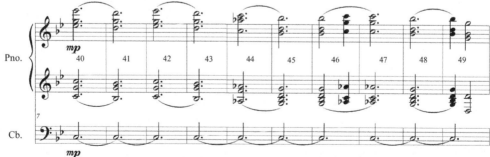

The wide voicing, parallel intervals, persistence of the pedal C, and the deceptive simplicity of the harmony recall works by Debussy and Satie. The progression is straightforward: Cm–Gm–Cm–Gm–Fm–Gm–(A-flatM7)–Gm. But it's not diatonic, despite the key signature, nor is it chromatic in the ordinary sense. The flatted A in measures 46–47 that seems to spell an ambiguous A-flat M7 chord (ambiguous, because it's missing the third), skews the feel toward the modal block progressions of Satie, and inserts an element of mystery. Following this interlude, the strings make a staggered reentry and we hear the "Cigarral" theme, octave doubled on piano at bar 58.

Figure 9.1D. *La piel que habito*, "Principio—La Cigarral," bars 55–59

Figure 9.1E. *La piel que habito*, "Principio—La Cigarral," bars 108–115

Now we may begin to have a sense of the palette from which Iglesias is drawing his colors. The key signature remains G minor, and there has been no modulation. The "Cigarral" theme, as outlined on piano, makes perfect sense in G minor, with the F-sharp at the conclusion of the second phrase as the raised seventh "leading tone" in an incomplete cadence. But this isn't what's happening at all. The entire string section is fairly unambiguously locked into a C minor harmony, and no dominant triad accompanies the F-sharp. Instead, we see in the first cello beginning in bar 64 a broken diminished triad, which—given the chameleon-like properties of diminished triads—can be read with a root of A, C, E-flat, or even F-sharp (in this case, it seems to be A). If this passage is not expressly bitonal, it certainly has that flavor. And it also leans toward something else: a sound we associate with Spain, and specifically with those areas of Spain that felt the strongest influence from the East (the location of the action is the city of Toledo). There is an element of flamenco in this cue, as in Isaac Albéniz.

The Main Title sequence is over two and a half minutes long, and it's a masterpiece of concision. Almodóvar establishes in short order that within the luxurious, high-security estate known as El Cigarral, a beautiful young woman is being held captive, not in a dank basement, but in a sparsely yet elegantly furnished upstairs room, complete with a dumbwaiter to deliver her meals, clean clothes, and reading materials . . . twenty-four-hour surveillance by an array of video cameras. When we first see Vera, she is doing yoga, and we get the feeling it's part of a daily routine: she has been in this room for a very long time (later, we see that an entire wall is covered with hash marks numbering the days of her captivity). She knows how to use the intercom system to summon Marilia, the older woman who manages the kitchen. Vera wears a dancer's unitard, flesh-colored and oddly stitched, almost as if she were a living dressmaker's mannequin—a work in progress, which is, in fact, exactly what she is. For Vera is Dr. Ledgard's grand experiment, his exquisitely beautiful Frankenstein monster.

Ledgard is an esteemed plastic surgeon whose specialty is restoring the faces of burn victims. In his quest to return the power of facial expression to his patients, he is both passionate and slightly messianic, and in his elaborate home laboratory, he has succeeded in synthesizing a new kind of skin, impregnable to fire and other damage, through a process called transgenesis. By the time we witness his first direct encounter with Vera, we know that she is wearing this skin.

In the scene underscored by the next cue, titled M206, "Estoy hecha a tu medida" (I'm made for you), Dr. Ledgard enters Vera's room, bringing her a gift of opium—presumably for both postsurgical pain *and* pleasure, since it comes with a pipe as delivery system. But Vera isn't interested in getting high—she's interested in getting out, and she's willing to offer herself as wife or concubine in return for freedom. "I know you look at me," she says, nuzzling him. "Since you brought me here, we practically live in the same room." She attempts to seduce him, but although he clearly finds her desirable, he has other concerns on his mind, both clinical and personal. He pulls away and leaves the room in a state of great agitation, locking her back into her designer prison cell, where she continues to stare at him via the video feed.

Figure 9.2A. *La piel que habito*, M206, "Estoy hecha a tu medida," bars 28–31 @ 21:23

Once again, Iglesias approaches the construction of his cue in a classical manner, with a clearly defined key center (C-sharp minor) undermined at first only by the D-sharp pedal in the bass, swelling and ebbing like Dr. Ledgard's edgy breathing. The solo violin plays a rapid-fire arpeggio, again in the high baroque style, the notes unaccented and separated, but given an anxious animation by the ostinatos in first and second violins. At measure 32, a dramatic shift into diminished harmony occurs as Ledgard frantically locks Vera in, fearful of her escape, and the first cellos enter with an agitato passage that runs chromatically through the new mode and includes such exotic inflections as this:

Although the passage in measures 32–35 is thoroughly chromatic (it includes enharmonic B-natural [as A-double sharp] and enharmonic C-natural [as B-sharp]), it also recalls the piano theme in "El Cigarral" with its descending augmented second (bar 68). We have heard modalities like this in Satie, Middle Eastern music, and flamenco, but their use in a piece that is otherwise completely diatonic is striking. Dramatically, the effect is to show us that although Vera is the one locked up, Ledgard is the real prisoner.

Figure 9.2B. *La piel que habito*, M206, "Estoy hecha a tu medida," bars 32–35 @ 21:32

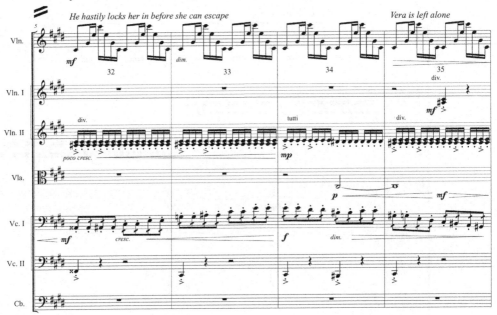

Dr. Ledgard, in a cold sweat, reenters his bedroom, which is just next door to Vera's "cell" and outfitted with the wall-size video display on which he "studies" her. As we've just learned, she *knows* he's watching, and takes full advantage of the paradoxical power this gives her by looking directly into the camera with an expression that's both enticing and heart-rending, a moment scored by the poignant asperity of the adagio passage for double-stopped solo violin in bars 41–43 (Figure 9.2C). This is the sort of bold gesture rarely allowed to film composers, but it works here because it matches not only the power of the image (a beautiful woman held in voyeuristic captivity on a video screen), but Almodóvar's sense of melodrama. Note how the wide voicing in measure 42 permits Iglesias to lay a first inversion B major chord over a C-sharp minor bed.

Figure 9.2C. *La piel que habito*, M206, "Estoy hecha a tu medida," bars 36–43

At the breakfast table the next morning, Dr. Ledgard is confronted by Marilia, the older woman who manages the household, and whom we suspect is more than what she seems. "You shouldn't have used her face," she insists. "The resemblance is too strong." Whose face? We haven't been told, but this is our first solid clue that Vera is also not what she seems. The captive upstairs has been transformed in some fundamental way by Dr. Ledgard's art. "You'll either have to kill her or keep her forever," Marilia warns.

Ledgard shrugs off the warning, but as a precaution, asks Marilia to dismiss the servants. It's clear the experiment he's conducting in his home is both dangerous and illegal. He drives off to work, and hasn't been gone an hour before Marilia's fears are borne out. The buzzer rings, and on the security camera she sees her estranged son, Zeca, a thief and hustler seeking sanctuary after a jewelry store robbery in Madrid. It is carnival time in Spain, and in true Almodóvar style, Zeca is disguised from whiskers to tail in a tiger suit, just like the one he had as a child when Marilia called him "El Tigre." Zeca is a true predator, and it doesn't take long for him to sniff out the alluring Vera on the closed-circuit video display. Furthermore, he seems to recognize her.

Figure 9.3A. *La piel que habito*, M207, "El Tigre," bars 43–50 @ 29:11

El Tigre is hungry for warm flesh, and when he spies Vera doing yoga on the video monitor, he licks the screen lasciviously. "She looks like—" he whispers. "It's not her," Marilia insists, pulling a gun from the drawer. "Now get out." Zeca wrestles her for the gun, which goes off, alerting Vera (Figure 9.3A). He then binds and gags his mother and goes off in search of his prey. The hunt and capture are dramatized in a scene running over seven minutes and through-scored. Figure 9.3A is the first eight-bar excerpt we'll look at from "El Tigre." The key signature is B minor. Notice the three elements in play: (1) a traditional two-voice suspense trope in violin and viola, opening from minor third to diminished fifth with stealthy tremolo; (2) a "tension pad" spanning an octave and a sixth in synth strings; (3) finally, and most perversely, a funky, syncopated gospel organ figure in parallel thirds that lends a "theater of the absurd" aspect to the costumed tiger's lust-fueled prowl.

Figure 9.3B. *La piel que habito*, M207, "El Tigre," bars 80–83 @ 30:00

Zeca's discovery of the location of Vera's room is signaled at bar 81 (Figure 9.3B) in the woodwinds by a polychord consisting of a diminished triad surmounted by perfect and augmented fourths. This leads us to the second of the cue's syncopated signatures, the pizzicato cello plus bass gesture beginning in bar 83, which uses the same rhythm as the gospel organ but reverses pitch direction. It's important to note what's going on here, because it echoes in some ways what David Newman did with his "Carmen" gesture in *War of the Roses*. Suspense and peril are being gently undermined by whimsical, almost cartoonish brushstrokes to underline the scene's bizarre qualities and perhaps to create a false sense of levity. Almodóvar's humor is, if anything, even darker than DeVito's, and this scene is *not* going to end well. El Tigre may be Marilia's "little boy," but he's also vicious, as men often are in Almodóvar's world. In measures 84–87 and 88–91 (Figures 9.3C and 9.3D), the cello/bass figure sustains the element of surreal menace.

Figures 9.3C and 9.3D. *La piel que habito,*
M207, "El Tigre," bars 84–87 and 88–91 @ 30:17

In measure 90 (Figure 9.3D), as Zeca arrives at Vera's door (30:17), the gospel organ returns, now riffing on a broken F-sharp diminished chord. This releases the tension briefly—but only briefly—because the scene is about to veer into genuine violence. Iglesias's choice to use an instrument/timbre that most people associate with schmaltz, early rhythm and blues, or roller-skating rinks as a "lead voice" in the prelude to a rape is an interesting and very distinctive one. It works precisely because of the freakish quality of the scene and the El Tigre character. Zeca is an animal, but he's also something of a buffoon—a parody of masculinity—and the sight of a grown man prowling hungrily up and down the wide marble stairs of an immaculately decorated villa in a full-body tiger suit is more than a little ridiculous. It's as if he's been recently released from a human zoo (or a mental ward) and set loose on the Spanish ruling class. Almodóvar and Iglesias tempt us to laugh in the face of the havoc that Zeca surely intends, and this is probably exactly the point.

Figure 9.3E. *La piel que habito*, M207, "El Tigre," bars 108–115 @ 30:50

In Figure 9.3E, Bar 110, as the gospel organ repeats and Zeca moves closer to Vera's door, a new gesture ups the level of peril for Vera: horns and trumpets, each with the lower voice of its section 2 a semitone off. The combination of that subtle dissonance, the staccato articulation, and the dramatic crescendo-diminuendo from *piano* to *sfz* and back again has a markedly unsettling effect, amplified by the bristling chromatic tremolo runs in the violas and celli that begin in measure 114. If the technique utilized so far in M207 emulates that of any other film composers, they would probably be Jerry Goldsmith and Ennio Morricone, whose work is treated in chapters 12 and 14. Those are very good role models. One of the truly notable things about the new generation of Spanish film composers (which includes Javier Navarrete, Roque Baños, and Fernando Velázquez, as well as hyphenate writer-director-composer Alejandro Amenábar), is how thoroughly and studiously they have absorbed the vocabulary of Hollywood film music (which, of course, has European sources) and made it their own.

Figure 9.3F. *La piel que habito*, M207, "El Tigre," bars 116–119

In the following and final excerpt from "El Tigre," Zeca enters Vera's chamber and beauty confronts the beast. In this scene, which culminates with Vera's rape, one of the film's mysteries is partially revealed. It turns out that there is a reason, beyond sex and beauty, that Zeca was so drawn to the image on the video display, and that his act of violation qualifies—at least in his twisted mind—as a kind of reunion. "How can you be alive?" he asks her incredulously. "I left you burning like a torch." She doesn't answer, but during the act itself, he taunts her by saying, "I used to drive you crazy." It's clear at this point that Zeca, and whoever he believes Vera to be, were once lovers, and that it's to this that Marilia was referring when she said, "It's not her." Iglesias's handling of this brutal but mon-strously madcap scene is a very different kind of action scoring.

Figure 9.4A. *La piel que habito*, M207, "El Tigre," bars 223–226 @ 33:25

At first glance, it may appear a little odd, or even primitive, to see an entire orchestra employed in ensemble to execute a single rhythm—and with every note accented! There is no counterpoint and no pulse, only jagged dissonance and equally jagged syncopation. (I should note that the reduction doesn't show the midi prelay elements, but they provide "tension pads" and atmosphere, rather than counterlines.)

What Iglesias seems to be doing here is scoring the struggle that precedes Vera's rape as an act of jungle predation. After all, the predator is costumed as a tiger and the sloe-eyed victim is wearing a flesh-colored one-piece that makes her look a little like a vulnerable gazelle. At 170 bpm, there isn't much room for active counterpoint, and the tempo becomes the pulse. It's a stripped-down approach to Stravinsky's "L'Adoration de la Terre," from *Le Sacre du printemps*, but without any of the elegance. El Tigre is not an elegant creature, and it wouldn't have been appropriate to give him Stravinsky.

Figure 9.4B. *La piel que habito,* M207, "El Tigre," bars 227–230

Dr. Ledgard returns home to find Marilia tied to a kitchen chair, helplessly watching the video display as her son rapes Vera. A cut takes us to Ledgard's holding a gun on both attacker and victim, uncertain of which more deserves the bullet. (He clearly knows Zeca, and may not be sure whether he's witnessing an act of nonconsensual rape or an act of betrayal on Vera's part.) Vera pleads with her eyes, and Ledgard, persuaded, unloads two rounds into El Tigre's backside, killing him instantly.

As we turn into the film's "second act," all but the darkest comedy is left behind and we are firmly on the ground of melodrama and noir. In the aftermath of the rape and revenge killing, we learn that Ledgard and Zeca, unbeknownst to either of them, are half brothers, both the strange fruit of Marilia's illicit liaisons as servant in the household of Ledgard *père*. We also learn the twisted reason Zeca was drawn like a moth to Vera's flame and felt he could ravish her with impunity. Vera's face, crafted with exquisite perfection by the cosmetic surgeon's art, is the face of Robert Ledgard's deceased wife, Gal, who was horribly burned when the car driven Zeca, who was her lover, crashed and burst into flame (this is what Zeca meant when he said, "I left you burning like a torch"). Later, when her husband's ardent efforts failed to restore her beauty, Gal flung herself out of a third-floor window, leaving her husband a widower and their daughter motherless. *So, who is the woman who now wears Gal's face?*

The next nearly thirty minutes of the film proceed via artful flashbacks, and with no music other than on-camera source, to reveal the tortuous backstory that answers that question. Ledgard worshipped his wife, despite her infidelity, and used every trick in his trade to repair her hideously disfigured face. When she took her own life, all he had left was the daughter they had produced together, Norma. In the wake of her mother's suicide, Norma became emotionally withdrawn, and Ledgard became the most protective of fathers. To "bring her out," he escorts her to a fashionable soiree at the home of a friend, where she manages to slip out of his grasp and into the arms of an attractive young man, Vicente, who takes her into the woods for a little amorous fooling around. Kissing escalates to fondling, and soon he has her on the ground with her dress half off. What Vicente doesn't know is that Norma has serious intimacy issues, and his sexual urgency triggers hysterics, whereupon Vicente panics and knocks her unconscious, then attempts to flee the scene of the crime on his motorcycle.

Ledgard, searching the woods, spots Vicente fleeing and only seconds later finds his stricken daughter, the apparent victim of a rape. He puts two and two together, holds the young man responsible for Norma's defilement, and proceeds to hunt him down.

Almodóvar has almost completed the circle that will lead us back to the story's "present tense," but to do so, he must bring back his musical collaborator, Alberto Iglesias. We learn that Norma, institutionalized after the sexual encounter with young Vicente (which, in convoluted Freudian logic, she blames on her father), has followed her mother out the window. On the day of her funeral, Ledgard, determined to avenge her, kidnaps Vicente from the dress shop where he works and holds him in brutal captivity, chained to a wall and deprived of all but water. Long after dark, he comes to visit his prisoner, and in a scene of both eerie tenderness and horror, shaves him with a straight razor. When a terrified Vicente asks, "Why are you shaving me?" Ledgard replies, "Interesting question." It is indeed, because in the following scene, we'll learn of Robert Ledgard's ingeniously monstrous plan, born of a husband's love and a father's grief: *he will transform Vicente into Gal.* This is vengeance served cold.

It's this scene that formally ushers the underscore back into the film's dramaturgy, with an extraordinary cue called "Afeitado" (which simply means "shave.")

Figure 9.5A. *La piel que habito*, M513, "Afeitado," piano intro @ 1:14:58

This hauntingly simple prelude for solo piano opens the cue, and its gravity turns the prosaic act of shaving into something closer to *Sweeney Todd*. Both hands are in bass clef, but the left hand is indicated 8vb, which gives us octave doublings an octave apart. It's somewhat reminiscent—if only in its starkness and register, of the "monotheme" used by Stanley Kubrick in *Eyes Wide Shut* (which may or may not have been the work of composer Jocelyn Pook). This time around, Iglesias gives us no key signature, but the voice leading suggests G minor. At bar 8/23, the right hand moves up another two octaves.

At measure 41 of the score, the strings enter with what appears from its spelling to be an A-diminished chord with a major seventh—an even more dissonant version of the *Psycho* chord. As we've seen, diminished chords are chameleons and can take on whatever tonal guise suits the composer's intentions, and this one is clearly not operating in service of any kind of functional harmony. At 42, the solo violin that has been a key character in Iglesias' score returns with an ultrarapid arpeggio on a C-sharp minor chord (the tempo is 141), and this becomes—for the moment—the new tonality.

Figure 9.5B. *La piel que habito*, M513, "Afeitado," bars 41–44 (@ 1:16:15

Once Vicente is clean-shaven, Dr. Ledgard suggests a splash of "after-shave" and clamps a chloroform-soaked rag to Vicente's face. Full brass enters sforzando with a rapid stab as Vicente struggles, while the violin continues its frantic sextuplets, raising the tension by moving the top note up a third. It's not clear why Iglesias opted for enharmonic spellings in the brass, though brass players often prefer to see flats. What's more mysterious, given the absence of key signature, is why the violin has an F-double sharp in bar 46. However, we saw this in Herrmann's work, as well, and note spelling is often a way to both insure performance clarity and reference a phantom key.

Figure 9.5C. *La piel que habito*, M513, "Afeitado," bars 45–48

The unconscious Vicente is moved into the operating room, where Dr. Ledgard's team has been assembled to perform what they've been told is a voluntary gender reassignment surgery. "He knows exactly what he wants," Ledgard assures his apprehensive colleagues. But when Vicente emerges from anesthesia a few hours later and is informed by Ledgard that he has undergone a *vaginoplasty*, it's clear from his horror that he's trapped in a living nightmare from which he can never escape—only find some way to accommodate, or possibly avenge.

The ensuing scenes track Vicente's gradual transformation into Vera and his installment in the high-security bedchamber that will become his prison for many long months. His skin is entirely replaced, like that of one of Ledgard's experimental burn victims, and his shaven head is masked in a post-surgical helmet that prevents us from seeing the alteration of his face into that of a replicant of Ledgard's late wife. On an afternoon when Dr. Ledgard brings Vicente/Vera a specially fabricated one-piece body suit to aid with the skin transplant, the captive makes a bold and desperate escape attempt, wielding a knife and threatening to slit his own throat. The cue is "Se rebela."

Figure 9.6A. *La piel que habito*, M516, "Se rebela," bars 7–10 @ 1:25:27

In a contrapuntal style reminiscent of the opening titles, first cellos and first violas enter with interlocking F minor and D diminished broken chords, or in another reading, an Fm6 harmony that resolves in measure 9 to C minor. As with the Main Title cue, the underlying architecture may recall Vivaldi, but the final design works more like the precisely meshing cells of a minimalist composition or even a sequenced piece of vintage electronica. A "four-on-the-floor" kick drum would make it almost danceable, and in fact a lot of Iglesias's music is strongly physical, even occasionally balletic. Another resemblance that is felt once all sections have kicked in is to arrangements for guitar of works by such Spanish composers as Albéniz or Villa-Lobos. When a composer marks his notes "staccato" as often as Iglesias does in this score, there is every reason to ask what "instrumental personality" he's aiming for, and here, it seems to be guitar.

Above all else, however, "Se rebela" is an action cue for chamber strings, something we don't hear a lot of, and it's difficult to imagine any other approach working as well for this scene. The low strings provide continuous propulsion, and the sense of panic and near hysteria expressed by the solo violin reminds us that Vicente/Vera is a person whose very "self" has been violated and will stop at nothing to escape—including the slitting of his/her own throat. The scene concludes with just that piece of drastic action, and with Ledgard carrying his patient into the operating room for emergency stitches.

Figure 9.6B. *La piel que habito*, M516, "Se rebela," bars 11–14

First escape attempts often fail, and long-term captives must sometimes devise a stealthier path to freedom. At the time of the climactic scene scored by the next cue, Vera has been in captivity for six years, and from all appearances, has either accepted her fate (and her gender) or succumbed to Stockholm syndrome, perhaps both. She is now Robert's lover, and they have exchanged promises: he will grant her the same freedom of movement that he would grant a wife, and she, in return, will never leave him. "Don't disappoint me," he tells her, and she replies, "It is all I have, Robert. I promise." Almodóvar films are always psychologically complex and provocative, and a composer can be no less in his or her musical portrayal.

The cue is titled M723 "Entra con el vestido," and begins at the close of a tense scene during which Ledgard is threatened with exposure by a member of his surgical team, who suspects that the young man on whom they performed the sex change was not, in fact, a willing patient but a kidnap victim. Just as the ax seems about to fall, Vera enters, looking goddesslike, and declares that she is there of her own free will and "has always been a woman." From all appearances, she has accepted her new fate.

As the cue enters, Almodóvar cuts to Robert and Vera in passionate prelude to lovemaking. When he penetrates her, she complains, "It still hurts," and bids him wait while she goes downstairs to retrieve some lubricant from her purse.

Figure 9.7A. *La piel que habito*, M723, "Entre con el vestido," bars 38–41, Bar 39 at 1:44:53

The achingly beautiful descant for solo violin in measure 39 has been heard just once before in the film (Figure 9.2C, M206, measures 41–42), in the same key but with a somewhat different phrasing. In this new iteration, there is a shift in harmony, on beat 2 of bar 40, from C-sharp minor to an A7flat5 chord, an especially biting way to allow the solo violin to hold onto its M2 dissonance. Other than the "Andalusian" piano line that first appears in the Main Title (Figure 9.1B, bars 58–67), this violin passage is as close as we have in the score to a recurring theme, so it's important to ask why Iglesias uses it here.

You'll recall that its first use (Figures 9.2A to 9.2C) occurred after Vera's initial attempt to seduce Robert into loosening the reins in exchange for a life of sexual reward and domestic bliss. He knew—and *we knew* then that this was a captive's ploy—*let me go and I'll make it worth your while*—and Robert fled to his room, only to see Vera gazing yearningly from the video display. The violin at that moment fused his desire and her longing to be restored to an authentic life. Now, minutes away from the film's climax, both characters seem to have what they want. Ledgard has "the perfect woman." Vera has won her freedom, and promised herself in return. Is it the consummation of what was hinted in the earlier scene? No, there is unfinished business, for Vera hasn't yet avenged Vicente. Even if she could forgive Robert, the pain she suffers in lovemaking is a reminder of the manhood—and personhood—that was taken from her.

Figure 9.7B. *La piel que habito*, M723, "Entre con el vestido," bars 42–45

A passage of silky Herrmannian dissonance ensues as Vera goes downstairs to retrieve the lubricant. Over a prolonged G-sharp7 chord (the third is chromatically raised), performed with tremolo by all strings, the solo violin descends in parallel sixths from D-sharp/B-natural to C-sharp/A, finally dropping chromatically to meet the bed of the harmony with B-sharp/G-sharp. The tremolo ceases at the end of the passage, but not the tension. With a fifth now in the bass, it's a tidy second inversion G-sharp chord—except for that dissonant E-natural in the first violins. In the following section, we see why there is dissonance, for Vera has just spotted the newspaper clipping of the missing (presumed kidnapped) Vicente with which Ledgard's colleague had threatened him in the previous scene. In this poignant moment, the woman is face-to-face with the man she once was, and though they are now divided, the attachment is as deep as that of separated twins. She kisses Vicente's picture. Vera may not have come downstairs with intent to kill her captor, but in the following section, Iglesias's job is to convince us that the memory of Vicente, and of the erasure of his existence, convinces her to do so.

Figure 9.7C. *La piel que habito,* M723, "Entre con el vestido," bars 84–87, piano in at 1:46:24

The key is nominally G-sharp minor, but the key signature is only mean-ingful for the piano. The chords, played without adornment, at a very som-ber tempo, are G-sharp minor "cadencing" to D-sharp minor, then C-sharp minor returning to D-sharp minor. All chords are triads. It's the voicing, with three pairs of octaves widely spaced—G-sharp (3), G-sharp (4), D-sharp (4), D-sharp (5), and B4/B5 in the first chord—that recalls earlier cues like those pictured in Figures 9.1C and 9.5, with their Satie-like spareness and sanctity. The interval relationships remain the same for the C-sharp minor chord, except that the wider spacing of a M6 is now on the bottom: E (3/4), C-sharp (4/5), and G-sharp (4/5). This evocative but entirely tonal progression occurs over what is probably the harshest dissonance in the score, a string stack composed of tritones and m2s and harmonically un-related to what the piano is doing. Iglesias is painting a musical picture of Vera/Vicente's cognitive dissonance. Simplistically put, the piano portrays the tenderness that Vera feels for her lost Vicente, the innocent young man she sees in the photo, while the strings eloquently depict both her inability to reconcile these two people and the rage that this confusion produces. In the second half of the passage, from 88–91, the strings are tacet, and the pi-ano repeats the progression, leaving the cadence hanging on C-sharp minor as Vera slips a handgun into her purse. Her head is now clear of indecision, if not entirely free of emotional conflict. In just eight bars, Vera has decided to become a murderess. When she heads back upstairs, we know the gun is more apt to be used than the lubricant.

Figure 9.7D. *La piel que habito,* M723, "Entre con el vestido," bars 88–91

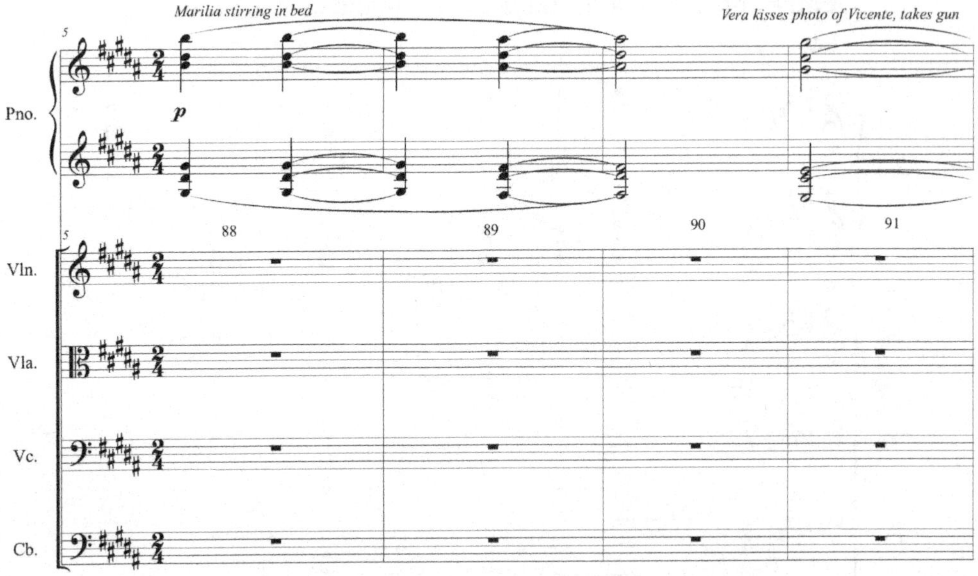

The earlier dissonance returns, along with a suspenseful chromatic figure in tremolo violins, as she enters the bedroom, tosses the tube of lubricant to an anxiously waiting Robert, and then calmly announces her intent to kill him.

"You are joking," he replies. *"Call it what you like,"* she says. "But you made a promise," he insists. *"I lied,"* she answers, and then puts a bullet through his heart.

Figure 9.7E. *La piel que habito,* M723, "Entre con el vestido," bars 92–95

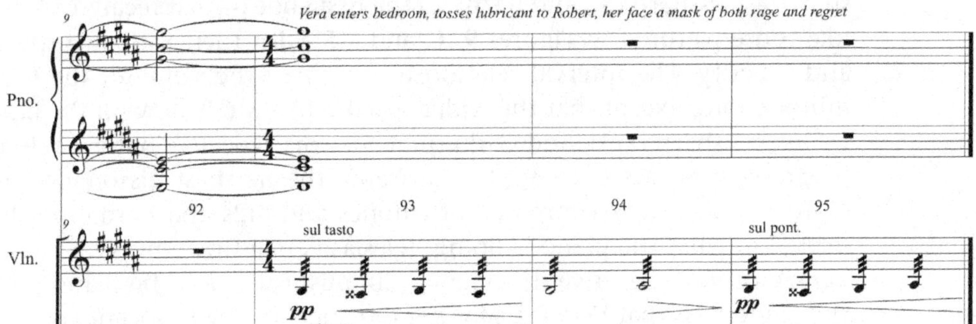

In a film that is otherwise unconventional, the scene that immediately follows is a classic in every good sense. Whether the film noir reference is *Double Indemnity* or *Body Heat*, there is a certain rhythm—and even a certain very caustic humor—in scenes of double-cross, betrayal, and table-turning revenge. (The dark humor in this case provided by the fact that Vera tosses Robert a sexual lubricant just before she kills him, as if to say, "Here's a little something to ease the pain.") Because such scenes frequently end with a trigger's being pulled, they also present the composer with one of his or her great challenges: how to play the gunshot. Since this particular sequence will end with not one, but two dead bodies, Iglesias gets the chance to have it both ways.

The reduction in Figure 9.7E ends before Vera issues her final words and squeezes the trigger. The first murder won't be shown here, but Iglesias opts for the "music out before the gunshot" approach, which is the safest and most frequently used. He handles it with great restraint: entirely with woodwinds, anchored by contrabassoon, on a jagged cluster that rises from *pp* to only *mf* before the shot is fired. It works because it graphs the energy of the scene: tension rises (something music handles very well) and is then broken by the release of a bullet. (When composers choose this approach, the shot is often followed by a single chordal statement, dissonant or elegiac, as if the gunshot had been the upbeat of a cadence, followed by a bitter resolution.) The shot awakens Marilia, who grabs her own pistol and heads for Robert's bedroom with a sense of dread.

Figure 9.7F. *La piel que habito,* **M723, "Entre con el vestido," bars 125–128 @ 1:48:12**

Vera warns Marilia away, calling out, "It was nothing. Go back to bed," but Marilia is not deterred so easily, and breaks through the bedroom door, to find Robert slumped on silk sheets saturated with blood and Vera nowhere to be seen. "My son!" she cries, followed by a curse: *"¡Hijo de puta!"* She enters the chamber with gun raised.

Iglesias scores this deftly with an eerie 8va chromatic line for high violins (Figure 9.7F, above) over a held open fourth in the second violins. The crescendo that precedes Marilia's discovery of the body is actually considerably more dramatic than the one that preceded his murder, rising to a dynamic of *sfz* in all sections before a hard cutoff. This is Almodóvar's feeling more for the mother's loss than the son's (deserved) death.

Figure 9.7G. *La piel que habito*, M723, "Entre con el vestido," bars 129–132

The excerpts that follow, and will conclude this chapter, pick up directly from Figure 9.7G and are played as subtly as the rest of the score. Marilia searches the bedroom for Robert's assailant, then joins him in death when Vera takes aim from under the bed and drops her with another bullet to the heart. Her aim is remarkably true.

Figure 9.7H. *La piel que habito*, M723, "Entre con el vestido," bars 133–142

Notice the difference in the way Iglesias has spotted the second gunshot/ murder in bars 147–48. This time, the gunshot occurs at the very peak of the crescendo in measure 147, and is then punctuated by the dead cutoff at the head of bar 148. We don't need for the second shot to be entirely in the clear. In fact, it might be somewhat redundant. What Iglesias and Almodóvar want is for us to feel Marilia's pain—and utter surprise—when she is hit, and by "scoring through" the gunshot and punctuating its immediate aftermath, this is accomplished. It's a riskier approach, but here, it works to great effect.

Figure 9.71. *La piel que habito*, M723, "Entre con el vestido," bars 144–148

There is some poetic justice—and a great deal of irony—in the fact that Robert Ledgard's vengeful and malicious act of gender identity theft has allowed his "Vera" to commit something approaching the perfect murder. The police are looking for Vicente, missing and presumed kidnapped or dead, not for a beautiful young woman of his age and size. Eventually, they will put the pieces together, but it will take some imagination, and that is the very least a clever killer—or a clever filmmaker—can demand. Until the crime is solved, Vera will return to the life she knew six years earlier as Vicente, working in a little dress shop, only now as the woman she has, perhaps, "always been" (Almodóvar's comment on the fluidity of gender).

Great filmmaking is sometimes a bit like a crime, or at least a good con job. And in the commission of this crime, Alberto Iglesias has been Pedro Almodóvar's very capable accomplice, and delivered one of the spiciest scores of the new century.

TEN THE STRENGTH OF THE RIGHTEOUS

ENNIO MORRICONE'S *THE UNTOUCHABLES*

Photograph courtesy Olivier Strecker/Wikimedia Commons

Ennio Morricone

**Figure 10.1A. Ennio Morricone, *The Untouchables*,
"The Strength of the Righteous," bars 1–12**

If film music is a language of signs and gestures, then "Il Maestro," Ennio Morricone, is its most literate practitioner of semaphore. No composer's gestures are bolder; no composer's signs point more clearly to meaning. One look at the opening motive of his Main Title theme for Brian De Palma's

1987 genre masterpiece, *The Untouchables,* is evidence enough. Five notes and a snare drum sum up the film better than any logline. It's almost impossible not to hear the *rat-tat-tat* of a tommy gun.

Figure 10.1B. *The Untouchables,* **Main Title, "The Strength of the Righteous," bars 13–18**

The only key elements missing from the reduction in Figures 10.1A and 10.1B are the trademark Morricone harmonica (not featured, incidentally, in the composer's score) and the muscular gated timpani hits that open the cue. The harmonica line will be picked up by soprano saxophone in Figure 10.1B, bar 13, which also introduces new voices in the brass and string sections (see red outlines). Harmonically, the cue could not be simpler, rawer, or more effective. A minor to G-sharp minor and A minor to B minor. But it's not about the chords.

Figure 10.1C. *The Untouchables*, Main Title, "The Strength of the Righteous," bars 25–30

Few opening statements in the film music canon—including the many standouts in Morricone's own catalog—are as unreservedly masculine as "The Strength of the Righteous," a title that clearly refers to the film's protagonist, Bureau of Prohibition agent Eliot Ness (Kevin Costner) and his relentless pursuit of gangster Al Capone (Robert De Niro) in late-1920s Chicago. It is a contender, along with Bernard Herrmann's *Psycho*, John Barry's *Bond* theme, Jerry Goldsmith's *Basic Instinct*, and a handful of others, for the distinction of being film music's most iconic opener.

The Untouchables is neither Ennio Morricone's best known nor his most transportingly melodic score. Those honors would probably go, respectively, to *The Good, the Bad and the Ugly* and to either *The Mission* or *Cinema Paradiso* (some might champion another Sergio Leone film, *Once upon a Time in America*). There's a case to be made, however, that of his more than four hundred film scores, *The Untouchables* has the most to teach us about the craft, because like *The Matrix*, *The War of the Roses*, *Vertigo*, and other examples in this book, it participates in a synergy of story, cast, and cinematic technique, all operating in top form, and thus drawing the very best from the composer.

As mentioned, the film was released by Paramount in 1987 and was considered a hit, if not a blockbuster, grossing $187 million worldwide against a budget of $25 million. It made Kevin Costner a star, and won Sean Connery an Oscar for his performance as the tough, soulful, and utterly incorruptible Chicago cop, Jim Malone. Brian De Palma (*Carrie*, *Scarface*) has never made a more visually stunning or narratively coherent film, and screenwriting credits go to Pulitzer Prize–winning Chicago playwright David Mamet. One of the film's most salient qualities is that, although neither De Palma nor Mamet were strangers to moral ambiguity and darkly antiheroic protagonists, *The Untouchables* casts its title characters in an unapologetically heroic light and makes no effort to shade its villains, Al Capone and his principal hit man, Frank Nitti, as anything other than classic bad guys. This moral clarity gives the movie an almost sagalike sweep that encourages Morricone's most unrestrained, anthemic, *and* tragic tendencies. "Morricone unbound" nearly always yields spectacular results, and has been doing so since he first exploded onto the scene with Sergio Leone's spaghetti westerns in 1964.

The fascinating thing is that nothing in Ennio Morricone's biography hints as to how this modest, unprepossessing, conservatory-trained trumpet player came to be capable of works both so staggeringly emotional and wildly flamboyant as to earn the devotion of artists from the rock band Metallica to bad-boy auteur Quentin Tarantino. The only clue may be that he came of age as a film composer in the mid-1960s, an era of "kitchen sink" composition when anything—jazz, rock, lounge, exotica, and avant-garde—could be thrown into the mix, and even traditionally trained musicians let their hair down. From 1964 until 1980, Morricone was a charter member of an ensemble known as Gruppo di Improvvisazione di Nuova Consonanza, which explored the use of free improvisation, "antimusical systems," "found sounds," and noise in pursuit of a "new consonance." In the arts, a mild manner can conceal a wild and antic creativity.

In this and a number of other respects, Morricone, born in 1928, stands as the European counterpart of another "conservative" film composer prone to marvelous excess in his music, Bernard Herrmann. These two men have probably done more to enrich the vocabulary of film music than any fifty of their peers, and the baseline reason seems to be this: while both were denizens of the classical world and composed numerous works for the concert hall [Morricone, by far the more prolific, has written over one hundred works of "absolute music" (*musica assoluta*)], in the realm of film music, they were pure *dramatists*. The importance of this cannot be emphasized enough.

The Untouchables is in many ways a Sicilian vendetta tale played out in the gritty streets of Jazz Age Chicago, and just as Morricone brought modal flavors of Mediterranean folk to the Wild West in the spaghetti westerns and made it feel "authentic," he bathes the most American of cities in the colors of the Old World while managing to make his score redolent of speakeasy jazz and bathtub gin.

Because the Main Title theme for *The Untouchables* is one of a dozen or so unquestioned exemplars of the form, a study of its construction is a film scoring course in itself. It's built in layers, and the foundation is that machine gun sixteenth-note motive, made from a four-note cell harmonized in parallel at a minor third below and anchored by the unyielding four-on-the-floor snare drum. Nearly all of Morricone's "action notes" are either accented or marked with a *staccatissimo* articulation, indicating not only a sharper, more detached staccato, but in Europe and among older composers, also implying a *thrust* as piercing as the quick in-and-out of a stiletto. This articulation is a hugely important element in the sonic character of the cue. In Morricone's handwritten score, the *staccatissimo* markings resemble angry slashes more than discrete little wedges, a good indication of his intentions. (Morricone's hand is even messier than Herrmann's, suggesting that his brain is moving well ahead of his pencil—not at all surprising for a man who composes directly to score without the intermediary of a piano!)

Figure 10.1D. Piano

I mentioned earlier that the chordal support for the opening gesture appears to be A minor to G-sharp minor, based on what happens in the horns and strings in measure 13. Yet the F-sharp in the bass of motive 1 suggests a different harmony (e.g., an F-sharp diminished triad). Nothing in the chart bears this out, however, and it seems more accurate to regard the first two sixteenths in each voice as a kind of anticipatory run-up or even, in a jazz sense, a *rip*. However we describe it, the fact that the statement opens with accented, nonchordal tones and then proceeds in a highly syncopated fashion only adds to its dramatic punch.

The second layer introduces a simple but very important line in the soprano sax (and harmonica), whose third phrase, the snaky four-note shape A/G-sharp/E/G-natural seen in measures 17/18 and 29/30, prefigures the Capone theme, its heart of darkness.

Figure 10.1E. Soprano sax

This layer also brings in stopped horns and a new counterline in violins and violas: a syncopated and highly chromatic series of triads, played *molto secco*.

Figure 10.1F. Violin/viola

If a single word describes Morricone's tonal vocabulary and chord-shifting, it is *chromatic*—not in a Wagnerian sense or even in the manner of Herrmann, but in a quirkier way that almost resembles the inflections of ragtime. Witness what he does next:

Figure 10.1G. Oboes

The "squawking oboes" that appear in bar 25 (doubled by horns) are one of the score's most indelible signatures. As if the *staccatissimo* articulations over every note aren't enough, he marks the entire passage *molto staccato*. The effect is like that of carrion birds pecking away at a fresh corpse, and it introduces an element of menace and frenzy to an already maniacal piece of music. And yet, like Herrmann's *Psycho* Main Title, it's all perfectly organized madness. At this layer of the cue, the main motive, having been well established, is temporarily abandoned and replaced by sinewy chromatic figures in clarinet and bassoon (see Figure 10.1C, 25–30). Now, all the elements are in play, and the cue finally comes to rest as it began: reverberant solo harmonica and resonant timpani.

The first major character we meet in *The Untouchables* is not the hero, Eliot Ness, but his nemesis, Al Capone, attended by his minions and interviewed by the British press corps as he enjoys a shave and a manicure at his hotel. In the original spotting of the film, Capone's theme was placed after the titles and is numbered M2 in the score, but the currently available version moves it back and instead kicks off the underscore with what Morricone has titled the "Ness and His Family" theme at 06:41, beginning on Mrs. Ness as she prepares her husband's brown-bag lunch. We'll hear Morricone's gift for heartfelt melodies that are unpredictable and harmonically daring enough to avoid excessive sentimentality.

In fact, Ennio Morricone has insured his immortality by writing gorgeous melodies that never feel hackneyed or cloying because he (1) frequently takes them in unexpected directions; (2) employs large and dramatic leaps, often in conjunction with striking changes in harmony, to break up the feeling of sequence; (3) makes use of parallel modes (i.e., modal exchange/ interchange); (4) utilizes chromatic tones not only in "passing" but on key downbeats; and (5) establishes a key center and then freely leaves it via chromatic voice leading. To see how he's able to take the most homespun of tunes, the "Ness Family" theme, and "mature it" like wine in a bottle, examine Figure 10.2. The almost perfectly stepwise melody is harmonized diatonically in the key of D major (D/G/A), followed by conventional departures to the vi and iii chords in bars 4–5 and a return to the tonic on the downbeat of bar 7. On beat 3, however, the melody suddenly leaps a minor sixth accompanied by a chromatic inflection in the harmony that steers us in the direction of a new, temporary key center of F major (bar 9).

Figure 10.2. *The Untouchables*, M3,
"Ness and His Family," bars 1–12 @ 06:41

The shift in harmony that occurs in measure 7 is what might be called a "Morricone modulation." The harmonic goal is the Fmajor7 chord on the downbeat of bar 9, and he gets there, classically, by way of a (secondary) dom-

A Word About Using Chord Symbols and Roman Numerals in Film Music Analysis

In general, harmony in contemporary film music doesn't lend itself very well to traditional Roman numeral labeling. Because its function is to shadow, highlight, or contrast drama, it can't really follow the rote rules of any system, whether tonal, atonal, or posttonal. Its modus operandi is more transformational than systematized. Much of Morricone's film music is unashamedly tonal, but as we've seen already, he isn't bound by that, and harmony in his work is a fluid, organic thing, seldom resting on block chords. The chord symbols used in the foregoing example are simply distillations of the various moving parts, frozen for just long enough to take a snapshot!

inant ninth chord. The pivot chord, however, is not a G7, but a *Gminor7*, which isn't "functional" at all. As quickly as he establishes a new tonic, he leaves it, briefly resting on a B-flat harmony before returning to D major by way of the traditional ii7–V7–I. He has taken us safely home, but on the way, we have learned that the connection between Ness and his wife is deep and abiding.

As mentioned, Eliot Ness in *The Untouchables* is very much "the man in the white hat." This isn't a case where hero and villain share attributes, other than perhaps ambition. They are polar opposites. Ness's essential goodness, and the way it's reflected in his relationship with his wife and daughter, is the film's moral center of gravity (along with the bond he shares with his men, in particular Sean Connery's Malone character). But De Palma, Mamet, and Morricone are sophisticated thinkers, and never for a moment does Ness register as a cartoon character, just a good man in a very bad place with an impossible job: the enforcement of Prohibition.

In stark contrast, De Niro's Al Capone, who essentially runs the city of Chicago like a fiefdom, ruthlessly removing any obstacle to his dominion, buying off the police force and the judicial system, is the film's nexus of evil. Unlike the archvillains of pulp, there is little about him that's charming. He's a thug, albeit a charismatic one. Whereas Ness and his men are "untouchable" (i.e., incorruptible), Capone is the embodiment of corruption. Morricone's theme for Capone captures him in all his imperial sleaze.

Figure 10.3A. *The Untouchables*, M2, "Al Capone," bars 1–4 @ 19:37

Morricone's "Al Capone" cue is a wonderfully perverse piece of music, anchored by the four-note chromatic cell (circled) we saw in the Main Title. Its first (and only complete) hearing in the film follows the public humiliation of Eliot Ness that occurs as his maiden crusade—a raid on a whiskey smuggling operation—goes awry when word is leaked to Capone. The cue is a mélange of jazzy, woozy chromaticism, outwardly simple but internally a small marvel of chromatic voice leading and counterpoint. In a mere eight bars, it paints a picture of a gangland empire at the peak of its power. What we remember about it is the sequentially descending series of two-bar melodic phrases in celesta, vibraphone, violin, and synth brass (and the nasty, wah-wah antiphonal responses in the trombones), but the hidden genius of the cue is in the wind and string parts, where Capone's reign is revealed as "rotten to the core." To see the harmonic grid, follow the top line of the clarinets, second violins and violas. Like the melody, it's sequential and descends chromatically, but in three-note groupings leading to the dominant seventh chord (E7-flat 9) and half-diminished seventh in measure 7 that return us to the tonic A minor. Note also how the horns in 1–4 quote the *Untouchables* motif (thanks to music editor Tom Drescher for pointing this out).

Figure 10.3B. *The Untouchables*, **M2, "Al Capone," bars 5–8 ꜛ 19:37**

The string parts in the Figures 10.3.A and 10.3B reductions are transcribed more or less directly from Morricone's autograph score, not from prepared parts. They are, frankly, a bit of a mess, but as mentioned earlier, this is in keeping with the modus operandi of a composer who writes directly from brain to page at breakneck speed (how else does one compose over 400 scores?). He doesn't stop to indicate divisi sections, much less to indicate how the section is to be split (sometimes a2 and sometimes a3), nor is he very clear with respect to articulation. Slurs and phrase markings are often entirely absent. One gets the sense that many of these choices are dictated directly from the podium, on the session, and probably only after he has heard the cue read through section by section a few times.

Once again, bear in mind that there are no chord symbols given in this cue, and that those I've indicated are the result of collisions of the moving, contrapuntal lines that are a feature of all of his scores. They are shown only to highlight the harmonic motion.

As has been true since he first burst onto the scene in 1964, Ennio Morricone is not afraid to "mix it up" stylistically and instrumentally. Here we have a cue for a film set in the late 1920s that perfectly captures the grimy glory of Capone's Chicago, and yet employs a very contemporary sounding drum kit hammering out a beat that would have been quite at home in a mid-1980s mainstream rock anthem à la Bruce Springsteen. Somehow, where other composers stumble over this kind of mash-up, Morricone gets away with it. Even at fifty-nine years old, "Il Maestro" was hipper than many younger rivals.

As noted, the numbering of the score cues does not, in every case, correspond to their final placement in the film. The failure of the Untouchables' first big raid on a Capone warehouse—a failure that threatens to derail their efforts almost before they've begun—introduces a very important secondary theme, one that poignantly portrays the loneliness of Ness's quixotic mission and his personal loyalty to the men who've enlisted in it. If Albinoni had written for alto sax with blue notes, it might have sounded like this. Morricone called the cue "Four Friends" and numbered it M6, thus it seems likely that its original placement fell a bit later in the story, after the Untouchables' A-team of Ness; Malone (Sean Connery); George Stone, a.k.a. Giuseppe Petri (Andy Garcia); and Oscar Wallace (Charles Martin Smith) has been assembled. Directors often find uses for cues that the composer did not originally envision, and in this case, De Palma showed great musical judgment, for the "Four Friends" cue becomes a leitmotif for sacrifice and heroism: for what it costs (family, friendship, community, and sometimes, life) when a man chooses to face down dragons. The cue is first heard in the current release version of the film at 15:56, as Ness heads alone for the bridge that spans the Chicago River, perhaps to clear his head, and perhaps with darker thoughts in mind. He has failed in his duty, and worse, he has failed to redeem the faith of his family and his government.

Figure 10.4A. *The Untouchables*, M6, "Four Friends," bars 1–10 @ 15:56

In the case of "Four Friends," Morricone wrote out the chord symbols himself, and here we see him in the "baroque" mode that is so much associated with such cues as "Gabriel's Oboe" from *The Mission*. Some of his most affecting pieces are essentially melodies over a ground bass, and here he modulates from A minor to C major as classically as any student of eighteenth-century counterpoint. Yet there is always something just slightly different about his harmonic language—note that the modulation in bar 12 is to a Cmaj7 (add 9), and that in bar 8, the Esus4 resolves not to E major, but to E minor.

Figure 10.4B. *The Untouchables*, M6, "Four Friends," bars 11–15

Two other things are worth noting about the "Four Friends" cue, both standard but essential weapons in the film composer's arsenal. Morricone's modulation to the relative major is not done for show, but to usher in the "Ness Family" theme at the very moment Ness is having his darkest moment on the bridge. Reaching for a cigarette, he finds the note his wife had tucked into his lunch bag, a note reading "I am so proud of you." He drops his head into his hands. That's when veteran beat cop Jim Malone walks into his life—perhaps just in time—and soon becomes "family," too. Finally, note that the cue closes on an incomplete cadence. The rule in film music is never to resolve until the story does—and it often doesn't until the end credits roll. In this respect, great film music can sometimes be a little like Messiaen's notion of an infinite series of suspensions without resolution.

Bringing Malone into his confidence changes the game for Ness, for Malone is an insider, a veteran of the gang wars who understands how to do things "the Chicago way" and has the fatalistic Irishman's weakness for lost causes. Soon they've enlisted two younger recruits, Treasury Department accountant Oscar Wallace (geeky, but a quick study with a pump-action shotgun) and police academy "prodigy" George Stone, whose aim is as disarming as his smile. Malone knows how the booze is getting into the city, and leads the team on its first successful raid, a triumphant scene that calls for a triumphant cue. Morricone delivers with a piece he calls, appropriately, "Victorious."

Figure 10.5A. *The Untouchables*, **M11, "Victorious," bars 6–9 opening fanfare @ 34:16**

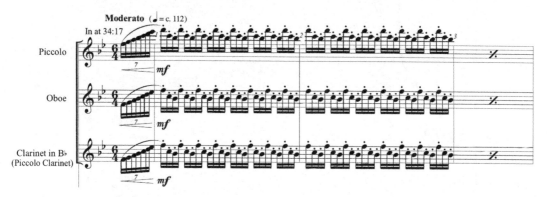

The cue enters on a grand crane shot of a busy La Salle Street at midday in Chicago's financial district, with a fanfare heralded by the woodwind statement above. (Please disregard the default "clarinet in B-flat" heading, as Morricone's score calls for a piccolo clarinet.) The combined effect of high reeds and piccolo playing staccato sixteenth-notes at a tempo of 112 bpm is quite striking, and this cue has been widely imitated. Here is a reduction of the same passage including the brass and strings. Note the clef change in the horns and the key signature of B-flat major. (European composers use key signatures more frequently than their American counterparts do, and are also likely to deliver transposed scores; here Morricone's scores have been reduced at concert pitch.)

Figure 10.5B. *The Untouchables,* M11, "Victorious," bars 6–9 @ 34:16

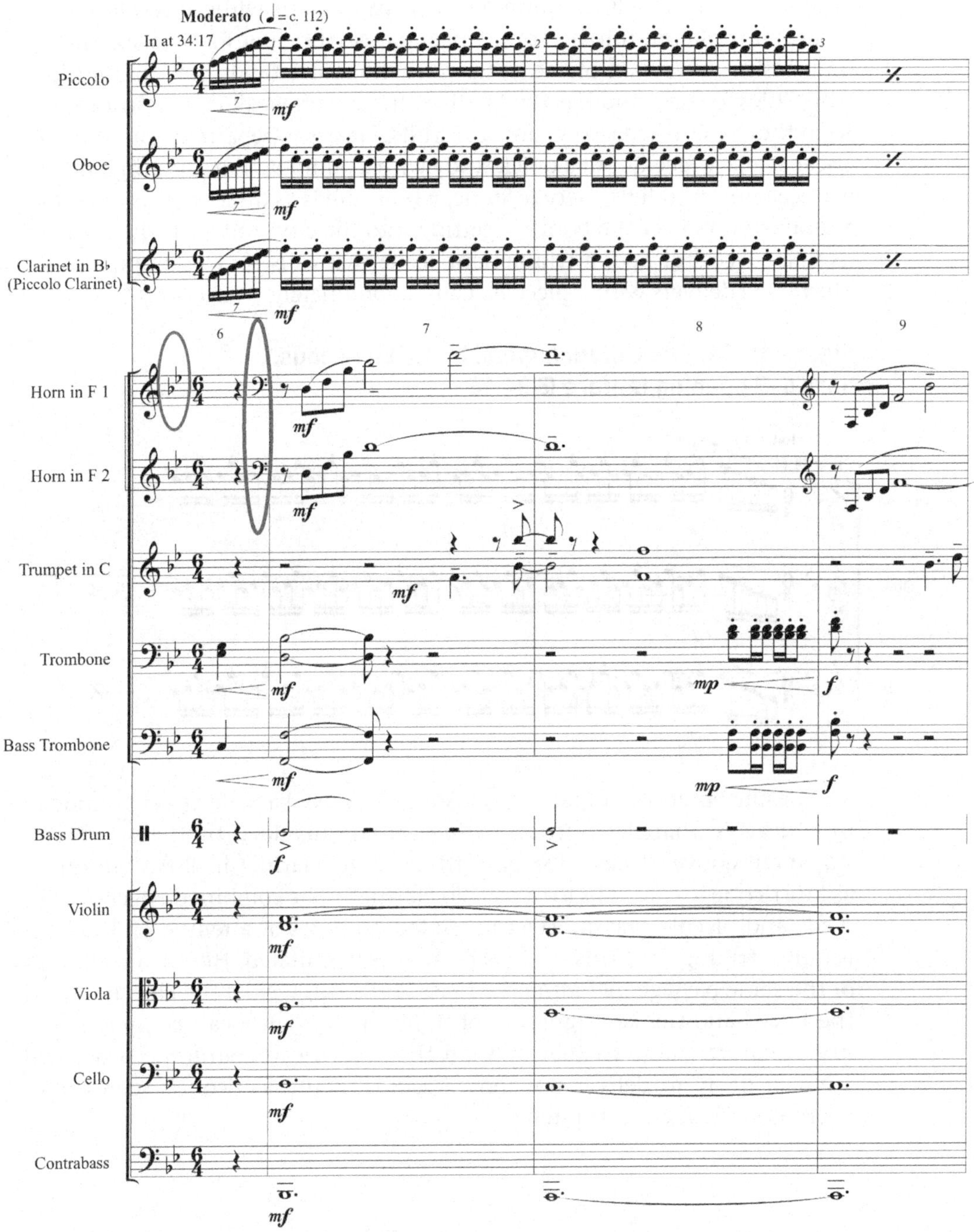

Figure 10.5C. *The Untouchables*, M11, "Victorious," bars 10–12

Other than the clarity and coherence of the various voices, there is nothing so far that expressly says "Morricone." This is anthemic writing through and through, and could as easily have been Erich Korngold. (Note the nice descant in horns and trumpets in bar 12.) When we arrive at bar 13, however, we are swept up in the sort of unbridled romanticism that bowled over fans of Morricone's music for Sergio Leone's monumental *Once Upon a Time in the West*, and suddenly, it couldn't be the work of any other composer. Not John Williams. Not James Newton Howard. Not even James Horner *imitating* Ennio Morricone. The question is: *why?* Part of the reason, undoubtedly, is that the melody, a 2+2 sequence in the high baroque style that the composer so admires, carries within it its own harmonic content. All you have to do is hum the horn line. And then there is that big octave leap in the violins at bar 15. It is a melody truly worthy of its title.

Figure 10.5D. *The Untouchables*, M11, "Victorious," bars 13–16

If any single thing defines Morricone's melodic writing—beyond its jazz-inflected classicism, such broad descriptive terms as *romantic* or adjectives as *emotive*—it is his fearless use of big leaps. Leaps of an octave, a ninth, and even a tenth aren't infrequent in his music. The principles of good melody writing have always been based upon the capabilities of the human voice, but in Morricone's music, that voice is often a coloratura soprano. His melodies begin with classic stepwise motion and then dramatically reach for the heavens. In Figure 10.5D, I've doubled the melody in the horns so that its shape is clear.

The Ness crew's first victory is followed by a second: the interception of another big whiskey shipment at the Canadian border, assisted (somewhat ineptly) by the Royal Canadian Mounted Police. Before the bust is made, however, there are some tense moments as the four crusaders await the handoff in a shotgun shack with a view of the international border. The timing is critical, and the boys are still new at this. Of the four, only Malone is a veteran, and only police academy grad Stone is an ace shot. Here, Morricone introduces what might be considered a variation of the Main Title: a dissonant, slow-motion fugue for winds that he titled "Electrocardiogram," but music editor Tom Drescher renamed "Waiting at the Border."

Figure 10.6A. *The Untouchables*, M18, "Electrocardiogram," bars 1–5/302–306 ⓡ 50:15

The cue begins with clarinets and horns over a sequence that recycles itself throughout the cue: an ostinato in electric bass and "gunshot" figures for his gated timpani, tom-toms, and *gran casa*. The score is something of a puzzle to decipher. There's no tempo indication (I've guessed at 58), and other than a few hairpins, the sole dynamic marking is the *p* at measure 1. The writing is highly chromatic, generally dissonant, and accidentals are by no means always clear. But from this chaos emerges something unmistakably Morricone. The core counterpoint can be simplified this way, with clarinets initially splitting the ascending and descending lines.

Figure 10.6B. *The Untouchables*, M18, "Electrocardiogram," piano reduction

Things, of course, aren't really so simple. Morricone experienced the rigor of the Italian *conservatorio*, receiving his certification well before the age of twenty, and spent time in his youth using serial technique in his composition. It's uncertain to what extent that practice has been employed here, but the cue does provide excellent proof of the fact that cinema audiences will tolerate even strident atonality as long as it's in service of drama. In many ways, "Electrocardiogram" is a standard piece of tension underscore—the sort that action composers are faced with on almost every assignment. But as has been mentioned, it can be very instructive to see how great composers handle routine assignments. Ennio Morricone is known as a melodist and a creator of iconic themes, but he is equally adept at the less glamorous but critical work of sustaining dramatic tension. Although M18 is not thematic or even especially remarkable as "pure music," it does its job so well that it pays to take an extended look at how it's developed over thirty bars without ever rising above a dynamic of *piano*, and largely without introducing new material after the first eight bars. Morricone, even in his concert work, is a composer who achieves great power through repetition and layering—not in the minimalistic sense, but like a painter painstakingly applying layer after layer of pigment on his basic sketch. "Electrocardiogram" underscores one of a trio of scenes of nailbiting tension in *The Untouchables*. Now that we've seen his major themes, we'll turn to how he integrates them into the drama.

Figure 10.6C. *The Untouchables*, M18, "Electrocardiogram," bars 6–10/307–311

In the second five-bar grouping, counterpoint in the clarinets becomes more active while retaining the same shape and pitch set, and the composer introduces a percussive piano gesture. The alternate measure numbers in the 300s are lifted from the recording score, and reflect Morricone's cumulative method of bar-counting, a method that allows him to keep track so that he can lift designated measures as *como sopras* in the same or subsequent cues.

In the next iteration, new colors of oboe and English horn emerge, and the horns split/double these parts. (For clarity, the reduction shows the higher part in trumpet.)

Figure 10.6D. *The Untouchables*, M18, "Electrocardiogram," bars 11–15/312–316 Woodwinds Only

Here is the full score for these measures. Note that the clarinet line, beginning in bar 13/314, begins to recycle. As indicated, Morricone shows this in the score simply by giving its original bar numbers. Watch carefully. This is how the cue develops its power.

Figure 10.6E. *The Untouchables*, M18, "Electrocardiogram," bars 11–15/312–316

We're going to skip the five bars from 16–20 that are largely repetitive, and move to the next development of the cue: the entry of the string section in measure 24/325. At this point in the film, Capone's trucks have reached the bridge with their cargo.

Figure 10.6F. *The Untouchables*, M18, "Electrocardiogram," bars 21–25/322–326

By now, it should be clear that Morricone is constructing a big, chromatic canon based on continual mutation of the same "genetic material." The same practice was very much a feature of Herrmann's work. The question is why we don't see more of it today. It's a relatively simple form of musical construction that yields an immersive and hypnotic texture that works very well with the fluidity of the cinematic image.

Figure 10.6G. *The Untouchables*, M18, "Electrocardiogram," bars 26–30/327–331

A partial answer to that question may lie in the fact that many contemporary composers evidence scant understanding of counterpoint. Offsetting note against note, especially in the quasi-atonal way that Morricone does here, requires a certain comfort with both eighteenth-century practice and the reformulations of that practice introduced by such modernist composers as Schoenberg and Stravinsky. The exercises in "species counterpoint" that were once standard practice in university music programs seem to have suffered "species extinction." Rhythmically speaking, most modern film scores utilize straight beat subdivision and very little syncopation: a big melody over an insistent "motor." In terms of harmony, they tend to be "blocky"; that is, based more on straight chord progression than the slippery and ephemeral harmonies created by the intermeshing of lines. It's too bad, because film music is an inherently "sneaky" form of composition. Cues must ease in and out of scenes almost invisibly, and skillful counterpoint can help to achieve this end. The sort of exercises provided in the original *Gradus ad Parnassum* by Johann Joseph Fux and Leo Kraft's contemporary treatment[1] can be great brain training for composers who wish to make better use of counterpoint.

A second successful raid by the Untouchables sets off alarm bells in the Capone empire. Money is being lost and—almost as damaging in gangland—so is reputation. "I want Ness dead!" Capone howls to his men. "I want his family dead and his house burned to the ground." The agent of his revenge will be his number one enforcer, the oily and odious Frank Nitti. Capone may be the movie's heavy, but Nitti wears its badge of evil. Ness is able to get his family into a safe house, but that leaves the most vulnerable member of the team exposed. The bespectacled shotgun-toting accountant, Oscar Wallace, dies ugly in a freight elevator.

But Nitti's next target takes a far greater dramatic and emotional toll. The machine gun murder of Sean Connery's Jimmy Malone is in many ways the fulcrum of the film, the hinge on which its two parts swing, and Malone's dying words to Ness, "What are you prepared to do?" drive the rest of the action. His death does not come suddenly like Wallace's. It's a long, tense, painstakingly choreographed, and gut-wrenching sequence, and its quietly menacing opening segment contains both some of De Palma's most dramatic camerawork and some of Morricone's most effective scoring. The cue is titled, "The Man with the Matches," and no one who has ever seen the film ever forgets why.

To set it up, we need to introduce "the Bookkeeper." This is the mousey little man who keeps track of the Capone syndicate's credits and debits, and because all operations are disguised by shell companies, Capone himself never seems to make any money. The key to getting him behind bars is proving that he has hidden his income from the Feds, and only the Bookkeeper can provide this evidence. Malone has learned through an informant that Capone is putting the Bookkeeper on a train at midnight, but the

---

1 (New York: W. W. Norton 1987), published in two volumes.

informant is a double agent, and Malone is marked to die before he can pass this information to Ness.

Figure 10.7A. *The Untouchables*, M14, "The Man with the Matches," bars 1–6/242–247 @ 1:18:33

An overhead shot on Nitti, backlit by a streetlamp as he stands in front of Jimmy Malone's apartment building at 1634 Racine and casually lights a cigarette. Violins bleed in on a high A, with the firsts dropping a semitone to G-sharp and violas (in treble clef) holding a B-flat, to create an eerily menacing cluster. That A to G-sharp descent is Nitti's signature, his austere leitmotif, and has been present since first voiced by harmonica and soprano sax in the Main Title. It returns again in the harmonica here, in measure 245.

Augmenting these sinister elements are the *Untouchables* motive, in the Main Title's key and once again in parallel m3's in piano and low pizzicato strings, and a new and very effective "tension figure" performed on what seems to be a prepared piano. Note that the top line echoes the first three notes of the full Capone/Nitti theme: A–G-sharp–E as seen in harmonica in bar 249. The bottom part begins as an 8ve and ends as an m2.

Figure 10.7B. *The Untouchables,* **M14, "The Man with the Matches," bars 7–12/248–253**

Nitti is joined by a second man at 248, a stiletto-carrying stooge who proceeds to climb up to the window ledge to get a fix on Malone, while Nitti disappears into the back alley. The knife man's first glimpse of Malone, apparently oblivious inside his Chicago flat, leads to the cue's first surge of tension in the crescendo that begins in measure 251.

The rest of M14 essentially reworks these materials in an escalating manner, leading to the moment when Malone, who steps out onto his back porch, thinking he has chased off the knife-wielding intruder, is savagely ambushed by Nitti. He takes a full round of machine gun fire, and is still—only barely—alive when Ness and Stone arrive at the scene. Before he draws his last breath, Malone manages to pass on the critical piece of information: the Bookkeeper will be on the 12:05 (midnight) train from Union Station.

Malone's death itself is scored by a variation of the "Four Friends" theme (Figure 10.4). There's some potent string voicing in this version, but the remainder of this chapter is probably best spent on the capture of the Bookkeeper in a scene that has become famous as both cinematic and musical tour de force: the Union Station "Odessa Steps" sequence. M31/32 "Machine Gun Lullaby" is a layered cue, recorded in separate passes, a method that will be familiar to many contemporary film composers. In this case, however, it had nothing to do with limitations of stage space. As with the rest of the score, it was recorded at the now defunct RCA/BMG stage in New York City, a room that was easily able to accommodate one hundred musicians. (*The Untouchables* is one of the very few Morricone scores to have been recorded in the United States.) Nor was Morricone obliged to provide his director with stems for the usual reasons. He was after something else.

The scene begins as Ness and Stone, the last remaining Untouchables, enter Union Station via the main doors at 11:55 p.m. (a large wall clock above the entrance provides a continual time reference). Just inside, a broad flight of marble steps leads down into the expansive waiting area, sparsely populated at this hour. The fact that the steps and station floor are of marble contributes significantly to the effectiveness of both sound design and score. The entire scene rings with cold reverberation, adding to the tension. Ness stakes out the upper level overlooking the steps, with a clear view of the entrance. Stone takes the lower sector near the platform doors. Two sailors ascend the steps. A baby cries. A woman rolls a baby carriage to the foot of the staircase. An ominous low pedal C is heard, followed by this:

Figure 10.8A. *The Untouchables*, M32/33, "Machine Gun Lullaby," celesta/music box loop @ 1:27:33

But for that low C, we might be inclined to hear this as source music, emanating from the baby carriage and echoing through the cavernous station, and that might seem a strange way to open a scene of high suspense. But this is Morricone. To accompany the lullaby diatonically as needed, he has written this simple string arrangement:

(Note: This can be faintly heard starting at 1:30:35 as Ness makes up his mind to assist the struggling mother.)

Figure 10.8B. *The Untouchables*, **M32/33, "Machine Gun Lullaby,"**
music box string accompaniment

The music box and its various string accompaniments will persist through much of the seven-minute cue. The music box itself will emerge intact when it's all over.

It's on the next cycle of the music box melody that things begin to get interesting, and we see Morricone's subversive intent. It is 11:57 by the big station clock, and passengers for the 12:05 train have begun to scurry through the main doors. One of them will be the Bookkeeper, doubtless escorted by a contingent of armed Capone henchmen. Ness has his eye trained on the doors, but he's also concerned about the woman with the baby carriage. She is struggling to figure out how to pull it up the steps, and further, may be in the line of fire if things go badly.

Another sailor, on leave for the weekend, takes a bench. The woman tries to calm her crying baby and position the carriage for the steps. A shady looking man in a fedora crosses the station floor, lighting a cigarette. A dissonant string and wind layer enters:

Figure 10.8C. *The Untouchables*, M32/33, "Machine Gun Lullaby," music box dissonant accompaniment, bars 147–150

In each of these passages as shown in the score (more than it's possible to show here), the numbering of the bars is identical: 147–154. These are his measure numbers for the first statement of the music box melody, and he's simply adding, layer by layer (through overdubs) increasingly dissonant elements with each pass. This creates an almost hypnotic tension, but also accomplishes an even more important dramatic task.

The scene is nominally about the capture of the Bookkeeper, but at a deeper level it is about Eliot Ness and what he is "prepared to do" to apprehend him. One thing he is not prepared to do, as a husband and father of an infant daughter, is let a mother and baby get caught in the crossfire. Almost from the moment Ness spots the woman, we know it's only a matter of time before he'll have to go to her assistance—possibly at risk to his primary mission. We know this through Costner's acting and De Palma's cutting, but more strikingly and intuitively, we know it because Morricone has made the lullaby the linchpin of his cue. This is the method to his madness!

Note in Figure 10.8C how, amid the dissonance, he preserves some tonal elements to draw our emotions toward the baby's plight. What we hear in the mix is a blend of the tonal and atonal accompaniments, with the mixer cross-fading between the two. When the camera is on Ness's face, the tonal chart emerges slightly from the mix.

Figure 10.8C2. *The Untouchables,* **M32/33, "Machine Gun Lullaby,"**
music box dissonant accompaniment, bars 151–154

In the autograph score, everything is stacked together almost in the fashion of a medieval palimpsest, making it difficult to parse. The entire seven-minute cue occupies just nine pages of score. The reductions provided here attempt to separate out the individual layers and provide a key to understanding this brilliant example of "concept scoring." Some adjustments have been required. For example, the music box melody is metered in 12/8 with the dotted quarter as a beat unit, while all the accompanying arrangement is in 4/4. To avoid multiple meters and ensure that tempos line up, I've allowed the music box to be the "governor" in Figures 10.8–10.8C and remetered the strings in 12/8, hence all the tied/dotted notes. Morricone is not terribly scrupulous in observing the usual rules about the subdivision of measures. It's not unusual to see a 4/4 bar filled nonsymmetrically.

As the station fills, the woman begins to ascend the steps, pulling the carriage with her. The clock strikes midnight. Ness can see she'll never make it before the bad guys arrive. He goes to her aid, but just as they reach the top of the stairs, the Bookkeeper arrives, accompanied by a phalanx of gunmen, and all hell breaks loose.

Figure 10.8D. *The Untouchables*, M32/33,
"Machine Gun Lullaby," bars 155–162

On top of the fact that Maestro Morricone has sandwiched three cues into a single nine-page score, he also omits articulations almost entirely, opting instead to give these instructions from the podium as we saw in some of the earlier cues. But they were clearly in his head as he wrote, and even more clearly in the performance, and I've tried to transcribe them here. Note especially the alternation of accents and tremolo as the strings ascend ever higher, sections "stepping" over one another (an especially effective contrast with the picture, in which all the motion is *descending* a flight of steps). Note also how he manages to create high drama and excitement without relying on dynamics: nothing in the section excerpted in Figure 10.8D rises above *mezzo forte* in the concert score (I've marked the "Untouchables" motif in low strings, percussion, and piano at *forte* for visual emphasis).

For the entire closing section of the scene, real time is suspended and everything moves into state of hypergranularity via slow motion, a technique first mastered in Sam Peckinpah's "blood ballets" (*The Wild Bunch, Straw Dogs*, etc.). This allows not only for the bad guys to die in spectacularly gory fashion, but for the key dramatic element in the scene—the descent of the baby carriage—to register with full impact. With each marble step it clatters over, and with each gunshot, we fear for the infant inside. Eliot Ness can do nothing: he's caught in a three-way crossfire and quickly running out of ammunition.

Almost anyone who has ever taken a film history class has seen Sergei Eisenstein's silent movie classic *Battleship Potemkin*. Its most iconic scene takes place on the grand steps of the city of Odessa, where the townspeople have assembled to welcome home and cheer on the mutinous crew of the *Potemkin*, much to the displeasure of the tsar. There are women, children, merchants, and schoolteachers, all completely unprepared for the nightmare they are about to face: a battalion of the tsar's infantry, who will mow them down in cold blood to teach the city a lesson. The scene is considered the premier example of Eisenstein's montage approach to editing (quick, rhythmic cutting and striking juxtapositions), and its central metaphor for the brutality of the Russian regime is the perilous descent and ultimate demolition of a baby carriage following the death of the mother. Brian De Palma, with obvious care, has fashioned his climax as an homage to this sequence. Fortunately, at the close of the breathtaking "Union Station Steps" scene in *The Untouchables*, both mother and baby are intact. George Stone (Andy Garcia) arrives in the nick of time and performs one of action cinema's greatest hero turns.

Figure 10.8E. *The Untouchables*, M32/33, "Machine Gun Lullaby," bars 163–170

Even here, at the climax of a shootout and the resolution of extraordinary tension, Morricone maintains superb control and respect for the priority of the image. The final crescendo is not a tutti gesture, but given only in the high strings. The percussion battery (not shown in this reduction) is tightly restrained. Winds have retired before the last bar.

There are practical as well as aesthetic reasons for playing it this way. The gunplay is ferocious, and taking place on marble steps in a cavernous building of nonabsorbent surfaces. No amount of musical bombast could compete with that, and he doesn't try. The great John Williams sometimes prances through dense patches of sound design as if he were writing for ballet, confident that either his director will see the wisdom of making music foremost in the mix—or if he doesn't, well, at least it will all survive in the concert suite. But a Morricone cue almost never risks getting "buried." Among his peers, living and dead, only Herrmann possessed an equal talent for finding breaks in the clouds for his musical light to pour through. Morricone's motto seems to be "If the director asked for music, then the music *must* have meaning"—even if it's a solo harmonica or the tinkle of a prepared piano. In the midst of sonic cacophony, his musical statements somehow manage to be iconic, and most important, *meaningful.* This isn't mere craft, it is artistic problem-solving, and the primary function of film music as an auxiliary art is to solve dramatic problems and to support the dramatic thesis of the film.

That leads to the other, and more salient reason for the way in which "Machine Gun Lullaby," and indeed, the entire score, has been constructed. *The Untouchables* is a film about a world: a place and a period—some might call it a historical aberration—during which the line between the forces of good and the forces of evil was more starkly drawn. Through this world walks a man with a family to protect and an oath to serve—the sort of man people once called, somewhat disparagingly, a Boy Scout. He's a young white knight, but his combat trainer is an older and far more seasoned knight who teaches him that principled reserve is no virtue in the face of rank evil. Ness learns his lesson well, yet manages not to lose his soul in the process: he puts Capone away *and* saves the baby. Had Morricone chosen anything other than the music box lullaby as the binding element of M31/32, we might have forgotten—*Ness might have forgotten*—what really mattered.

Ennio Morricone won't be with us much longer. And when he goes, the film music world will have lost its last unreservedly emotional voice. *The Untouchables* isn't his prettiest score, or even his most moving, but in its dramatic scope, sweep and total command of its milieu, it remains a monumental contribution to the canon.

ELEVEN TOWARD A NEW AESTHETIC OF MUSIC FOR THE SCREEN

Mention *aesthetics* to a panel of professional film composers and you are likely to see a lot of eye rolling. They will humbly insist that they are, at best, artisans, there to serve the project and its producers. The notion of music as a mere handmaiden to cinema has become so prevalent that thousands of novice composers now seek counsel in books, Internet forums and "webinars" that traffic more in entrepreneurial and people-pleasing skills than artistry. This feeds a cycle: composers discount the importance of their contribution and are, in turn, devalued by the industry they serve. (The average portion of a film's overall budget allocated to original music, never large, has fallen drastically since the turn of the century) Humility is an admirable quality, and so is esprit de corps, but neither one is in conflict with artistic integrity. Likewise, while no single standard can set the artistic aims of music for the vast array of visual media now extant, the absence of *any* standard seems a recipe for mediocrity. Good music requires every bit as much rigor as good screenwriting, editing, or cinematography, and deserves every bit as much credit.

The phrase *toward a new aesthetic* calls to mind artistic movements and manifestos of past centuries, and artistic movements—like religious and political reform movements—have often been about the restoration of purity to an enterprise seen as having fallen from its original purpose. While some in the film music profession would argue this is precisely what has become of the once-noble craft of Rózsa and Tiomkin, the diagnosis offered here is less damning, and the cure less drastic than a purge.

Film music has never been "pure." It's a crossbreed, a hybrid: a loveable mutt. It is a citizen of no nation (other than perhaps the imaginary nation of "Hollywood") and owes allegiance to no flag and no culture (other than the "culture" of cinema). Whereas once (pre-1940), it might have been asserted that film music owed whatever pedigree it had to Viennese and Italian opera and the late romantic composers, that hereditary thread had already begun to fray when the radio *mélodrames* of the 1930s encouraged such mavericks as Bernard Herrmann to experiment with music that stood apart from the action as opposed to merely miming it. This is the musical language that film scholars came to refer to as *nondiegetic*; that is, outside the created "reality" of the film's narrative. Its classical expression was the "symphonic film score" as exemplified by composers from Max Steiner to John Williams.

Such films as *Sunset Boulevard, Lawrence of Arabia*, and *Star Wars* lent themselves beautifully to this kind of score, and their directors fully accepted the "intrusion" of nondiegetic music—even if occasionally they asked, "Where exactly is this music supposed to be coming *from*?" I will argue here that the right answer to that question is, "It's coming from *within* the story—from its emotional and 'mythical' subtext."

In terms of harmonic language, probably 80 percent of the film music recorded between 1931 and the end of the twentieth century would lend itself comfortably to the sort of *Schenkerian analysis*[1] that is still done in university music classes—at least to the degree that such analysis can parse the vocabulary of Wagner and Mahler. The remaining 15 percent comprised such outliers as Toru Takemitsu (*Woman in the Dunes*); early electronic composers, such as Louis and Bebe Barron (*Forbidden Planet*); the handful of scores that employed serial technique (e.g., Leonard Rosenman's *The Cobweb* and *East of Eden*); jazz scores (e.g., *In Cold Blood*); and finally, a new strain of theatrical composition that's attributable almost entirely to the tempestuous genius of Bernard Herrmann.

THE EMBEDDED SCORE

This last sliver of the genome points the way toward a mutation that will ensure the survival of the craft and its purveyors, because Herrmann at his best wrote from inside the film, and this is where today's filmmakers want the music to live and breathe. Beyond the rarified commercial realm of $100-million-plus "tentpole" movies, today's leading directors have little interest in traditional symphonic scores. They want something *new*: something that moves like an ocean current beneath the narrative, supporting it and gently pushing it forward. When you're searching for something genuinely novel, counterintuitively it's often best to search first in the archives of the past, and especially in the music that exerted and continues to exert the most potent psychic force. There are good examples of this "retrospective innovation" in concert music: Debussy's embrace of archaic harmonies and non-European forms, such as gamelan; Satie's quasi-mystical (and often whimsical) meditations for piano; and more recently, Arvo Pärt's evocation of medieval organum and Renaissance polyphony.

The psychological trigger that makes this "new use of the old" work is closely related the one that made something as bold as John Adams's *Short Ride in a Fast Machine* a concert hit: the appeal of the *familiar-unfamiliar*. Or, to crib an acronym from the father of twentieth-century industrial design, Raymond Loewy, MAYA (most advanced, yet accessible). That approach can

---

1   Heinrich Schenker (1868–1935) developed a method of analyzing the underlying structure (ursatz) and fundamental line (urlinie) of tonal music of the common practice period. Roman numeral analysis of harmony is one form of this.

be summed up as: to sell something surprising, make it familiar; to sell something familiar, make it surprising.[2]

Bernard Herrmann wasn't afraid to look back in time or to raid the collective unconscious, and his music—though deeply conceptual—set off triggers in the most ancient parts of the brain. From the opening measures of *Citizen Kane* (1941), he sounded like no one else, and for seventy-five years, few have ventured to follow his path (the major exception being Danny Elfman, whose influences come mostly from Herrmann's body of work in sci-fi/fantasy). Herrmann's technique is sui generis, but shouldn't be.

What's interesting is that Herrmann's groundbreaking musical "gene splicing" happened almost inadvertently. He was a classicist and an Anglophile who longed to write pastoral works in the manner of Frederick Delius. But nothing he wrote for film sounds like Delius, and the reason seems to be that Herrmann, who cut his teeth scoring the aforementioned *mélodrames* for CBS and the Mercury Radio Theater, was a dramatist and a storyteller even before he was a composer. After 1950, he simply could not and *would not* violate the dictum that the form of the diegesis should determine the function of the nondiegetic. This is actually a pretty radical notion, because its ultimate expression could be music that doesn't sound like conventional "music" at all.

This isn't to say that Herrmann's scores would play well in today's cinema. Many would strike us as anachronistic. But a contemporary application of Herrmann's way of thinking about music in film could lead to some very interesting places. The film music of the future may function as an embedded element of the diegesis—an organic part of the film's imaginary world—if not joined with it, then at least enfolded *within* it.

For those who fear that I'm talking about music as "sound design" or pure texture (pejoratively: "wallpaper"), let me be clear: film music will remain worthy of serious study and stature as an art form only if it continues to satisfy certain basic criteria:

- It must offer the audience significant *insight* with respect to character psychology, emotional subtext, and/or the *nature of the world* the film/television show/video game inhabits. If it does not in some way *illuminate* the images on screen, it fails.
- It must achieve this in a way that isn't *redundant* with pictorial information or dialogue, i.e., it should "speak" from its own unique place or perspective.
- To retain its integrity as a craft deserving of awards and accolades, it must adhere—in some manner—to universally recognized principles of good composition, which include fundamentals such as melodic invention (however we define *melody*), theme and variation, symmetry, repetition, and development.

2   Derek Thompson, *Hit Makers: The Science of Popularity in an Age of Distraction*, (New York: Penguin, 2017).

- There must be an authorial voice behind the music that is identifiable at least to those in the visual media professions and to students of the craft.

If these standards are met, it doesn't make a great deal of difference whether the medium of delivery is a symphonic ensemble, electronic chamber group, a capella vocal consort, "ambient" composition or solo *duduk*. In every case, the successful practice of the art will demand musical literacy, compositional rigor, study of the "repertoire," and especially, a mature understanding of the mechanics of drama. No composer without an understanding of story can hope to make the A-list, and no composer without equal measures of curiosity and musical discipline will ever be more than a flash in the pan.

THOMAS NEWMAN'S REVOLUTIONARY ROAD

If we ask ourselves which composers have taken Bernard Herrmann's fundamental approach of "scoring from the inside of the film" and developed it further, we come up with a very short list. Dozens of composers qualify as superbly talented melodists, arrangers, producers, emulators, and imitators, but only a few have truly advanced the integration of music with picture in a way that serves to make music an *indispensable* ingredient of visual storytelling. Music must be, to paraphrase the brilliant orchestrator Conrad Pope (John Williams, Alexandre Desplat), not simply something filmmakers "need" (to fill space, mark time, smooth transitions) but something they *want* (to say all the things that images and words alone can't say and increase the value of the product). If composers can't provide this, they may soon find themselves supplanted by algorithms.

With this high standard in mind, one name on that short list deserves special recognition in any discussion of the present and future state of the film music art: Thomas Newman. Brother of David (see chapter 5), son of Alfred (*Anastasia, The Song of Bernadette*), cousin of Randy (*The Natural, Toy Story*), he is probably best known to cineastes and students of film music alike for his work in such films as *The Shawshank Redemption* and *American Beauty*, and for an extraordinary four-year period, 1991–95, when, for all intents, he reshaped the rules for the scoring of drama and in the process altered filmmaker expectations regarding the role and character of music.

When people attempt to describe Thomas Newman's music, certain expressions and descriptors tend to come up repeatedly: *contemplative, reflective, hip, dreamy, deep, moving, elegiac, otherworldly*. Most of these words are suggestive of qualities we mark as spiritual or profound. Yet the music itself is often seemingly weightless, floating like a vapor over the screen. Common analyses of Newman's work are likely to stop short at "I can't really figure out what he's doing, but he seems to be breaking a lot of rules" or "There's something exotic, something quirky, something *nonstandard* about his harmonies." Curiously, these are the same sort of comments that might have been made about someone like Debussy in his time. J.A.C. Redford, who took over duties as Newman's principal orchestrator after the departure of longtime collaborator Thomas Pasatieri, describes Newman's ear for harmony as "very sophisticated," and it is, though not in quite the sense that Debussy's was. There is something idiosyncratic going on in Newman's charts, and it accounts largely for why his style was so passionately embraced by filmmakers and why—for at least ten years following his emergence in the early nineties—his music found its way into hundreds if not thousands of temp scores.

One thing is certain: he scores from the inside.

It simply can't be coincidental that Thomas Newman's arrival as the most sought-after new voice in film music coincided with the emergence into the public sphere of the Estonian "holy minimalist," Arvo Pärt, and in particular, those pieces he composed between 1977 and 1983, after his self-imposed period of silence, contemplation, and intensive study of medieval and Renaissance forms. The most cinematically ubiquitous of these pieces is *Fratres*, a string quintet written in Pärt's *tintinnabuli* style. It has been featured prominently in films by such major directors as Paul Thomas Anderson (*There Will Be Blood*), Terrence Malick (*To the Wonder*), Derek Cianfrance (*The Place Beyond the Pines*) and Tom Tykwer (*Heaven*), and has served as the temp score model for dozens of "knock-off" cues over the past decade. Clearly, something is going on, because *Fratres*, as a work of music, is as *internal* as music can be. It transports us to a world of interiors, and to a sensation the modern world rarely affords: that of the sacred.

This is not to say that Thomas Newman aped Arvo Pärt. If it were that simple, we'd all be multiple Academy Award nominees. Newman has his own voice, and his influences come equally from sources as diverse as Indonesian gamelan, Appalachian folk, and Charles Ives (see, in particular, the opening movement of Ives's Third Symphony). But the simultaneity of their emergence into the cinematic zeitgeist suggests that "something was in the air," and that both of them deliver an ineffable something that filmmakers very much want in their movies. And if we look deeper, we see that there is indeed a common thread, for Newman's use of harmony, sophisticated as it may be, is a perfect example of reaching back to the old to derive something entirely new. Its haunting qualities result from the way it evokes the familiar-unfamiliar, and the same can be said of Pärt's music. In very similar ways, Newman's music draws us inside.

Newman often seems to write like a brilliant but self-taught jazz pianist transported back to early fifteenth-century Europe. A good illustration of this is his essentially monothematic score for the adaptation of Richard Yates's novel *Revolutionary Road*, directed by Newman's now loyal collaborator, Sam Mendes, and released in 2008. At first glance, it may appear to be one of his lesser scores, perhaps not as emblematic of his style as *Scent of a Woman* or *American Beauty*. But it enfolds a musical mystery, the "solution" of which may help explain why he has entranced a generation of leading filmmakers. Figure 11.1 is a reduction of the first ten bars of the End Credit cue, which consist entirely of the simple but enigmatic cadence that lies at the heart of the score. The "ethnic flute" and synth pad parts are simplifications of Newman's multilayered patches and motion sequences, which are among the best in the business.

Figure 11.1. *Revolutionary Road*, End Credit, bars 1–10

The first and most obvious question to ask about these five measures is: is this "tonal" music, and if so, is there a "key?" The answer is a sort of musical conundrum. The pad and the landing chord of the cadence suggest an E major tonality. And in one sense, that perception is exactly right. But

using a flat-VII chord (D major) over an E pedal in place of a dominant or subdominant chord creates immediate tonal ambiguity. The E major chord will never feel fully resolved to, as indeed it shouldn't, given that the central relationship in the film is in a state of persistent irresolution and the final frame will fade without any reconciliation of the film's major (and fairly tragic) themes. In that sense, *Revolutionary Road* is a very modern film, and Newman's is a very modern score.

In fact, the D-E axis creates what might be described as a "Lydian quandary." The memory of the G-sharp continues to resonate within the Dsus2 chord, and as we saw in *To Kill a Mockingbird*, the Lydian fourth is a chameleon: it can function modally as the raised fourth, or it can act like a leading tone (in which case, Newman's D major and E major chords could function as the IV and V chords in an incomplete cadence in the "phantom key" of A major!) This ambiguity is classic Tom Newman: we almost never hear a straight dominant-tonic juxtaposition in his music, which means that nothing aims at a definable tonal center. This has been the case at least since *The Player*, the score that signaled his emergence as a truly distinctive voice.

That his *Revolutionary Road* theme is modal isn't in doubt, but it's a mode of his own making, more in the manner of modal jazz composers. Look at the climb back to the E chord in measure 6. The parallel fifths in the left hand are as straightforward as any piece of medieval plainchant, but they "resolve" in an E major harmony, with the flavor of the Picardy thirds in Renaissance polyphony. And hidden in this ascent is another Newman trademark. Note the wide voicing of the B minor chord. There is an interval of a minor tenth between root and third. Parallel tenths are a key feature of Thomas Newman's piano scoring, particularly noticeable in the "Long Gray Line" cue from *Scent of a Woman*, and the "Brooks Was Here" cue from *Shawshank Redemption*.

Before looking at the next ten measures of the cue, notice the highlighted harmony shifts in bars 8–10. In any E major modality, we'd expect the sixth scale degree to be C-sharp, and its chord to be a C-sharp minor. Instead, Newman pulls out a C major chord (a flat VI)—once again, a *mixture chord* and a color of both early and "posttonal" music—cadences to a Gsus2, and then moves through A major to A minor before falling in bar 12 (Figure 11.2) to a temporary resting place on D major. This sort of progression remains relatively rare in modern-era orchestral music, but it *is* heard in folk and rock, and it *is* heard in the Renaissance piece "The Coventry Carol" (see Figure 11.3). In one sense, Thomas Newman seems to have found his way into film music's future via the past. But it gets even more interesting than this. Let's take a look at what comes next:

Figure 11.2. *Revolutionary Road*, End Titles, bars 11–20

The section from 13–16, when strings join, is especially powerful, and again, evades any single modality. At times, the cue feels bimodal, if not polymodal, but these are, at best, academic labels, of little use to the work-

ing film composer. It doesn't seem likely that Tom Newman sat down at the keyboard and said to himself, "I think I'll write a polymodal cue." This is music that's evolving through a *transformational process*. By the time he lands satisfyingly on the E major chord in bar 20, he has observed all rules of good voice leading without having once utilized "functional harmony." And here is at least one clue to how he did it: although the music isn't diatonic in any conventional way, the chords are related by common and neighboring tone/s and are, in a sense, "diatonic" to the musical world of the cue. If we assemble them into a "set," we have: E major, F major, G major, A minor and A major, B-flat major, B minor, C major, and D major. All but two are major triads, and all but one (the B-flat) have "'white key" roots. Even the suspended seconds are incidental rather than stacked in the manner of jazz chords. This is triadic writing,[3] and yet, it does in fact employ a "sophisticated harmonic language."

Figure 11.3. Excerpt from "The Coventry Carol" (16th-century Christmas carol, author unknown)

In a hauntingly similar way, and across six centuries, the unknown author of "The Coventry Carol" (Figure 11.3) led his four voices (the tenor and soprano voices largely in parallel sixths) through a series of transformations

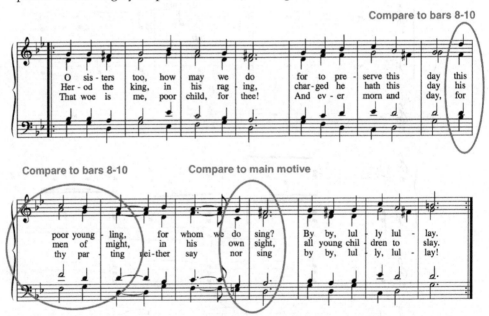

which take this plaintive G minor tune convincingly to resolution on a G major chord. Of course, he was doing this within the operative rules of his time and largely through the use of the leading tone and Picardy third, but the emotional effect—of longing for some measure of grace in the midst of tragic events—in this case, the murder of the innocents by King Herod—is not unlike the effect of Newman's theme.

At first glance, the music of Thomas Newman and Bernard Herrmann seem to have little in common. Newman's music is reflective and ethereal, while Herrmann's strikes us as eerie, astringent and even jarring. What they

---

3   See Richard Cohn's *Audacious Euphony: Chromatic Harmony and the Triad's Second Nature* (New York: Oxford University Press, 2012).

share is a sense of harmony whereby successive chords relate and refer to each other but not to any common key center. In other words, the harmonic language is *contextual*. Despite this absence of a "home key," there is a generalized feeling of tonality—even in Herrmann's most assertively dissonant scores (e.g., *Psycho*).

TRIADIC POSTTONALITY (OR PAN-TRIADICISM)

In comparing these two harbingers of what may be to come in film music, we may want to return briefly to two of the keystones of posttonal music theory: *Neo-Riemannian Theory and Transformational Theory*. Hugo Riemann was a German composer and music theorist of the late nineteenth and early twentieth centuries who, like many during this period, sought to derive some coherent theory from the new harmonic language created by Richard Wagner, Franz Liszt, and other late romantic composers. Building from the triad, or *Klang*, as the fundamental unit of harmony, he argued for a posttonal understanding of harmony that related triads *only to other triads* (he also subscribed to some rather arcane notions regarding the derivation of the minor scale, but these have landed on the dust heap of history). The fundamental idea, adopted in the mid-1980s by musicologist/mathematician David Lewin and theorist Richard Cohn, was that harmonic language consisted in "something one does to a *Klang* (triad) to obtain another *Klang*."[4] In other words, a transformation. This was a shift in music theory that reflected the general abandonment of serialism and the return to what Cohn calls "triadic post-tonality," a term that could conceivably embrace composers from Wagner to John Adams, as well as Arvo Pärt and Thomas Newman. In 1987, Lewin published an influential work called *Generalized Musical Intervals and Transformations* in which he carried Hugo Riemann's torch onward and introduced what has become known as *transformational theory*. As mentioned, Lewin is a mathematician, and some of his headier ideas about harmonic change occurring as the result of "operations" (as in algebra) may strike many composers as overly academic, but the core assertion that modern harmony results from operations, such as (1) chromatic voice-leading; (2) linkage by common tone/s, and (3) inversion and mirroring, suits film music beautifully. Lewin summed it this way: "If I am *at* s and wish to get to t, what characteristic *gesture* should I perform in order to arrive there?"[5] Each of these "characteristic gestures" or operations was given a letter name, such as P (Parallel), R (Relative), and L (Leading Tone). In combination, they may yield this analysis of a transformation utilized by Wagner, Herrmann, and Newman alike:

Figure 11.4A. Neo-Riemannian transformation of triads

The "Tarnhelm" L-P transformation of a minor triad (fifth up a semi-

---

4   Richard Cohn, "Introduction to Neo-Riemannian Theory," *Journal of Music Theory* 42, no. 2 (1998). Cohn is here quoting David Lewin.

5   David Lewin, *Generalized Musical Intervals and Transformations* (Oxford University Press, 2010), 159

tone/root down a semitone), named after a leitmotif from Wagner's *Das*

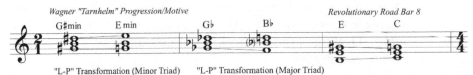

Rheingold, will be familiar to anyone who has ever loved a Bernard Herrmann or Danny Elfman sci-fi score. The major triad version of this is a feature of almost every Thomas Newman score since *Scent of a Woman,* and in the third example (Figure 11.4A), we see an inverted version of the same transformation, drawn from the *Revolutionary Road* cue.

To take this a step further, begin with the G-flat to B-flat mediant transformation in the second bar, and continue, using the principals of "parsimonious voice-leading"; that is, wherever possible, no voice should move by more than a whole step, and there should be at least one common tone carried over from the previous chord. There is more than one way to "skin this cat," but Figure 11.4B is one attempt. After six transformations, we "cadence" on an Fm6 chord in the first inversion, a very different place from where we started. But this is not modulation. It's something else.

Figure 11.4B. Triad transformation example

In this light, examine anew the excerpt from Bernard Herrmann's well-known "Temptation" cue from *Psycho* (Figure 11.5).

Figure 11.5. Bernard Herrmann, *Psycho,* "Temptation"

The four little bars excerpted in Figure 11.5 are a living example of Richard Cohn's "triadic post-tonality." They are likely seared into the memory

of any student of film music who has made a study of Herrmann's paradigmatic score for Alfred Hitchcock's *Psycho*, perhaps even more than the famous shower scene glissandos. Marion Crane is preparing to drive north to see her lover, having promised to first make the weekly cash deposit for her employer. The stack of fresh bills is on the bed, wrapped in brown paper. Should she be a good girl and put it in the bank, or should she take the money and run?

We all know her decision and its dire consequences. At this early stage of the film, however, we barely know her character, and the choice could go either way. The music needs to tell us something that the picture alone cannot: what's going on inside her head. *Psycho* is a fretful, agitated, neurasthenic film in which every scene bristles with anxiety, but the jagged dissonance of its score is often contrasted with a kind of languor that is frankly quite erotic. Marion wants the money so that she'll no longer have to meet Sam in cheap hotel rooms. She wants it to buy off his ex-wife, and the temptation is killing her.

So, what does Bernard Herrmann do? Time is the key element in anxiety, since the clock always plays against us. He creates a little ostinato figure to show the passage of time, the kind of sequence a young piano student might practice ceaselessly. Alone, it suggests a simple elaboration of D minor and C major chords with neighbor notes. But what are the strings doing? Second violins, divisi, begin on a high C (doubled an 8ve below) dropping to a B-natural. Violas open on A-flat and step up to an A-natural. A M10 closes to become a dissonant M9, confounding our recognition of the chords. What are the harmonies? It's only when we step back and read the cue in the context of the entire score, and indeed, Herrmann's entire body of work, that we see it. A first inversion F minor chord (with the M6 and M7 as ornaments) is being transformed into a root position A minor chord with a biting M9 in the violins, and it is the same transformation we see in the *Tarnhelm* progression of Figure 11.4A: minor triads/root movement by an M3.

Students of Herrmann know how fond he was of this harmonic device, and of its putative originator, Richard Wagner. But what's most fascinating here is the way the score functions almost as a diegetic sound element: a ticking clock, a beating heart, a pulse slowing as blood ebbs from the body. Herrmann has created a musical picture of *temptation* and its consequences, without which the scene would not work.

FINDING THE MUSIC INSIDE THE MOVIE

How do we score systematically "from the inside," embedding music so thoroughly in the story that no filmmaker would ever think of forsaking it and no producer would dare relegate it to the low end of the budget? How do we practice the craft in a way that ensures the deepest possible integration of music and story—a way that could never be characterized as "wallpaper" or "window dressing?" How do we create new Bernard Herrmanns and Thomas Newmans?

Maybe it begins with an admission that may, at first, seem to fly in the face of what contemporary filmmakers want. No matter how integral to story it becomes, film music, by its very nature, is *artifice*. It can never be other than that without losing its value as music in and of itself. The other crafts—cinematography, set and costume design, art direction, editing—even when at their most fantastical or baroque, all seek to convince us of the physical "reality" of what we're seeing on the screen. Nondiegetic music—i.e., score—just can't do that. Music cannot *denote* things. The only reality that pure underscore can underpin is the reality *behind the images*, the reality of feeling and impulse, and the full range of psychological states from calm sanity to raging psychosis.

But this practical "handicap," far from making music nonessential, is its ace in the hole. Despite attempts by French new wave and Dogme 95 filmmakers, it is almost impossible to create a convincing mimesis of the most primal emotional states—fear, panic, love, longing, etc.—without the aid of music. It *is* possible, however, to do so without the aid of traditionally composed music, as we've seen with the triumph of scores for such films as *Babel, The Social Network, Gravity* and *The Dark Knight*.

With all credit to the enormous ingenuity of their composers, however, the aforementioned scores aren't essential additions to the repertoire. Each of them is important as a transitional stage in the development of the form, but only as a chrysalis is to a butterfly. We will have to go farther if film music is to survive as an art.

I have an idea what a young (and perhaps less cantankerous) Bernard Herrmann might do if faced with such a challenge. He'd sit down with *his* director—with *his* Hitchcock—and say something like this: "Look . . . let's imagine that a movie really is what it pretends to be. A four-dimensional microcosm that enfolds human experience. How do I *draw* those elements from the film *into* the score, as if I were drawing oil from a seed or water from the ground? How do I synthesize music from cinema?"

Here's how we might hope a thoughtful director would respond:

- *Listen to the film.* What kind of sound world does it describe? Is it an industrial world, full of clanking and groaning and grinding of metal against metal? Is it a pastoral world, where the soft but insistent buzz of crickets at nightfall is the dominant soundscape? Or is it a world in which the chief "sound" is the flow of information through integrated circuits? Take those elements, transmute them, and lift them into your score. Make the music feel as if it's of a piece with the sound world of the film, while still maintaining its uniquely *musical* qualities.
- *Read the beats in the story like Braille.* Let that reading determine what you write. Don't *impose* anything gratuitous or intended purely to show off your skill. By all means, use strings, winds, percussion, and electronics if they're the most effective "voices," but let that Braille card be the score you keep referring back to.

- *Score the entire film, not individual scenes.* Just as every film has a production design and a cinematographic look that are consistent throughout, so should the music—in its instrumentation, style, complexity or simplicity, and attitude—be congruent with the film's identity. If the musical choices are right, we don't mind hearing them repeated with minimal variation. In this way, the audience becomes accustomed to the presence of music as an integral part of the film's sound world.
- *Think like a filmmaker.* Consider the "species" of the film, its literary and dramatic referents, its links to mythology and legend. There are only so many essential human stories, and this is one of them. Chances are, that story has been scored many times before, and if you allude artfully to those forebears, your score will be successful. Novelists and painters and filmmakers do this. So should you.
- *Make it immersive.* When we attend a concert, we're there for the music, and we want to be transported by it. When we see a film, we're there to live in a different world for two hours, and once we're in, we don't want anything to take us out. When a score works, it's like an enchantment—it's the spell that will allow the audience to suspend disbelief. This is why music is so mysterious to filmmakers—and also so frightening.

The writing, of course, is up to you. Converting these imperatives to "notes on paper" (or more likely, to MIDI data) requires technique. The approach of this book has been "show, don't tell," and the preceding three hundred pages have offered abundant examples of how it's done. But if a single truth can be distilled from all of those examples, it is probably that composing music that truly lives inside the film and offers the audience the most emotionally immersive experience has a great deal to do with employing the right kind of *harmonic language*. It is a language whose syntax is rooted in tonality but not in any sense anchored by it. To hammer the point one last time: the harmony is contextual. The harmonic linkages are chord to chord, bar to bar, or phrase to phrase, "functioning" as integrated units faithful only to themselves and to story. Their nature is that of a transitory (but passionate) hookup rather than a long-term relationship. They are very often, as in life, unresolved. Except in cases where the story expressly calls for it, almost nothing will pull an audience out of a film faster than a predictable ii–V7–I (or the like) chord progression. Been there, done that. It is simply too familiar, and to hammer another point: great film music demands the unfamiliar-familiar. The somewhat paradoxical corollary to this is that chord sequences lacking internal logic, fluid voice leading, and "sense of place" will rarely if ever move an audience to tears or goose bumps. This may be one reason why serial technique and, to some degree, free jazz harmony have seldom resulted in emotionally effective film scores. They demand too much of the ear at a time when our mind wants to be captivated by story, and were never designed to entrance, to seduce, to mystify or immerse. This in no way means that the harmonic language of film music must be "dumbed down" to suit an unsophisticated audience. Ligeti and Penderecki, in the right place, have powerful applications in cinema. (Pierre Boulez—not so much). John Adams's practice of *harmonic gating* isn't the least bit dumb, nor is the language of Hindustani raga, nor the approach utilized by Icelandic composer Jóhann Jóhannsson in such films as *Arrival* (2016). What all three do share is a fidelity to "narrative" and to full emotional engagement. There are exciting times ahead.

ON THE CURVE: BENSI AND JUURIAANS

With all these points in mind, we will consider a more recent score, one very different in character from most of those examined in this book, yet very much aware of its predecessors. The film is *Enemy*, and its director is one of the new century's most distinctive talents, Denis Villeneuve, the French-Canadian auteur responsible for *Incendies*, *Prisoners*, and *Sicario*, as well as *Arrival* and the *Blade Runner* remake. The composers are Danny Bensi and Saunder Juuriaans, former college roommates who in the second decade of the twenty-first century have already carved out an impressive niche.

Enemy is a postmodern thriller, one of a number of recent films dealing with the idea of the doppelgänger, and loosely based on José Saramago's 2002 novel *The Double*. It contains elements of political allegory and dream/nightmare imagery that recall Franz Kafka and Jorge Luis Borges, and also boasts what David Ehrlich of film.com called "the scariest ending of any film ever made."[6] It stars Jake Gyllenhaal in both principal roles.

For a composer, a film like *Enemy* can offer both delight and danger. Its meanings are left deliberately obscure; there are no "good guys" and "bad guys," and we can't always be sure of what we're looking at. It is perilously easy to fall into melodrama on one extreme and droning understatement on the other. Bensi and Jurriaans get it right.

---

6   "TIFF Review: "Enemy," http://www.mtv.com/news/2771092/enemy-review/, accessed September 13, 2013.

Figure 11.6A. Danny Bensi and Saunder Jurriaans, *Enemy*, "The Dark Room" (excerpt/reduction)

Like the Mica Levi cue from *Under the Skin* excerpted in chapter 4, a conventional reduction of this kind of hybrid scoring can only hint at what it sounds like. Structurally, it's quite simple, and on the face of it, not harmonically sophisticated. Everything happens over a low pedal D, and the canon-like counterpoint in cellos and first violins that form the principal melodic line couldn't be more straightforward. But as with much of Thomas Newman's music, the devil is in the detail of the elaborately constructed loops and pads that underlie the horizontal movement of the line—detail that cannot be shown very effectively on paper because it wasn't conceived on paper.

To hear this cue against the opening scenes of *Enemy* is to know that something hideous is lurking beneath the hazy, malarial surface of this deeply disturbing movie. It isn't a "synth score" with a few acoustic brush-strokes, but an immersive soundscape that pulls us almost immediately into the film's surreal diegesis. What is shown in the reduction as a "synth pad" is, in fact, a dense pudding of sound elements that are as carefully assembled as those in a traditional orchestral score, but given organic life by the acoustic instruments. It's the sort of writing that Hans Zimmer has been experimenting with in such films as *The Dark Knight* and *Inception*, but here in the service of a motion picture that was truly made for it. Bars 5–8 (Figure 11.6B) show the introduction of a second line (I've made a cut between measures 4 and 5 to eliminate the intervening atmosphere). Here, we see something closer to a conventional melody, but there is nothing conventional about the way it's presented.

Figure 11.6B. Danny Bensi and Saunder Jurriaans, *Enemy*, "The Dark Room" (excerpt/reduction)

The line is initiated by the cellos, then imitated by the violins in a fashion that, as in Bernard Herrmann's most enduring cues, can almost be described as romantic. That expressiveness never gets out of hand, however, because—again, as Herrmann did in *Psycho*—the violins are in mutes. The notation here of the aleatoric pizzicato figures in the third violins is only an approximation. Neither the rhythm nor the sequence is at all regular. In other cues in *Enemy*, the bass clarinet (and other low woodwinds) play a far more active role in carrying the haunting fragments of twisted melody. Low woods are indeed the score's most evident signature, and this, too, seems an homage to Herrmann. Contemporary film composers look to Herrmann not necessarily because the subject is macabre, but because he remains the gold standard for the musical depiction of aberrant psychological states, alienation from self, moral ambiguity, and other qualities that are abundant in the cinema of the twenty-first century. The music isn't atonal. It's posttonal.

THE HORIZONTAL ELEMENT AND THE FUTURE OF MELODY

Notwithstanding the importance of harmony, there's an impression held by many that the screen music of our time has become too "vertical": overlayered, rigidly metrical, and unmelodic (all qualities that are abetted by the principal mode of composition: the digital audio workstation). Let's focus for a moment on the matter of melody, because its threatened extinction has been a long time in the making. Among the most highly-regarded concert composers of the last century, and especially in academic and conservatory settings, melody earned something of a bad rap, perhaps because it was difficult to conceive of a melody that wasn't spawned from a purely tonal matrix. Exhaustive attempts were made to subvert, invert, and render obsolete traditional melodic invention through such devices as serial technique. Modern jazz improvisation transgressed the notion of "tune" by coming at the melody from above, below, around, and outside. By and large, the general audience never embraced this flight from tunefulness, which may account for why concert programs continued to consist mainly of Mozart, Haydn, Brahms, Dvořák, et al., and why film music, during its so-called Golden Era (roughly, *Gone with the Wind* to *Lawrence of Arabia*) was virtually synonymous with the idea of "the big theme."

So, why did so many filmmakers, beginning in the 1970s, signal a retreat from melodic statement[7] that has led us today to a place where some question whether film music should sound like *music* at all. First, it should be acknowledged that filmmakers drink from the well of culture and aren't immune to trends. They, too, want to be on the cutting edge. But more critically, *thematic* film music is associated with a glossy, highly packaged studio product that is the antithesis of the edgy immediacy that contemporary filmmakers seek. Their fear is that a "pretty" melody may undercut these values.

But melody, if redefined as purposeful linear movement through the score, can never be entirely absent from great music for the screen—whether or not it gives us anything to hum as we leave the theater. Because the word has such strong associations with old-school style, I favor term *line* over *melody*: the horizontal as opposed to the vertical; the thing that carries through. Why is it essential? Because *line* is the musical counterpart of *dramatic development in time*. If a given scene is mutating—with characters experiencing such things as surprise, realization, trauma, grief, or transformation—and the music is static in time, then the score is no longer functioning as an emotional auxiliary of the drama.

As an exercise, choose any highly dramatic movie scene, preferably one that includes dialogue. Take a piece of graph paper and draw X and Y axes: the X (vertical axis) represents dramatic tension, rising or falling, and the Y (horizontal axis) represents linear time and, hence, *change*. Now get a pencil, and as you watch the scene, graph the increase and decrease of dramatic tension over time (Note: Tension isn't always a negative thing—it can also precede a kiss or a great discovery.) The resulting trace is your "throughline." It may take the form of a conventional melody, or it may be purely dynamical, but one thing is certain: it will change in response to the drama.

---

7   The obvious exceptions were such directors as Spielberg and Lucas, who quite deliberately sought to recall the epic cinema of another era, and engaged John Williams to help them do so. Likewise, such composers as John Barry and Alan Silvestri continued through the 1980s and into the '90s to write in the classic Golden Era style.

Some will counter that this is a recipe for old-fashioned underscore; that in the current era, music in film is mostly about mood or—in action movies—momentum. But sooner or later, everything old is new again, and the challenge for visual composers in the years ahead will be to re-establish the importance of *development*, and to find innovative ways to integrate fundamental things like theme and variation into the weave of immersive scoring, even if these take a very different form from that employed by Mozart or Max Steiner.[8] After all, screenwriters do this. So do art directors, in their own fashion. Linking the score to the both the central ideas and the emotional subtext of the story will insure that film music never becomes simply another branch of sound design.

THE FOX MUSIC SYSTEM

Speaking of making the "old" new again, another Newman—David, whose work was explored in chapter 5, has recently found himself drawn to a reexamination of the underscoring style developed into high craft by the 20th Century Fox music department during the period of his father Alfred's stewardship. It was known as the *rubato style*, but that label hardly does it justice, for the conductor (usually Newman himself) sought to follow the rhythms of drama so fluidly that, in effect, "the bar line was effaced"[9] and the audience became unconscious of meter—an ideal "state of suspension" for the prolongation of cinematic illusion, and not altogether different from what such composers as Debussy and Delius were attempting to do in the concert hall.

From 1939 to 1960, when Alfred Newman held the baton, Fox had a contract orchestra that he was able to mold no less methodically and lovingly than had such contemporaries as Stokowski or Ormandy. Having an ensemble of highly trained symphonic musicians at one's disposal allows for experimentation, trial and error, and boldness of approach. Most of all, it allows for the emergence of an extraordinary unity of voice. This unity in turn allowed Newman to employ his orchestra in a far tighter and more organic synchronization with picture, and in particular, with the continuous stream of dialogue that was a hallmark of "talking pictures" during this formative era. The underscore weaves freely in and out, unhitched from fixed tempo, punctuating when necessary, keeping a low profile when other elements predominate. It is a creature that lives—if not inside the film—then very closely alongside it.

The goal, as Newman explains it, was that from the orchestral choir there would emerge a single strain, "the sound inside the sound."[10] The Fox orchestra spoke as one, and if you listen to cues such as "I Saw a Lady" from

---

8   Ryuichi Sakamoto did this very effectively in his otherwise highly immersive score for *The Revenant* (2015).

9   Interview with David Newman, August 6, 2015.

10 *Journal of Music* (April 26, 2016), http://journalofmusic.com/focus/bleeps-and-bloops-epic-theme-rise-video-game-music.

The Song of Bernadette (1943) or "Eve's Narration" from *All About Eve* (1950), you can hear something very close to the arioso style used in vocal/choral works and opera, where all the elements of composition conspire to support a single, apparently free-floating line.

In our own time, when—to cite just one example—the treatment of harmony in the Berklee College of Music's film scoring program is essentially a study of chord progressions, the Fox Music approach reminds us that the notion of harmony emerged originally from the confluence and intersection of lines. The horizontal precedes the vertical. It's sometimes difficult for our ears to appreciate the beauty of this approach, because the recordings are old, usually monaural, plagued by the wow and flutter that was intrinsic to the recording apparatus of the time, and because we tend to dismiss as old-fashioned what hasn't been recorded with high-impact digital samples for 5.1, 7.1, or 11.1 audio systems.

When it came to the integration of music and picture, the Hollywood studio aesthetic embraced by Alfred Newman and his contemporaries hewed closer to that of the *mélodrames* of previous centuries (and revived by the Mercury Radio Theater) than to the tradition of "incidental music" that was adopted by many European composers, in that music was conceived to be a "character" and not simply a mood-inducing accompaniment or broad thematic statement. There is no reason why contemporary film music—orchestral or otherwise—cannot also profit from this point of view.

INTERACTIVE MEDIA AND VR

One more avenue of development demands space in this book (some may say too little and too late!), and that's the rapid escalation in the level of artistry brought to the creation of music for interactive media. Cultural awareness is a slow-moving curve, even in the age of the Internet, and for many people, game music is still something best appreciated by adolescent boys. It's been eighteen years since Nintendo's release of the 3-D Ocarina of Time edition of its Legend of Zelda series, and for most of those years, game music and its composers were consigned to stepchild status in much the same way film music originally was. It's understandable why this might have been the case in the "early days," when sound quality was poor and composition extremely rudimentary. In the early years of the 2000s, quality improved significantly, but most game music remained derivative: aiming for the unabashedly anthemic à la *Back to the Future* and/or the epic grandeur of *Gladiator*, and usually falling short of both. Around the turn of the first decade, however, the ante was raised by such composers as Garry Schyman (e.g. BioShock, 2007), Austin Wintory (e.g. Journey, 2009), and Russell Brower and his team at Blizzard Entertainment (World of Warcraft, Diablo) and under the influence of Moore's law and unrelenting consumer demand, the industry made giant advances. Top games are now scored by first-tier composers with live symphonic ensembles that are, in many cases, beyond the economic reach of low to midbudget theatrical films.

Writing in Ireland's *Journal of Music*, Eimear Noone, the leading conductor of live performances of game music (and a game composer herself), writes: "Some may argue that this music is written for the purpose of being in the background. However, in-game music has great freedom for expression, which is giving rise to ever-more complex compositions. Furthermore, with the opening up of technological possibilities, we now have a new, modern vehicle for those of more classical leanings—artists, writers and composers—to express themselves, whilst having a support structure that supersedes the kings and churches in the feeding of artists' families!"[11]

The two salient qualities of interactive media affecting music composition are, of course, (1) nonlinear narrative; and (2) player/participant *agency*. If an observer (in this case, the player) can make choices that influence the outcome, then it isn't possible to compose the score with a single vector of development. If each player's game experience is somewhat different (within the limits of the game design), then optimally, his or her musical experience will also be different. Game composers and sound supervisors have devised a host of layering, looping, and triggering functions and programmed them into game engines to reflect player choices, but despite the great improvement in audio and writing quality, the musical response to player agency is still primitive. That's to be expected. The first generation of interactive composers have opened only the first room of a many-roomed castle. It's in the related but vastly broader area of virtual reality (VR) "experience" that composers will be challenged to ascend to the next levels. For here, we face something like the media counterpart of the many-worlds hypothesis in theoretical physics, or—for a literary reference—Borges's *Garden of Forking Paths*.

An article published in the *Wall Street Journal* (March 4, 2016) imagines Cary Grant's iconic crop duster encounter in Alfred Hitchcock's *North by Northwest* reconfigured as a VR experience in which we are sprinting alongside Grant and free to veer off into the cornfields or turn and aim a rocket-propelled grenade at the attacking aircraft. The original sequence was scored, of course, by Bernard Herrmann. Let's take it a step further and ponder how a latter-day Herrmann might handle the assignment for *multiple outcomes*, some triumphant and others tragic, and what sort of musical transitions and switching technology would be required to reflect our choices and their consequences. One thing is certain: we'd emerge from the experience with a great deal more empathy for Cary Grant, or for anyone facing a life-or-death scenario.

And therein lies the most exciting potentiality of VR for visual composers: the capacity of music to evoke empathy may finally be put to full and transformative use.

Shari Frilot, who curates the *New Frontiers* section of the Sundance Film Festival, put it this way when speaking of the VR entries in the 2016 edition: "This medium . . . engages our very survival instinct [and] it creates an enor-

---

11 Journal of Music; (April 26, 2016)

mous opportunity for connection and understanding . . . what we're seeing here is artists' understanding of VR as an empathy machine."

An empathy machine. Come to think of it, that's also a very good description of the role and function of music in motion pictures.

TWELVE THROUGH A GLASS, AND DARKLY

ANATOMY OF A CUE FROM JERRY GOLDSMITH'S *PATTON*

Jerry Goldsmith

General George S. Patton, as depicted in Francis Ford Coppola and Edmund North's Oscar-winning screenplay, was the very definition of psychological complexity. He was a brilliant military tactician and scholar; a martinet, a bully, and a self-glorifying egoist; an avowed Christian who nonetheless believed in reincarnation. He also wrote poetry. That complexity is at the epicenter of *Patton* and of George C. Scott's portrayal (also an Oscar winner), and if composer Jerry Goldsmith had failed to capture it with such eerie precision, the movie would almost certainly not have achieved the stature it enjoys.

At the time Jerry Goldsmith composed his *Patton* score, there were only a few precedents for the musical limning of complicated historical figures. The best-known among them was Maurice Jarre's *Lawrence of*

Arabia, which had aimed to depict psycho-sexual conflict and the seesaw between vaulting ambition and crippling modesty within the same character. But as innovative and memorable as Jarre's epic score was, it never reached the depths of complexity that Goldsmith, with his command of orchestral color and harmonic vocabulary, reaches in *Patton*. The achievement is all the more remarkable given that the *Patton* score occupies a scant thirty minutes of the film's three-hour span. It can be said without exaggeration that Goldsmith almost *never* wrote a note more, or less, than what the drama required. His writing was astoundingly concise, and as sensitive as an EKG. In fact, as this chapter will argue, the entirety of General Patton's psychological imprint is registered within a single cue: "The Battleground." Everything else in the film refers back to this scene.

The cue occurs at 28:13, shortly after General Patton, having taken Morocco from the Vichy French, is dispatched to Tunisia to lead the campaign against Hitler's Afrika Korps and its formidable leader, Field Marshall Erwin Rommel, following the Allies' humiliating rout at the Kasserine Pass. En route to the battlefield to assess the loss, Patton asks his second-in-command, Omar Bradley, to detour their jeep to the nearby site of a far more ancient conflict: the Battle of Zama in the Second Punic War, 202 BCE, when Scipio and the Romans overcame Hannibal and the Carthaginians, in what's now Tunisia. "It was here," says Patton, with the certainty of an oracle. "The battlefield was here."

But there are no fresh corpses, no carrion birds, no bomb craters, and no gutted tanks on this battlefield: only empty, sunlit meadows, the ruins of once great Carthage, and the echoes of war cries issued more than two millennia before. Bradley and the jeep driver are perplexed. What is their new commander talking about? Is he suffering from dementia or battle fatigue? They know that the site of the Allied defeat is miles away.

Patton indeed knows whereof he speaks, but he speaks from a perspective few men can comprehend. He sees history as an onion skin, not a linear progression, and he perceives himself as having played a decisive role in each layer. He is the eternal soldier, and war is the eternal truth. As he steps from the jeep, eyes fixed and riding crop in hand, the still air shivers with sound. Sixteen muted violins, in divisi pairs, execute a rapid and simultaneous descending chromatic run from G-natural, distilling in the following bar to a pitch stack spanning a doubly diminished eleventh (enharmonic m10). Each pair of violins (sharing a stand) trills pitches a whole-step (2s) apart, the upper part going a semitone up and the lower part a semitone down (in general), yielding a vibrating cluster of seconds, a musical gesture that is an almost perfect analog of the idea that history is alive and its ghosts roam in this hallowed place. Moreover, it places us squarely *inside* Patton's head.

The enharmonic spellings appear to have nothing to do with tonality and everything to do with the precise execution of the trill. In fact, the cue seems to be entirely nontonal, the only indication of "key" sealed within the iconic motif that enters following a four-octave glissando on the harp.

That motif, written for two C-trumpets in parallel fifths, both of them fed through an Echoplex tape delay, is both the heart of the cue and the heart of the score, and the single best known museme in Jerry Goldsmith's oeuvre.

Figure 12.1. *Patton*, "The Battleground," bars 1–3

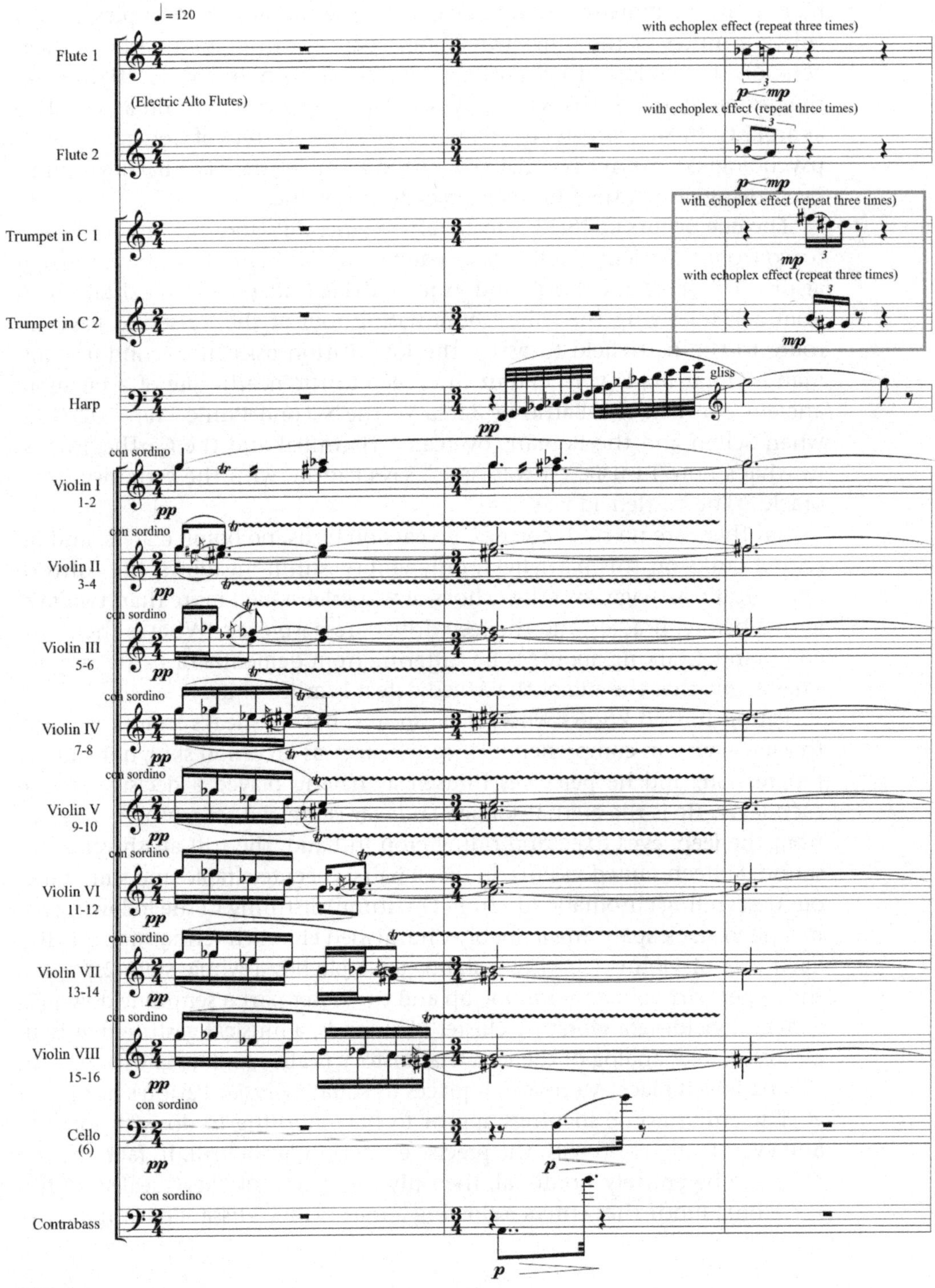

The trumpet motif, a triplet figure that the Echoplex renders as a gradually fading series, is as famous among film music aficionados as John Williams's *Jaws* motive or Bernard Herrmann's *Psycho* gesture, and far more subtle than either. It is the echo that George S. Patton hears as he stands on a field watered with the blood of his heroes: the echo of his own past lives. That echo is the source of both his vainglory and his greatness. Big men have big ideas, and those ideas are often touched by more than a bit of madness. It is the music's task to support this conceit.

Goldsmith doesn't downplay the madness. In fact, the film's portrayal of Patton, while giving ample screen time to his victories, is distinctly unflattering. Released in 1970, the year that Nixon expanded the Vietnam War into Cambodia, it was viewed by many as an antiwar statement, in the vein of Stanley Kubrick's earlier *Paths of Glory*. Time has lent the film a more multilayered meaning, befitting its title character's view of his place in history. It isn't really a "statement" at all. It's a portrait, and the portrait—like that of Dorian Gray in the Oscar Wilde tale—reveals its ugliness over time.

Not every film composer is capable of filling in the details of such a portrait. In fact, those who can are a distinct minority. Franz Waxman could (e.g., in *Sunset Boulevard*). Alex North could (see *The Bad Seed* and *A Streetcar Named Desire*). Others—including some, such as Max Steiner, John Barry, and even John Williams, whose command of symphonic form is unquestionable—seem less sure-footed when the terrain is the human psyche. A different part of the composer's skillset—less intuitive and more analytical—is being employed. This is Shostakovich territory. Goldsmith, at his best, was able to summon this facility without ever seeming clinical. He was able to read the emotional tremors running through a drama like a human seismograph. In another classic seventies film for which he delivered a similarly compact, streamlined score, *Chinatown*, he navigates some of the darkest psychological territory imaginable without ever letting us forget that what the damaged and world-weary protagonists want more than anything else is to be safe from harm. His portrayals were never less than fully human, even when they were cyborgs, as in some of his sci-fi scores.

In the section that follows, Patton will step from the jeep onto the ancient battleground, and into his personal myth. The score will go with him. At first, it will illuminate him from the perspective of the clearly rational Omar Bradley, and the music will be as mystified as Bradley is. But as Patton's vision takes on more and more poetic authority, new colors will enter the musical portrait, and although the cue will remain discordant and multilayered, by its finish we may find ourselves a little hypnotized.

Figure 12.2. *Patton,* "The Battleground," bars 4–8

The architecture of this section of the cue is so rigorous and the special techniques used so clearly that it reads almost like a treasure map, complete with map coordinates. The flutes speak and are answered by the trumpets, all in triplicate because of the tape echo. Beneath, as if inside Patton's trance, a stack of tightly voiced strings spanning a minor ninth quiver in quarter-tones. A harmonium enters with a jarringly dissonant cluster. Then a soft swell of string harmonics. Patton surveys the battlefield, totally in the moment, and announces, "It was here."

Figure 12.3. *Patton,* **"The Battleground," bars 9–12**

Now, recalling the original Battle of Zama from the perspective of one who was there, Patton relates the story of Hannibal's defeat at the hands of the Roman army. The tempo is dramatically halved, as if time had gone into retrograde, and the triplet figures are now fully articulated by alto flutes and French horns. Both sections are voiced in parallel fifths, but a P4 apart, creating a haunting evocation of past intruding on present. On the second statement, they're transposed up a minor third. Something strange is happening. Patton is no ordinary crackpot. But he's not entirely sane, either.

Figure 12.4. *Patton*, "The Battleground," bars 14–17

The piano—a new color—in two growling octaves of the bass clef, sounds a cluster of m2's/M7's, wholly dissonant, while the organ holds a high pedal C as its lower voice ascends the C minor scale's lower tetrachord. That slightly more anthemic tone is bolstered by the timpani and matching pizzicato basses, strongly registering a C tonal center. The effect is cognitive dissonance: the hero as demigod and madman; the urge to battle noble, but also a sickness in the blood. Only rarely since Herrmann had a "mainstream" film composer so deliberately used the orchestra as a semiotic machine.

Other composers, operating in less time and commerce–driven circumstances, had done similar experiments. There had been Charles Ives, of course, and Béla Bartók, with whom Jerry Goldsmith from the beginning had seemed in kinship. There was no time, in fact, during the first fifty years of film music, when its composers did not keep one ear cocked to the explosion of modernism and its streetwise cousins in jazz. In fact, such film composers as Goldsmith and Alex North had what you might call a "jazz head" about their work. Music should be just difficult enough to challenge its audience to think. Just enough of a puzzle to leave some missing pieces for the audience to fill in.

In the measures from 27–30, the cue unfolds further. Having set the stage with history, Patton now moves into myth, and opening with, "You know what the poet said . . . ," begins to recite the lines of an epic verse. To suit the more reverential tone, Goldsmith's harmonic grid coalesces around an E-flat-B-flat axis, creating a kind of false tonal center. The triplets played by the strings are as precise and parallel as a military tattoo, but the overall effect of the section isn't regimented at all. It's impressionistic. There are glimmers of Copland's quartal harmonies, emerging from the offset between the strings and the signature trumpet figure (which aims toward A-flat rather than E-flat), and while the strings in motion are animating an E-flat voicing, at rest they sound an open fifth on G-flat, giving the section an archaic, modal feel. The clarinet and organ double a meandering line that is divorced in tonality from the strings and seems to follow the rhythm of the elegiac poetry more than the memory of battle. "Midst the pomp and toil of war . . ." Patton intones, and the clarinet-organ descends from high-B-flat to F, then ascends again to B-natural in a way that quite deliberately clashes with the prevailing E-flat center of gravity. It would be accurate to call the passage bitonal, except that the tonality of the clarinet-organ line itself isn't clear. The mood is stirring but disturbing; reverent but also revealing of Patton's grandiosity. And once again, we see the unfamiliar-familiar and its uncanny effect. Goldsmith is using tonality as a cloak of deception.

Figure 12.5. *Patton*, "The Battleground," bars 27–30

"As if through a glass and darkly," he continues, paraphrasing Scripture, "the age-old strife I see." The strings depart further from the E-flat center and more strident dissonances enter the voicings. Patton is out on a psychic limb.

Figure 12.6. *Patton*, "The Battleground," bars 31–34

"I fought in many guises, many names," he boasts. "But all was *me*." And on the word "me," at measure 36, Goldsmith inserts a wonderfully off-balance gesture in the strings: a strongly slurred—almost portamento—descent from D to C-sharp to C coupled with an ascent from E-flat to E-natural. This is the musical equivalent of mania.

Figure 12.7. *Patton*, "The Battleground," bars 35–39

The virtuosity on display in "The Battleground" is not of the showy sort. In fact, the cue is mixed so low in the film that without access to the score, it would be very difficult to figure out precisely what's going on, and one might almost be inclined to think it had been assembled from diverse elements by a clever editor. But it wasn't. It's a completely realized musical statement, and its dramatic impact and rank in the canon of film music is as great as anything in the John Williams oeuvre. Goldsmith was never a showy writer. Although his technique was peerless, his work was never ornamental. With every note, he evidenced a commitment to making music serve a substantive dramatic function in motion pictures. It's more than a little ironic that his "showiest" score, for *The Omen*, is the one that finally earned him an Oscar. Behind this, in a rank stretching from 2003 back to

1962 (and a little beyond if you include his TV credits), stand such works as *L.A. Confidential, Rudy, Basic Instinct, Star Trek, Hoosiers, Alien, Chinatown, Papillon, Planet of the Apes, A Patch of Blue, Seven Days in May, Freud,* and *Lonely Are the Brave.* With the exception of Ennio Morricone, no film composer of the modern era can boast such consistency. In future editions of this book, I hope to offer more of his catalog for analysis. He was a film composer's film composer.

THIRTEEN STAND UP!
TWO CUES FROM ELLIOT GOLDENTHAL'S
MICHAEL COLLINS

Elliot Goldenthal

In contrast with such prodigiously prolific composers as Morricone and Goldsmith, dyed-in-the-wool New Yorker Elliot Goldenthal has been very selective about the projects he offers his considerable passion to. Some would contend that Hollywood has also been selective in what it offers him, since Goldenthal is perceived as an artist, and hence—almost by definition, "difficult." The credit list may be lean, but as Spencer Tracy said of Katharine Hepburn's character in *Pat and Mike* (1952), "Not much meat on her, but what there is, is choice." Elliot Goldenthal's cinematic collaborators include Neil Jordan, Michael Mann, David Fincher, and most notably, his longtime partner and partner-in-creative crime, Julie Taymor. He, like Goldsmith, is a composer's composer.

Goldenthal's musical pedigree is 24-karat, but he grew up gritty in Brooklyn before it became a fashionable address. He worked his way through a master's degree at the Manhattan School of Music, mentored by the likes of Aaron Copland and John Corigliano (the latter of whom had a profound influence on the development of Goldenthal's own voice), and has authored operas, ballets, and most recently, a symphony—but the sting of his youth has remained in his blood and in his music. This synthesis of maverick cerebrality and mean streets authenticity may well have been among the things that drew the major Irish auteur of the nineties, Neil Jordan, to Goldenthal and fostered their most celebrated collaboration, *Michael Collins* (1996).

The story of the founding of the Irish Republic and the years between the 1916 Easter Rising and Collins's violent death in 1922 is one soaked in blood, tears, and Irish fatalism, but it's also driven by a rousing and infectious fervor embodied by the title character, played by a young Liam Neeson. That fervor is evident throughout the score, and earned it one of the film's two Academy Award nominations. Goldenthal claims that he found the key to the score's identity in the feminine perspective, a fascinating angle given that the film has only one prominent female character, and she is somewhat marginal to the plot. What he may be referring to is the spirit of the country itself, and the metaphor of Ireland as a mother weeping for her children. The conceit is presented right up front: the first major cue, "Easter Rebellion," is performed poignantly by Sinéad O'Connor. But the cue most closely associated with the film, "Raid on the Police Station" (2M7), is stirringly masculine, and climaxes with Collins's telling his ragtag group of volunteers that he'll "make a fuckin' army" of them yet. Here's how it opens.

Figure 13.1. *Michael Collins*, 2M7, "Raid on the Police Station," bars 1–4

A cue that begins at a dynamic of *ff*, with virtually every note accented, is going to make a statement or die trying. This one succeeds. The 12/8 time signature, strong D minor tonality, pumping low strings and assertive percussion are all signifiers of Celtic culture and temperament, and so immediately Goldenthal takes command of the terrain and puts us in the right place, both geographically and emotionally. This is the setup of the cue's rhythm and modality, so no development is necessary, save for the syncopated upstroke in the violins in bar 3 (doubled by the oboes). The fledgling

Irish Republican Army is about to make its first strike under Collins's leadership: a raid on the provincial police headquarters in search of weapons and ammunition. The scene takes place at night, with most of the light provided dramatically by flaming torches of gas-soaked sod.

The form adopted by Goldenthal for this cue is basically a jig (these are always in compound meter), but it's a jig by way of Beethoven. In Figure 13.2, we see the first full statement of the cue's jig melody for piccolo, harp, and high strings.

Figure 13.2. *Michael Collins*, 2M7, "Raid on the Police Station," **bars 41–43A @ 16:35**

Elliot Goldenthal almost never allows his melodies to simply lie on a bed of chords. His compositional style is not that of a songwriter-producer, but of a symphonist. His music, even when it's slow and heavy, never feels inert. Some kind of movement in the lower parts always keeps the upper voices aloft. This may sound like basic orchestrational technique, but it's surprising how few film composers bother with it, relying instead on motion sequences and loops, or dispensing with motion altogether. These propulsive rhythms give Goldenthal's music a distinctive vigor.

One of the cue's most thrilling gestures occurs at 16:52 and bar 58, following a reprise of the jig tune. The raid has been successful and the raiders have come away with a cache of weapons. Now that they have guns, Collins' mission is to turn his ragtag cohort into a real army. Back at the barracks, he gives the troops their marching orders: "You'll engage the enemy on nobody's terms but your own. And I want you to account for every bullet. D'you understand?" "Yessir!" they shout, to which Collins replies, "Stand up!"

Figure 13.3A. *Michael Collins*, 2M7, "Raid on the Police Station," bars 54–59

Woodwinds, brass, percussion, and high strings all respond on the heels of his command with a musical salute that cements in an instant the bond between Collins and his men, and makes credible their willingness to commit mayhem for him. In the scant half-second it takes to deliver this two-note gesture, everything promised by the marriage of music and image is delivered, and the moment is electrifying. That may seem hyperbolic, but how often do we see a filmmaker and his composer working together in such tightly choreographed fashion?

If we examine the score, we find that this "Stand Up!" gesture is foreshadowed not once but twice during the preceding fifty-seven measures, and this is another reason that its final statement is so effective. The musical ear responds to repetition, especially in threes. The first instance, in bar 3, has already been mentioned. Here is the second:

Figure 13.3B. *Michael Collins*, **2M7, "Raid on the Police Station," bar 5, prefigured motif**

7M2, "ROSIE'S LETTER"

Later, in the film's second act, between roughly 56:39 and 1:02:12, there are five minutes of sustained tension accomplished by expert cross-cutting, evocative nighttime cinematography, and a single, continuously conceived and composed cue (split into three separate recording "starts") and titled 7M2, "Rosie's Letter." It is the kind of underscoring associated more with the masters of the old school than with contemporary film composers, but it doesn't sound dated at all—in part because Goldenthal, as steeped as he is in Wagner's *Gesamtkunstwerk* concept and in the symphonic and operatic traditions of the mid- to late nineteenth and early twentieth centuries, is neither a late romantic nor a modernist, but something "curiouser." The peculiar kind of angst and agitation expressed in his best work is a very contemporary thing. For lack of a less overused term, it might be called postmodern.

The Rosie of the title is a Dublin chambermaid working for the man who comes closest to being the movie's villain, Soames, head of the elite MI5 British Intelligence unit dispatched to Ireland to assassinate Collins and the rebellion's leadership. "Rosie's Letter" is, in fact, a list of all twelve members of the hit squad and their whereabouts in Dublin, and all twelve will be marked for preemptive execution on what later became known as Bloody Sunday. The sequence scored by 7M2 is the nail-biting prelude to this event.

In what remains of this abbreviated chapter, we'll take a look at a few key sections of this long musico-dramatic sequence. The first and shortest of these offers something of a Rosetta stone for the encrypted contents of Elliot Goldenthal's composer psyche. It includes a motive, or more properly, an *idea*, that shows up repeatedly in his work (including concert pieces). All composers of note have these "fixations," and the fact that they keep coming back to them is part of what makes composer study so interesting.

The idea is first heard at 57:32, shortly after Collins has told his men, "And none of us tonight stays in the usual places. If we're lifted, we're dead." Each pair has been assigned a target, and each target will be hit. Here is the essential cell:

Figure 13.4A. *Michael Collins*, 7M2, "Rosie's Letter," agitato phrase

Notice that, as with many of Bernard Herrmann's cells, harmonic implications are ambiguous. Let's see if the other instruments give us a clue.

Figure 13.4B. *Michael Collins*, 7M2R, "Rosie's Letter," part 1, bars 23–25

The simple answer is: they do not. The two isolated pitches in the contra-bassoon could mean many things. This uncertainty may be serendipitous, because it forces us to look beyond the usual conventions for an understanding of what's going on. The issue is clearly not one of harmonic function. Nothing here is "functioning" as anything. Nor can set theory be applied to a passage such as this one. An analysis in this case requires something closer to the neo-Riemannian approach alluded to in previous chapters.

There is a triad—in this instance, D minor—that sets the tonal identity of the passage. That triad is then transformed by "parsimonious voice-leading" (i.e., movement by the smallest possible interval) into something else. The root drops a semitone to C-sharp. The "invisible" fifth (A) may drop a semitone (to G-sharp) or rise a semitone (to A-sharp), forming, respectively, either a C-sharp major triad or an A-sharp minor triad. Goldenthal leaves this a mystery. The third of the D minor triad (F) stays put, giving us the all-important common tone. Without the common tone, the idea loses its quirky, haunting quality.

This quirkiness is only reinforced by the fact that both clarinets are playing at the very bottom of their compass. Almost more grunt than note.

This may seem to be overthink for an incidental passage of underscore that is so sparsely arranged, but there is an essential lesson about film music's harmonic vocabulary to be had here. As mentioned in earlier chapters, film music can be tonally very unstable, but it is almost never atonal. Conversely, it can have a very strong key center, but except for major thematic statements like love themes and main titles, it is rarely tonal in the pre-Wagnerian sense. Instead, it seems to occupy a third sphere that neo-

Riemannian scholar Richard Cohn calls "triadic post-tonality." Due to some earlier debunking, neo-Riemannian theory is only now finding a place in university music departments despite having been around for a century, but academia is slow to change, and the music academy is slowest of all.

We'll now move deeper into the sequence to illustrate something mentioned earlier: that Goldenthal maintains restless motion even under broad melody. The film's love triangle (Neeson, Aidan Quinn, and Julia Roberts) is often pointed to as its weakest element, not least because Roberts, a thoroughly American actress, is cast as an Irish colleen, Kitty Kiernan, complete with brogue. But this pivotal scene, played by Neeson and Roberts in the semidarkness of Kitty's hotel room against the backdrop of the ongoing Bloody Sunday executions, further illuminates Goldenthal's technique.

Figure 13.5A. *Michael Collins*, **7M2R, "Rosie's Letter," part 2, bars 1–3 @ 1:00:34**

Notice that he has carried forward the agitato cell from Figure 13.4, lowered it a semitone, and placed it in the strings, specifically, viola and cello. There, it can continue to exert its ominous effect without calling so much attention to itself. The tension is building, as Collins has hurried back to Kitty's hotel to move her to safer quarters before the executions begin. She's tied to him and therefore in great danger. On top of the rolling ostinato, we now have unison flute and violins well above the staff and sounding a very cold m3 above C-sharp. Once again, we have a clearly defined locus of tonality (C-sharp minor), and an altered triad, but no indication as to whether that alteration can be called a chord. C major? C augmented? Or A minor? Any of them are eerie.

Notice that in the alternation between viola and cello, the cello keeps its C-sharp, while the viola drops to C-natural. This obscures harmonic identity even further.

Figure 13.5B. 7M2, *Michael Collins*, "Rosie's Letter," part 2, bars 4–6 ⓐ 1:00:35

The low string pizzicato in measure 5 shouldn't be ignored. It comes in reaction to a knock at the door of the hotel room. Collins is a man with a price on his head. Some composers—and some directors—might have stopped short of answering a knock with a *knock*, thinking it too much of a "mickey mouse" gesture, but *this* composer and *this* director appear to be on the same page with respect to the choreography. And with the "Stand

Up!" gesture, they have already signaled their intent. It's an operatic story in many ways, and it only becomes more so with a little operatic treatment.

Now Kitty arrives, distraught and more than a little put out by Michael's brusque urgency. Watch how Goldenthal keeps their feelings for each other (the English horn solo) on edge. The scene never goes all the way to romance. It can't. There's no time for romance. The sequence in the string section is a beautiful piece of musical architecture.

Figure 13.5C. *Michael Collins*, "Rosie's Letter," bars 19–22 @1:01:05

Once Kitty has calmed and the two of them are truly alone, the agitation ceases and the scene moves into another register altogether. As Michael and Kitty lie together in a bedroom cloaked in predawn blue, sheltered—for the moment—from the terrible events outside, the Bloody Sunday reprisals commence against a cross-cutting design that may remind some of the famous

"Michael Corleone settles all scores" sequence from *The Godfather*. Through-scoring this sort of scene requires a deft hand if it is not to come across as overspotted or melodramatic, and yet a theatrical weight is called for in view of both the gravity of the events and their climactic place in the story.

Elliot Goldenthal knows opera (he has written a well-received one, *Grendel*, based on the Beowulf legend). He knows this isn't the place for a big aria. He also understands cinema's intimacy. He opts to keep the score in that bedroom with Michael and Kitty, but to acknowledge the violence of the executions by way of subtle dynamic changes, instrumentation, and harmonic unpredictability. Although geared down and simplified as befits background score in a dramatic film, there is a Wagnerian quality in the way Goldenthal employs the brass (Figure 13.6C; only horns are shown in reduction) and in the chromaticism employed in moving from section to section. It begins with Kitty's fraught, and rhetorical, question to Michael: "You've sent your boys out, haven't you?"

Figure 13.6A. *Michael Collins*, 8M1, part 2, bars 1–6 @ 1:03:19

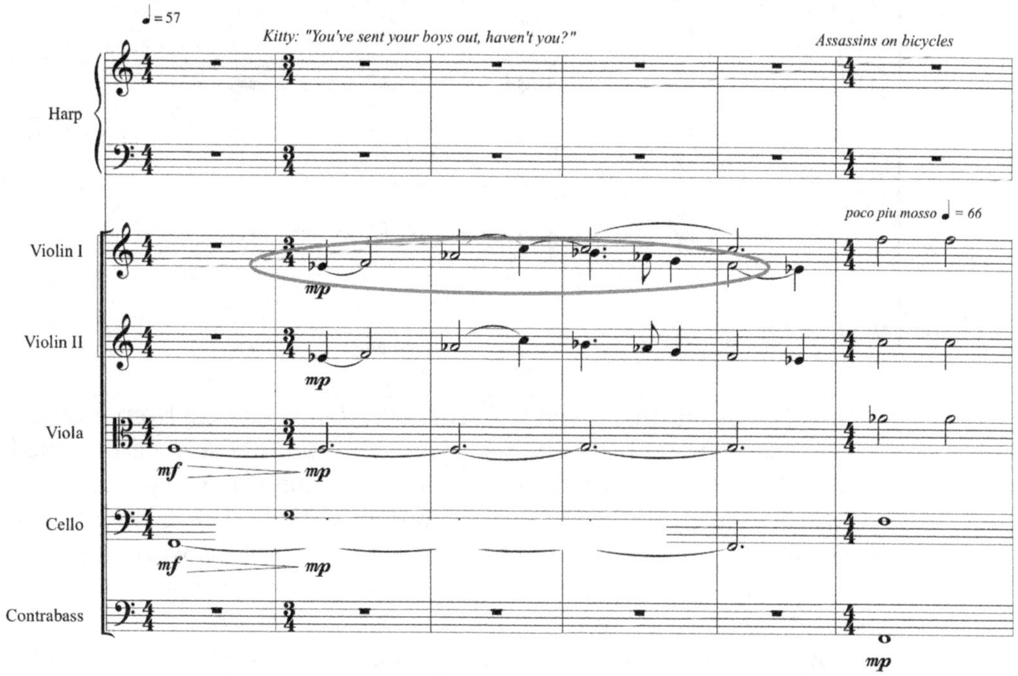

The minor mode melody line etched out by the violins is the theme most closely associated with the Irish homeland and the noble but heartbreaking efforts required to obtain her freedom. When heard next, it will be in the horns, its most fitting instrument. But before that happens, there is an exchange in which Kitty mordantly compares the bullets of Michael's assassins to Valentine's Day bouquets and seems to question whether anything he could win is worth the cost in blood. This is an especially interesting moment for our study, because it's the one place in the film where the performances and direction don't quite rise to 100 percent. What we're supposed to feel, I think, is emotional resistance and erotic desire in direct conflict within Kitty, since it's clear that she wants "Mick" to make her his woman, but also that he'll likely make her a widow. If ever there was a moment for the aching irresolution of Wagner, this is it, and Goldenthal delivers, landing on his own Tristan chord in bar 12 with a tritone leap in the violins and violas.

Figure 13.6B. *Michael Collins*, 8M1 "Bloody Sunday," part 2, bars 7–12 @ 1:03:35

Directors as skillful as Neil Jordan don't often need help from music, but this is a case where the composer has taken hold of a scene and pulled it up to a higher level of intensity. The drama of that dim5 leap is important because, as Kitty's words still linger, Jordan will crosscut to the first team of assassins riddling a restaurant window with automatic weapon fire on a foggy Dublin morning, as the Celtic "Homeland" theme heard in the previous example now sounds in the brass, over a Gm7 bed.

Moving ahead sixteen measures and past the second of the murders to 1:04:26, we hear a further development of the "operatic" movement. Kitty and Michael are silhouetted against the lace curtain, she with a blood red rose in her hand as she searches for some poetry in the awful events. Extending the conceit of the "love note," she asks, "What does it say?" and he answers, "It says: 'Leave us be.'" "Not very romantic," she observes dryly.

Here, over a moody F-sharp minor7/9 wash, broken delicately by harp, the horns and violins (sul G) outline a version of the "Homeland" theme in a "new key" of C-sharp minor/Aeolian. The melody line is chromatic only with respect to the surrounding F-sharp minor harmony, but the contrast of tonics gives this passage an impressionistic and unresolved feel. It can't be otherwise, because another terrible killing awaits just four measures ahead in bar 32.

Figure 13.6C. *Michael Collins*, 8M1, "Bloody Sunday," part 2, bars 28–33 ℗ 1:04:26

Crosscut: Two more IRA gunmen hold their weapons on a trembling young British couple, still in pajamas and sleeping in on this quiet Sunday. "You could at least spare my wife this spectacle," the husband, a junior MI5 officer, says, and the lead gunman agrees, saying, "Get her out of here." At this point, the quasi-tragic "Homeland" theme makes its most emotional statement yet and the score rises to one of its most dramatic moments. The doomed British agent pulls a gun, a fusillade of shots ring out, and the young wife screams in despair, accompanied by woodwinds and brass. It's a fittingly operatic close to the sequence.

Figure 13.6D. *Michael Collins*, 8M1, "Bloody Sunday," part 2, bars 36–41

Following the onomatopoeic scream of dissonance from the combined winds (39–41), the cue makes a final dramatic turn with the entry of a female choir and a new, more elegiac mood. The penultimate execution takes place in a green park with the tone of an awful sacrament. Then, with the death of the villainous *Soames*, the Bloody Sunday sequence comes to a close.

Not too long ago, a composers' roundtable took place as part of the yearly Film Music Festival (FMF) in Kraków. The discussion featured Hans Zimmer, Dario Marianelli, Garry Schyman, and Elliot Goldenthal, among others. At one point, Goldenthal had to leave to attend a rehearsal, and Zimmer quipped, "Now there goes the only *real* composer." Although the observation wasn't fair to either Zimmer himself or the other composers on the panel, it demonstrates the level of respect that the film music community reserves for their rebellious New York colleague. Goldenthal is widely regarded as a *serious* composer, and that's a characterization that is all too seldom applied to writers of music for the screen. He is perhaps the only living film composer whose work elicits the sort of admiration once shown to such men as Alex North.

Why is this, and what does it say about the state of the art? It isn't simply the depth of his training or the tutelage he received from such people as John Corigliano, although these things lend weight to his reputation. Nor is it his longtime association with the formidable Julie Taymor, though there is certainly a belief that any man who can keep pace with a talent like hers deserves the title of "artist." There is a general consensus that Elliot Goldenthal is a composer who tackles ideas of real substance and that he doesn't shy away from a fight if it's called for, but moreover, a sense that he is a film composer who has never once thought of what he does for a living as frivolous.

Interviewed in a crowded bookstore shortly after the premiere of his Symphony in G-sharp Minor, Goldenthal was asked whether any single theme or event had inspired the work. He reflected for a beat and then replied, "I think a lot about death these days." The audience chuckled somewhat uncomfortably. This was not the kind of answer expected from someone who labors in Tinseltown. Yet we wouldn't be surprised in the least to hear it from a writer like Jonathan Franzen or Michel Houellebecq, or for that matter, from film directors like Stanley Kubrick or Martin Scorsese. There is a place in the craft of music for the screen, notwithstanding its commerciality and compromise, for serious composers. With luck, there will always be someone like Goldenthal to fill that place.

FOURTEEN JOHN POWELL SLAYS A DRAGON

Photograph by Melinda Lerner

John Powell

Since 1989, the year that Walt Disney Studios released *The Little Mermaid* and kicked off a renaissance of the form, the world has seen a glut of animated feature films. DreamWorks Animation, under CEO and former Disney studio chief Jeffrey Katzenberg, has released more than forty of them. How many of these titles hold as enduring a place in the hearts of children and parents as such films as *Bambi* or *Dumbo* or *Aladdin* once did and still do? A case could be made for the Shrek franchise, and some might argue for *Kung Fu Panda*, but soaring far above these in terms of sentimental attachment (and on a par with them in box office receipts) is the 2010 release, *How to Train Your Dragon*. A common factor in the success of all three (as well as their respective sequels) is UK-born composer John Powell, a protégé of the redoubtable Hans Zimmer, who has carved out his own very special place in the genre.

The scores for the Shrek and *Panda* films were collaborative endeavors (with Harry Gregson-Williams, in the first case, and Zimmer himself, in the second), but *How to Train Your Dragon* belongs to John Powell alone, and it earned him an Academy Award nomination for Best Original Score (an honor won for animated film only during the Alan Menken streak in the 1990s and by Powell's mentor, Hans Zimmer, for *The Lion King* in 1995.) The *Dragon* score is many things: bold, stirring, highly colored and deliciously tuneful, but its most singular quality is *heart*. That may seem almost a given in a genre that aims directly for the emotions, but it's surprising how rarely it happens. Contemporary animated film scores are typically witty, referential, and sometimes sweet to the point of toothache, but except in cases like Menken's *Beauty and the Beast*, Zimmer's *Lion King*, and the Randy Newman *Toy Story* scores, they don't often inspire leagues of young composers to declare, "That's what I want to do."

John Powell's music for *Dragon* is the object of genuine love among people who cherish great film music, and it's well worth looking at how he managed to implant a warm, beating heart in the most "artificial" of cinematic categories. All the more so given the hi-res gloss of digital animation, which can leave some people cold.

The skeleton of the story will be familiar to any devotee of hero lore, and anyone who's seen a Disney film in the last twenty-five years: *from he/she of whom the least is expected comes the greatest achievement.* Young King Arthur pulls the sword from the stone when even the strongest in the realm cannot, and young Hiccup will tame the fearsome Night Fury, a dragon with the evasive powers of a Stealth fighter jet, and win the heart of Astrid, the comely village girl who is a badass dragon fighter in her own right. Based on the series of books by Cressida Cowell, the story opens and unfolds in Berk, a Dark Ages Viking hamlet that—considering the accents of its inhabitants (all but Hiccup, of course, who sounds like a typically irreverent teenager)— would seem to be in the vicinity of the Scottish Hebrides or remote Orkney Islands (once, in fact, Viking territory).

But before Hiccup begins his voiceover narration, and even before the Dreamworks Animation SKG logo appears, John Powell has made his opening statement. In a sense, music provides the story's "once upon a time." It's given as a stately brass chorale:

Figure 14.1. *How to Train Your Dragon*, 1M2, "Bonding" theme, bars 24–27

This phrase, and its development as a hymnlike sixteen bar theme, will thread throughout the story, reaching its most triumphant expression at just over forty-three minutes, when Hiccup finally mounts and pilots the dragon he names Toothless. Its use here, at the very top of the film, prefigures not only that bonding of boy and beast, but the boy's growth into a man worthy of his father Stoick the Vast's admiration—and Astrid's.

The "A" theme excerpted in Figure 14.1, which might also be called the "Bonding" theme, is paired with a secondary idea, in Dorian mode and almost always in either 6/8 jig or 4/4 reel form, illustrating the mist-enshrouded village life and lot of the Vikings of Berk (though, as with the characters' burrs, the accent is more Scottish than strictly Scandinavian). When first heard at :25 and introduced by a brief tattoo rhythm on field drum, it's marked *legato e tranquilo*, in contrast to its high-energy use less than a minute later during the film's first dragon attack. At any tempo or dynamic, it links us to the land and the storm-tossed life of its people, who must continually rebuild the houses incinerated by dragon breath in a place "twelve days north of hopeless." This lilting but plaintive little pentatonic melody, opening with a typical "Scottish snap" (according to the composer, a gesture peculiar to Scottish idiom), keeps the film's fable rooted in folk reality and the right amount of Gaelic wistfulness—a quality that is a signature of Dorian.

Figure 14.2. How to Train Your Dragon, 1M2, "Village" theme (alt 1d), bars 37–41

A third idea, more virile and "Viking-like" than the others, makes itself heard at 2:27, making 1M2—the very first cue in the film—something of an overture. This theme, voiced by hearty brass and percussion, and underpinned briskly by triplets in violins and violas, seems to represent the true Norseman's strength that Hiccup longs to have.

**Figure 14.3. *How to Train Your Dragon*, 1M2,
"Viking Strength" theme, bars 83–86**

STATING THE THEMES

Before we move deeper into the story of Hiccup and Toothless, let's look at how Powell elaborates his "A" and "B" themes—both initially stated as simply as possible—within the framework of the same cue. We may find that it's their simplicity, in fact, that allows him to do so much with them. A tune that is too busy or too harmonically rich will not permit the composer to expand, compress, abridge, or "fit things into its cracks." Again, all one has to do is think of Bernard Herrmann or, for that matter, Beethoven and Brahms. Another fine example would be the first three notes of Henry Mancini's "Moon River" (the theme song for *Breakfast at Tiffany's*). An entire score could be (and, to a large degree, was) based on that single motif. Complexity belongs in *development*.

The second iteration of the "A" or "Bonding" theme follows immediately upon the first statement of the "B" or *village* theme, maintaining the latter's 6/8 meter and unifying them as elements of the same overarching composition, almost in the manner of song.

Figure 14.4. How to Train Your Dragon, 1M2 (alt. 1d), bars 46–49

Take a look at the chord progression as given in the harp staff of the Figure 14.4 reduction. All chords are diatonic to the key of A-flat major (and its relative, F minor), but the movement from F minor to D-flat major (vi–IV) involves a "borrowed chord." It's familiar to us from countless great folk and rock ballads, but in the sometimes abstruse argot of posttonal theory, it's known as an L-transformation (two common tones persist, and the fifth of the minor triad moves up a semitone to become the root of a major triad). This is the smoothest kind of "parsimonious voice-leading" and a staple of film music, particularly in the postrock era (it's the same transformation that constitutes the signature of Don Davis's *Matrix* score). It also allows Powell to repeat the A-flat in his melody, which along with the added sixth in the lower voice, enhances its poignancy. In contrast, the next movement from D-flat major to E-flat major involves no common tones, and is more striking. It serves to restore some functionality and closure to the progression by leading us to the tonic: A-flat major.

Finally, take note of the alteration of the "A" theme melody. Because the phrasing is identical, we hardly notice the change. It still begins on the third of the chord (though now the chord is F minor rather than F major, another case of mode mixing), but its shape differs. It's a straight ascent instead of an upper neighbor–lower neighbor "loop."

We'll look now at the second—and far more bracing—iteration of the "B" theme. It enters at 1:12, just after Hiccup has barely managed to slam the door of his workshop on the flaming breath of one of the attacking ". . . dragons!"

Figure 14.5. How to Train Your Dragon, 1M2, "Village" theme development, bars 45–48

It's a little hard to believe that this is the same lyrical melody we saw in Figure 14.2, now presented as a classic, rousing Scottish Highland reel as the stalwart villagers of Berk fight off the latest dragon attack. Notice the horn staves. There are indeed twelve French horns, all on the same tune. When this kind of brass muscle is paired with strong percussion (timpani and bass drum, both at *forte*) and Celtic melody, it's hard not to be reminded of the wind arrangements in the late, great, and slightly mad Malcolm Arnold's Scottish Dances, Op. 59.[1] Arnold, who died in 2006, also scored over one hundred films, including *The Bridge on the River Kwai*, which earned him an Academy Award.

---

1 Composed in 1957 for the BBC Light Music Festival, an especially good recording is Lyrita SRCD.201 (1979).

TRAINING OUT THERE

The brilliant Dreamworks animators offer us a multitude of dragon breeds, from gargantuan and terrifying to pint-size and comical, but as mentioned, the breed most feared by the villagers is the Night Fury, impossible to see in the black of night until it's too late. During the opening melee, Hiccup, who as the weakling of the clan is forbidden to leave his post as apprentice to *Gobber the Blacksmith* to engage in combat, sneaks off in darkness with his own invention, a sort of machine-operated *bola*. Against the starry sky, he tracks a Night Fury as its shadow eclipses the stars, and manages to bring it down in someplace beyond the horizon. The next cue to be examined, 1M7, "Training Out There," takes Hiccup into the deep woods, where he discovers his fallen prey, ensnared and wounded but very much still alive. It's a very important cue.

The function of this book isn't biography, much less psychology, but when we look at a score that *affects* people, as Elfman's early work, such as *Edward Scissorhands*, and John Williams's Spielberg projects do—and as *Dragon* certainly does—it aids our investigation to know something about the composer, and how he or she saw the project through the lens of his own predilections. Is there something about John Powell that made him uniquely suited to this particular task? It does seem that way.

Powell was born in Crowborough, East Sussex, and was a self-described "classical music snob" until he reached young adulthood, but interestingly, he had a grandmother in the Hebrides (those same misty Scottish isles where *Dragon* author Cowell spent her summers) who was a practitioner of *puirt à beul*, or mouth music, a relative of both Pakistani *qawwali* and African-American scat. The orchestral music that spoke most strongly to him included the folk-tinted work of such Scandinavian composers as Grieg, Nielsen, and Sibelius. The chapter on Elfman's *Alice* highlights the importance of a composer's early emotional experience of music. These experiences form kinks—or, as John Powell likes to call them, "fetishes"—in a composer's personality, and there's a strong case to be made that those with the most distinctive "fetishes" evolve into our most distinctive composers. The converse also seems to be true: those who lack these defining qualities are unlikely to introduce new vocabulary to the craft. Filling out and complimenting John Powell's musical profile was a great love of Latin jazz and dance forms, such as mambo, and this rhythmic vitality is heard everywhere in his work.

At the center of the cue numbered 1M7, "Training Out There," comes a moment that is absolutely critical to the development of the story and Hiccup's character. It may be the single most important dramatic turn in the film. Hiccup has already told us by way of his narration that a Viking is not a Viking until he's killed a dragon, and that by this measure, he may never be fully accepted by his clan—or by his father. Now he has brought down a Night Fury and the dragon is at his mercy. "I'm going to kill you, dragon," he says, taking his knife from its sheath. "I'm going to cut out your heart and bring it to my father." The reduction in Figure 14.6 begins at 13:24 of the video release. Note the horn line in 72–73: this is the "Viking Strength" theme we heard introduced in Figure 14.3. Watch what happens to it.

Figure 14.6. How to Train Your Dragon, 1M7, bars 72–75

Once again, the voice leading is parsimonious; that is, movement in semitones around a common tone/s. The chord progression isn't functional harmony, and the modulation to F minor that occurs in Bar 78 isn't approached in the conventional way. The movement and weight of the harmony recalls such nationalist composers as Mussorgsky and Sibelius. In the context of an animated film, these are pretty dark colors. The big crescendo through bars 78–79 occurs just as Hiccup is about to plunge his knife into the dragon's heart. According to Powell, the filmmakers were very concerned that the music not "telegraph" Hiccup's choice (which, as we'll see in Figure 14.8, is to show mercy). And it doesn't. Right up to the peak of the crescendo, it's played as if the murderous deed was a fait accompli.

Figure 14.7. How to Train Your Dragon, 1M7, bars 76–79

Note the dramatic 8ve leap of the violas in bar 79 to very nearly the top of their range. The crescendo takes us to a dynamic of *ff* and to the pivotal four measures of the cue, when Powell brings in his beloved trumpets. With knife raised, Hiccup makes the classic mistake of looking his quarry in the eye and sees another sentient creature looking back. Hiccup, who is no natural born killer, hesitates. At bar 83, with the commencement of a rallentando, the Night Fury rolls its eyes back and accepts fate. But that fate is not death. The descending melodic sequence that brings us to this crucial turn (see violins/trumpet/oboe in Figure 14.8) has an almost tragic trajectory, and yet . . .

Figure 14.8. How to Train Your Dragon, 1M7, bars 80–83

Figure 14.9. How to Train Your Dragon, 1M7, bars 84–87

Figure 9 shows the emotional denouement of the cue, as the rallentando concludes with bass drum rolls into a gradual diminuendo. The choice is made. The Night Fury will live, and Hiccup will have to live with his choice. He'll have to find another way to prove his worthiness as a Viking. We all know what that will be, as did John Powell when he was writing the score. And therein lies a bit of its genius, and the "Russian egg" construction it shares with many great film scores.

The heartbreaking melody line introduced in the four measures from 80–83 conceals the seed of Hiccup's eventual triumph, for its shape and sequence are identical to the stirring Highland pipe intro to the film's most joyful cue, 3m20 "Test Drive." This cue doesn't makes its appearance for another thirty minutes, but jumping ahead as John Powell probably did, let's take a quick look at it in Figure 14.10.

Figure 14.10. How to Train Your Dragon, 3m20, bars 3–6

Compare the highlighted sequence for pipes and harp (Figure 14.10) to the first violins, trumpets, and oboes in measures 80–83 of 1m7 (Figure 14.8). The line still loops around the pitch class of A, but the mode has shifted to a triumphant major, and the key center from A to D. It's as if the sunlight hidden behind the storm clouds of 1m7 has broken through in 3m20, and the close musical kinship creates a strong sense of what we've elsewhere called the *familiar-unfamiliar*, and makes for an indelible moment. Contemporary live-action film only rarely allows for these big, "Wagnerian" gestures, but animated tales invite us to return to a world where the true of heart can overcome physical limits, emerge as heroes, and even wind up with the girl.

WOUNDED

Keeping our focus on the relationship between Hiccup and Toothless that is the film's emotional center, we'll move to the pair's next encounter and the cue that enters at roughly 20:40 into the video release. It's numbered 2m10 and titled "Wounded." Here Hiccup learns that in bringing down the Night Fury, he has damaged its tail fin.

Figure 14.11. How to Train Your Dragon, 2m10, "Wounded," bars 6–9

Cue 2m10 stands apart from most of the other cues in *How to Train Your Dragon* as a piece of musical exotica (a dubious word choice, but widely understood). This exoticism is a factor not only of instrumentation and articulation (flutes, clarinets, and harps executing rapid ascending and descending scalar passages; breathy choral voices and strings employing harmonics and trills), but also—most strikingly—of Powell's choice of mode. The pitch set he's using seems to come closest to the Middle Eastern *maqam* known as *Hijaz-Nahawand* (a *Hijaz* tetrachord on D interlocked with a *Nahawand* tetrachord on G).

Figure 14.12. *Nahawand maqam*

The emblematic features of this mode are the Phrygian m2 between the first and second scale degrees, and the augmented second between degrees 2 and 3. That augmented second gives it the unique property of being a major mode with minor second, sixth, and seventh. But that's not all that accounts for the cue's mysterious emotional pull.

The plot content is simple: Hiccup has returned to the scene of the crime and found his dragon wounded and unable to escape from the canyon. He watches, not without compassion, trying to understand the Night Fury's flight mechanism. As he watches, sketching in his notebook, a kind of fraternity is established between boy and beast.

Now, take a closer look at the choral part:

Figure 14.13. *How to Train Your Dragon*, 2m10, "Wounded," choral part

The first thing we notice is the similarity in shape and phrasing to both the "Bonding" theme (Figure 14.1/Theme A) and the "Viking Strength" theme (Figure 14.3/Theme C). The two themes are, in a sense, merging as Hiccup discovers a new sense of purpose: a new way to be a Viking. But harmonically, something very different is going on. The chords are drawn directly from the exotic mode, and that makes the "II" chord an E-flat major (a little like a Neapolitan sixth, but over a D pedal) and the "VII" chord a C minor. (I've put the Roman numerals in quotes because this is not functional harmony). There is something eerily familiar about that progression.

Figure 14.14. Arvo Pärt, *Fratres* (excerpt/reduction)

The strong attraction that the music of Estonian "holy minimalist" Arvo Pärt has for contemporary filmmakers was discussed in chapter 11 in relation to the work of Thomas Newman, as was the fact that none of Pärt's compositions have been more ubiquitous than the spellbinding *Fratres*, originally scored for string quintet plus wind quintet in 1977. *Fratres* is a prime example of Pärt's *tintinnabuli* style; its ghostly parallel tenths in the upper (or "M") voice and its puzzling ambiguity of mode (the upper voice uses the M3, m2, and m6 of *Hijaz maqam*, while the lower "T" voice is a broken minor triad) have an immediate psychological impact on listeners.

In fact, the opening 7/4 measure of *Fratres*, with its austere four-note upper line (E–D–F–E), is as close to perfect an example of a *museme* as we're likely to see, right up there with Monty Norman's *Bond* theme guitar lick or Morricone's *Good, Bad & Ugly* ocarina. The shape of John Powell's *Wounded* choral line is clearly drawn from his own themes, but its harmonization and sparseness strongly recall Pärt. *Fratres*, of course, means "brothers" in Latin, and in this scene, that's the relationship that's being forged between Hiccup and Toothless. Is it a stretch to think there is a connection? And even if there is, was Powell consciously aware of it? This is the marvelous thing about thinking of film music as a language of shared signs. These connections exist, whether we're aware of them or not.

Of all the cues in the *Dragon* score, 2m10 is the most purely impressionistic. It utilizes an array of exemplary articulations and ornaments: staccato, tenuto, tremolo, both natural and artificial harmonics, glissandos, and trills. That's a lot of expression for a single cue. It all works here because the setting and *meaning* of the scene are so poetic: a canyon in an isolated wood, a boy coming of age, both terrified and fascinated by the creature he has brought down, as well as moved by its plight. This will be the last "resting point" before the plot begins to accelerate and action takes over.

Figure 14.15 takes us up to the dramatic shift in harmony in bar 13, at which point Hiccup begins to understand what is inhibiting the dragon's flight. Bars 10–11 repeat the haunting choral line, but now resolve it more sweetly to the nominal tonic of D major (this *is* Dreamworks Animation, after all). But the astringency of the exotic mode is retained: note the B-flat in bar 11 that creates a passing diminished harmony against the chromatically altered E-natural. Powell stays true to his materials beginning to end.

Figure 14.15. *How to Train Your Dragon*, 2m10, "Wounded," bars 10–13 @ 21:06

GETTING TO KNOW TOOTHLESS

The cue that follows, 2m11 "Dragon Book," continues to develop this evocative new variation of the "Bonding" theme, adding further layers of mystery and what seems like a clever homage to *Peter and the Wolf*. Hiccup, along with Astrid, Snotlout, Tuffnut, Ruffnut, and the other adolescents of the clan, has been undergoing dragon training in the tutelage of Gobber the Blacksmith. Here, he's left alone in the mess hall to study *The Dragon Book* by the light of a single candle, and discovers that the chapter profiling the fearsome Night Fury offers nothing more than a stark warning: *hide and pray it does not find you*. Figure 14.16 shows the "Bonding" theme variation as expressed in string harmonics in measures 3–6 of 2m11, and Figure 14.17 excerpts the brass writing in bars 17–24.

Figure 14.16. *How to Train Your Dragon*, 2m11, bars 3–6 @ 23:14

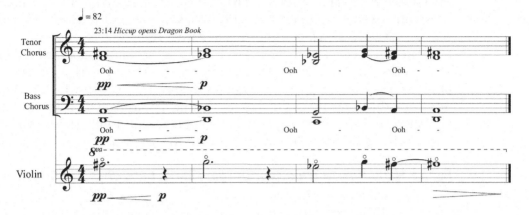

Figure 14.17. *How to Train Your Dragon*, 2m11, bars 17–24

The enchanting Phrygian twist that Powell has given to this fusing of his "A" ("Bonding") and "C" ("Viking Strength") themes in the foregoing cues is a beautiful example of "scoring the sequence, not the scene." And what *is* the sequence about? It is about Hiccup *getting to know* his dragon, coming to understand its exotic and alien ways (which turn out to be not so very different from his own). Composers must look for "story arcs" no less diligently than screenwriters and editors, and when it is seen that two or three (or more) consecutive scenes are linked thematically, it's both logical and artful to treat them, in a sense, as one. The rightness of Powell's approach is affirmed in the final cue in the set: 2m15, "New Tail," which, although it follows two intervening cues—2m12, "Hiccup: Focus," and 2m13, "Offering"—is properly part of the same sequence. 2m15 underscores the pivotal scene in which Hiccup brings Toothless the prosthetic tail fin that he has fashioned for him in the workshop, and which he hopes will allow his dragon to fly. Here is what's Powell's strings do when Hiccup begins to fit the new tail.

Figure 14.18. *How to Train Your Dragon*, 2m15, bars 29–32 (@ 35:29

Notice once again the wavelike motion from D major to E-flat major, requiring a shift of only a semitone in all but the first cellos. In the language of neo-Riemannian theory, this is another example of transformation, but it has a lineage far more ancient than postmodern music theory. In 1567, Thomas Tallis, the great English Renaissance composer, created nine tunes for the English Hymnal, one of which (#3, "Why fum'th in fight") was known as the "Third Mode Melody." The third mode is the Phrygian mode (C–D–E). In 1910, the equally great English composer Ralph Vaughan Williams adapted and cinematically expanded this little "tune" into the genuinely awe-inspiring piece for double string orchestra he called Fantasia on a Theme by Thomas Tallis (featured on the soundtrack of both Peter Weir's *Master and Commander* and Terrence Malick's *Knight of Cups*, among others). This is one of an essential list of pieces from the twentieth-century repertoire for film composers to study and allow to percolate into their own musical vocabulary. Here is its opening statement, reduced to just four of its many voices. Notice the striking kinship between the divisi viola parts here and the first and second violins in Figure 14.18. If this is coincidence, it has supernatural origins!

Figure 14.19. Ralph Vaughan Williams, Fantasia on a Theme by Thomas Tallis (1910) (excerpt)

In the science of semiotics, as touched on earlier in this book, allusions within a work to *other works* thematically or structurally connected to it are called *intertextual references* (semioticians characterize all works, whether literature, art, or music as "texts"). This is not cribbing if it's done well and integrated respectfully: it's a critical element of art making, because no work of art subsists entirely on its own without reference to others. In fact, it's a way of acknowledging your sources and tapping into their emotional well-spring. After all, Vaughan-Williams did it. It happens all the time in symphonic works, but the references are often more obscure or transfigured. When these referential gestures are as effective as they are in *How to Train Your Dragon*, they open doors of perception that allow the audience a deeper and richer understanding of the story.

In previous chapters, we've seen how masterfully such composers as David Newman, Don Davis, and the *Perfume* trio made use of such allusions, and this was no less true of Brahms and Stravinsky. Intertextual reference and homage should never be confused with the sort of borrowing that some lesser composers are prone to under the pressure of deadline, writer's block, or producer pressure to mimic a temp score.

The artificial tailfin is a success, as an unexpected aerial trial demonstrates, but there is work to be done before the triumphant test flight of 3m20 can occur. Meanwhile, Hiccup is expected to continue his dragon fighting sessions under Gobber with Astrid and the other teenagers, leading ultimately to his rite of passage: the killing of one of the captive dragons, bullring style. As we've already seen, this is a task Hiccup has no desire to perform. Over the ensuing five to six minutes, he begins to apply some of the dragon psychology he has learned in working with Toothless to the beasts in the ring, pacifying them without violence and in the process gaining a reputation as something of a "dragon whisperer." Astrid, for one, is intrigued by this new talent, and begins to watch Hiccup with more interest. Meanwhile, he continues to work on the harness and tack that will eventually allow him to mount Toothless for some of the film's most thrilling scenes.

PREPARING FOR FLIGHT

In cue 3m18, "See You Tomorrow," marked *Tempo Celtico*," we observe Hiccup in the workshop as he tools his riding gear, and Astrid observes both his growing prowess in the ring and his strange comings and goings from the woods. In this sequence, Powell introduces the first of two entirely new themes, a pentatonic melody, modally and melodically related to the "Village" theme, that has both the depth of Celtic song and the breadth of a classic Western theme. Because of the latter, I'll call this the "Ready to Ride" theme. Figure 14.20 is a reduction of its fullest tutti statement in 3m18.

This long cue (nearly 4:00) accomplishes more than the introduction of a new melody, however. Opening at 39:05 with an infectious Scottish Highland reel as Hiccup fashions his riding gear in the leather shop, it exuberantly reprises most of the key ideas presented so far in the score, and for good reason. It is setting us up for the movie's joyous high point, when Toothless gives Hiccup the ride of his life. 3m18 twice prefigures the Highland pipes fanfare (shown in Figure 14.14) that will open 3m20, "Test Ride," and which, as we saw, was built from the elements of Hiccup's fateful choice in 1m7. It offers a number of variations on the "Bonding" theme. In terms of story, John Powell aids his directors in carrying along one of the film's most important subplots: Astrid's growing admiration for and attraction to the village weirdo, Hiccup. And even the following reduced orchestration illustrates the orchestrational panache employed:

Figure 14.20. *How to Train Your Dragon*, 3m18, "See You Tomorrow," bars 26–29

With the completion of his saddle and stirrups, and the perfection of his dragon-whispering skills, Hiccup is now ready for his first test drive. But although the scene depicts a maiden voyage, the cue of the same name that underscores it (3m20) is a consummation and synthesis rather than a new statement. Powell has been preparing our ears and heart for it for nearly forty-four minutes. Experts on the psychology and neurology of music, such as Daniel Levitin,[2] write of the brain's remarkable ability to retain musical

---

2   Daniel J. Levitin, *This Is Your Brain on Music: The Science of a Human Obsession* (New York: Penguin, 2007) and *The World in Six Songs: How the Musical Brain Created Human Nature* (New York: Dutton, 2009).

patterns and pitch sequences (often in the original key), and the importance of familiarity in triggering an emotional reaction to a piece of music. There is almost no musical information presented in 3m20 that we've not already been exposed to, albeit in a far more understated way. In fact, it's been with us since the very first frame of picture. As a consequence of this methodical "sowing of seeds," when six trombones and a tuba enter at *ff* with an open fifth on D accompanied by a mighty timpani roll, and the winds carry Hiccup and Toothless high above the sea and the jagged coastline of Berk, we experience an instantaneous frisson.

Figure 14.21. *How to Train Your Dragon,* "Test Drive," 3m20, Bars 5–8

After this rousing introduction, we hear both "A" and "B" statements of the "Bonding" theme, followed by a grand reprise of "A," shown in reduction in Figure 14.22, minus percussion and low woodwinds. At this point, after a few pilot errors, Hiccup takes Toothless on a straight vertical toward the stratosphere in a moment that recalls test pilot Chuck Yeager's (Sam Shepard) fateful breakthrough flight in *The Right Stuff.*

Figure 14.22. *How to Train Your Dragon*, 3m20, "Test Drive," bars 32–35 ⓐ 44:30

This is the score's fullest orchestration of the simple five-note theme that opened the film (it consists of just three pitch classes: F-sharp, G, and E), and its realization is entirely diatonic. Twelve horns, split evenly between melody and lower harmony, are the only members of the brass family to speak on the antecedent phrase, but twelve horns are a mighty force. Powell reserves his trumpets and trombones for the consequent phrase, shown in Figure 14.23. Notice how in both four-bar phrases, he keeps the melody aloft by means of the sixteenth-note figures in clarinets and violas, with flutes joining at measure 36. Without this motion, Hiccup's flight would be far less exhilarating. It is, so to speak, the wind beneath his wings. Equally important is the decision to save the trumpets for the back four bars, and to give them the melody at that point. These are the small touches that make a film cue feel anthemic and insure that the energy level continues to rise along with its visual counterpart. The sextuplet runs in flutes, second violins, and violas on the last two beats of bar 39 are isomorphic, as Hiccup has flown Toothless a little too high and a little too fast, and stalls out, losing control of the reins at the zenith of his flight. We can see that the other instruments cease their motion here. The clarinets, in fact, come to a pointed stop.

Figure 14.23. *How to Train Your Dragon*, 3m20, "Test Drive," bars 36–39

Chordally, the densest section of the cue is the tutti statement of the "B" half of the "Bonding" theme in measures 21–28 (this occurs at 44:06, 24 sec/11 bars earlier than the passage shown in Figures 14.22 and 14.23). Once again, it's a statement we've been waiting for since the opening cue of the film, and it underscores a thrilling dive toward the sea and through the arches of rock on the craggy shore, after which Hiccup cries, "Yes! It works!"

Figure 14.24. *How to Train Your Dragon*, 3m20, "Test Drive," bars 21–24

Animators think about the details, sometimes obsessively so. How can they not, when every frame has to be painstakingly rendered? As a result, the picture hits they ask for are quite specific, and for composers who are new to the genre, can sometimes feel like a latter-day version of "mickey-mousing" (e.g., "add a cymbal swell here . . . a trombone blat there . . . a woodblock on that hit," etc.). But John Powell is hardly new to scoring animation. *Dragon* was, by my count, his thirteenth animated feature film, and so the gestures he makes to match picture are not simply flourishes or add-ons, but integrated elements of the orchestration. Notice the tuplet woodwind figures in Figure 14.24. These are the winds buffeting the dragon's wings as he dives toward the sea.

Figure 14.25. *How to Train Your Dragon*, 3m20, "Test Drive," bars 25–28

Notice once again the voice-leading in the progression B minor–F-sharp minor–A–E, where Powell has his first trombones split (or with 2,3 on the inner voice of the triads). Each successive chord has at least one common tone until we arrive at the final E major chord. The rock solid foundation provided by the bassoon, brass section, and percussion allows the strings to glide and sweep through the stirring, Celtic melody line as effortlessly as Toothless rides the air currents, and again, the high woodwinds provide the voice of the wind.

Hiccup has now tamed his dragon, and must now turn to "taming" the other object of his affection: Astrid. He has won her attention with his dragon-whispering skills, but has also piqued her suspicion—and perhaps her envy—with his unexplained trips to and from the woods. To face the greatest obstacle of all—persuading his father and the Vikings of Berk that the dragons are "not what we think they are"—he will need allies among his classmates, and none is more important than Astrid. How is he to win her over to his side? By taking her for the ride of her life.

ROMANTIC FLIGHT

Cue3m25, which John Powell has titled "Romantic Flight," is the last one we'll examine. It enters at 54:14, and the section we will look at begins at 54:36. There are still thirty minutes left in the film—the critical and action-packed "third act"—and the score handles them with aplomb. But third acts in adventure/fantasy films, as we've seen in others examined in this book, are noisy, and don't generally allow for the introduction of new musical material or even much development of existing motifs. By this point at the end of act two, Powell has introduced all his key musical characters, and could easily have rested on his laurels, reconfigured existing material such as the "Village" theme, or let Dreamworks plug Hiccup and Astrid's "Romantic Flight" with a pop song. The scene is, after all, reminiscent of the magic carpet ride in Disney's *Aladdin,* and that yielded an Academy Award–winning song.

Instead, Powell gives us an entirely new theme, and one every bit as stirring as those that have come before. Fittingly, it's a waltz, and would have made Johann Strauss proud, if Strauss had been a Scotsman! The melody is first heard on solo violin, played in the highly ornamented style of Celtic fiddle, and with the marking *"molto espressivo,"* accompanied only by choral voices at the hushed dynamic of *p.* The chord progression is folk-like, based on I, IV, and V and plagal cadences in a B major key center. The cue enters almost literally as the calm after the storm, since only seconds before, Toothless has gotten a little sweet revenge on the dragon-killing Vikings of Berk by taking Astrid on a zero-gravity roller-coaster ride, complete with spins, swoops, loop-the-loops, and hair-raising dives. Now, however, having shown off his stuff, he breaks through the clouds and rides a thermal, soaring serenely above the sea. Astrid is duly impressed.

Figure 14.26. *How to Train Your Dragon*, 3m25, "Romantic Flight," bars 15–19

When the orchestra joins at bar 15, the melody leaves the solo fiddle and is picked up by six French horns and the first cellos, both at *mf* and marked *"con amore."* There is no doubt that love is in the air. As the *Aladdin* sequence mentioned earlier, and perhaps even more reminiscent of the Meryl Streep–Robert Redford flying scene in *Out of Africa* (scored wonderfully by John Barry), this is an experience to win the heart of even the toughest village girl. Notice the crescendo-decrescendo markings in the melody. These are part of what gives the tune its aerodynamic "lift."

To provide forward momentum, Powell gives us the lilting contrary motion of the second violins and violas. Finally, the meshing rhythm of woodwinds and pizzicato basses provides stability and assures Astrid (and us) that she is riding a "good machine."

Figure 14.27. *How to Train Your Dragon*, 3m25, "Romantic Flight," bars 20–24

In measures 20–21, of all those in the score, we hear most clearly the evidence of John Powell's period of study with Hans Zimmer. In that big climb up and crescendo from the second inversion I (Badd9) chord to the first inversion IV (E), with the line beginning, technically, on an appoggiatura (C-sharp), we hear the Zimmer of *The Lion King* and other landmark scores from his early career. It feels like a fitting homage to John Powell's musical mentor, and there would have been a lovely poetry had Powell won his own Oscar for *How to Train Your Dragon* (it went instead to Trent Reznor for *The Social Network*). In bar 26, a single oboe joins the first violins for the closing phrase of the romantic theme, followed by an emphatic and unified I–IV cadential gesture as the camera pulls way back and Hiccup and Astrid soar upward into the clouds. The cue continues on to a Disneyesque fantasia before reprising the theme one last time.

Figure 14.28. *How to Train Your Dragon*, 3m25, "Romantic Flight," bars 25–29

Speaking of Mr. Zimmer, he is quoted as having said that John Powell's artistry is "underpinned by a moral stance." It's a telling statement. Film composers are moral beings, but the nature of the business compels compromise and can take a piece of one's soul. How has Powell avoided that fate? *How to Train Your Dragon* codirector Dean DeBlois has said that "music did the heavy lifting" in the film, particularly "in places where (it became) too difficult for picture to communicate an idea or indicate a moral shift in character." If one thinks about it, that's about as high a compliment as can be paid to a film composer, and to an art form—*music*—that many theorists have contended is incapable of signifying or depicting anything beyond its own form and emotional color. But music does indeed signify, and film music *is* a language—one of the most widely understood languages on the planet. In *How to Train Your Dragon*, and in John Powell's hands, it signifies many things: courage, ingenuity, humor, and most of all, the redeeming power of empathy.

FIFTEEN AGAINST THE ODDS
THE ROAD TO KRAKÓW

I once invited an industry insider to speak to a postgraduate scoring class. When I gave him the floor, he took a moment to compose himself, then looked out at the dozen or so students, and said, "One of you . . . if everything goes your way . . . might actually make a living in this business. The rest of you can probably forget about it."

That sort of pronouncement disheartens me every bit as much as the one cited in the foreword to this book—that film scoring is to "serious music" as prostitution is to serious romance. It turns the pursuit of a passion into a zero-sum game: you win or you lose; you're either virtuous or not. But life, like drama, is a whole lot more complicated.

If you persevere in your study of music for the screen and in your efforts to build a career, you're going to run into a certain number of "veterans" who'll want to tell you the "hard truth" about how few people make it in this field. Some will speak from wisdom, others from bitterness, and a few, from genuine concern about how your heart will handle rejection. Regardless of where they're coming from, it's good to listen, take whatever lesson can be had, and then continue doing exactly what you were doing before, only with redoubled commitment. The only way to beat the odds is to keep playing.

George Miller (*Mad Max: Fury Road*), perhaps the greatest action director of our time, once told me that the wonderful Australian actress Naomi Watts had her bags packed and her ticket home from Hollywood purchased when she decided "for the hell of it" to answer one last casting call for David Lynch's *Mulholland Drive*. She had already reached an age at which many an ingénue actress's stock begins to fall, and had seen peers, such as her friend and fellow Aussie, Nicole Kidman, race past her. But she was a pro, and pros answer the call. Needless to say, the rest is history. She turned in one of the most incandescent performances in recent cinema, and hasn't stopped working since.

This book isn't a career manual, but it wouldn't be fitting to conclude it without acknowledging that, for most of you, career is at the heart of your reasons for reading it. As much artistic satisfaction as we may get from the pure study and appreciation of great film music, it can't compare to the satisfaction one derives from being involved in the making of it. The global proliferation of visual media (soon to be augmented by virtual reality) has opened up numerous paths to such involvement. For those whose wish is to follow the path set by the composers treated in this book, there really are just four cardinal rules:

- Develop your craft to the very highest level of which you are capable, and develop it in multiple directions. If you can score a little indie feature, play in a string quartet or rock band, write a ballet, and produce tracks for a production library all at the same time, keeping your eye on the prize, your creative engines will get used to running at full throttle, and the world will hear you coming.
- Never forgo an opportunity to connect with a kindred spirit. If a friend invites you to a poetry night, or a cold reading of a play, go. If the poet or playwright uses words, expressions, or themes that resonate with you, introduce yourself afterward and make it clear to her or him that you "got it," because *you,* too, are fascinated by many of the same things addressed in his/her work. That poet or playwright might be the next Tracy Letts, Martin McDonagh, Wes Anderson, or Christopher Nolan. The same advice applies to film festivals.
- Stay healthy in mind, body, and spirit. You can't win a road race on deflated tires, and you can't win someone's confidence with low energy.
- Confidence is critical, but at the same time, don't oversell yourself. You don't need to prove that you're the smartest person in the room. You just need to be *in the room,* and be ready to stand up when called. Most important, never stop asking, "How can I help? How can I make it better?"

Because composers of music for the screen operate broadly as independent contractors and without the umbrella of protection afforded by trade unions or guilds, often working out of their homes or small commercial rentals with minimal support staff, and because they offer "goods" (i.e., music) in exchange for an agreed upon price, it has become conventional in some quarters of the industry to label them as "entrepreneurs." This redefinition was, I suppose, inevitable in an era of increased commodification. Without denying the need for media composers (who, truth be told, function nowadays as producers more than artisans) to market themselves and maintain good business practices, I take a somewhat different view. Let's see how the dictionary defines *entrepreneur*:

> businessman/businesswoman, enterpriser, speculator, tycoon, magnate, mogul; dealer, trader, dealmaker; promoter, impresario; informal wheeler-dealer, whiz kid, mover and shaker, go-getter, high flyer, hustler, idea man/person.

This broad definition would seem to apply equally to the owner of a falafel stand, a chain of dry-cleaning outlets, or a billionaire real estate developer like Donald Trump. It does not, except in certain respects (dealmaker, idea man, etc.) describe the role of a composer very well, and taking it as your handle may lead you down avenues very different from the ones traveled by the people in this book. Screen composers—like illustrators of children's books, architects, designers, choreographers, etc.—are "hired guns." There is a job that needs doing, and someone (usually the producer) has decided that you're the person to do it. You are being hired first because you are an *artist* and second because you are a *problem solver*. The first is a prerequisite for the second: if your art isn't up to snuff, you won't be able to solve many problems. It has also been presumed that your contribution will add to the value of the production, as gold plating adds to the value of a watch or a beautiful fresco enhances the value of a public space. Most important, you've been chosen because it's believed that your artistry will bring a certain, ineffable "something" that will raise gooseflesh on the arms of the audience.

None of these things are especially related to your ability to hustle. Sure, you have to hang out your shingle, build your website—and at some point, a good publicist may be of real value to your career. But these are only the scaffolding erected around the core of your talent. You are not a "brand." Rather, you are an expert in your field who has been trusted to guide the production through the uncertain waters of musical expression. It's an honorable occupation. Maybe even the "greatest gig in the world."

Music for the screen has come of age, and enjoys far greater respect than it once did, but there are also challenges that didn't exist in Elmer Bernstein's era. These are, in many ways, "the best of times and the worst of times." On the negative side of the ledger is the fact that music no longer enjoys the immunity it once had from the sausage factory aspects of motion picture entertainment. It's on the factory floor along with all the other entrails. Elmer once confessed to me that he was glad he hadn't come up in this period, when "everyone's an expert and composers are more like order takers." It is indeed harder to develop the kind of distinctive signature that such composers as Bernstein, Herrmann, and Goldsmith had with a committee of people looking over your shoulder.

On the plus side, however, is the undeniable fact that—to quote Lucasfilm's THX tagline—"the audience is listening." Zimmer, Elfman, Williams, and Shore are far better known to the general public than Rózsa, Tiomkin, and Waxman were in their day. Their music is being heard not only in cinemas, but in concert halls and arenas, as well as on smartphones and game consoles. And a book like this one could not have hoped to find wide circulation were it not for the growing number of festivals in Europe that have expanded the audience and enhanced the international cachet of film music—such festivals as Fimucité (in the Canary Islands), Film Fest Gent (in Ghent, Belgium), Transatlantyk (in Poznan, Poland), and the Film Music Festival (FMF) in Kraków, Poland, where the fifteen-thousand-seat Tauron Arena is filled to capacity for live performance to picture of such scores as *Gladiator* and *Star Trek*, and where scores featured in this book, such as *Perfume* and *The Matrix*, as well as new works by composers like Elliot Goldenthal, have received receptions normally reserved for rock stars. For me, and for many others in the profession who have attended FMF, Kraków has come to symbolize the recognition of film music as both serious art and modern spectacle.

With that said, this closing chapter's subheading can be explained. "The Road to Kraków" is not only wordplay on "The Road to Dubno," the title of a rousing Franz Waxman cue from the 1962 costume epic *Taras Bulba*, well known to aficionados of classic film music. It's also a metaphor for what such events as Kraków's FMF represent: the ever-broadening avenue toward the serious study and wide appreciation of motion picture music, a language of signs that take the shape of notes, figures, motives, and phrases, and, in complement to picture, reveals the hidden contents of the human heart.

AFTERWORD

CONSPICUOUS BY THEIR ABSENCE

There are two substantial sins of omission in this book—sins that I hope to expiate in future editions.

For some, the most glaring omission may be the work of John Williams. After having served as the standard bearer of the craft for better than four decades, why isn't he in here? The principal reason is this: I resolved that in writing *Scoring the Screen* I would work only from original recording scores, not from suites, medleys, arrangements, or compilations cleaned up and published after the fact. The rationale for this lies in the fact that my analyses are all "note-against-picture," and the original score is the only document (even if there have been edits made) that can be laid against the film and used to measure the composer's dramatic intentions and back-track through his writing process. I was not able to obtain an original score manuscript from Mr. Williams, but I to catch up with him in future editions of this book.

Another major composer not represented here (but for the excerpt in chapter 3) is Hans Zimmer. Hans has indeed been a game-changer on many levels, and again, I hope to remedy this omission, with his help, in a later edition.

For me, the more painful lapse is the absence of a score written by a woman (other than the Mica Levi excerpt, also in chapter 3). Here the reasoning gets a little more complicated. The central idea advanced in the book is that film music is a language with its own distinctive vocabulary, and so I determined to include only scores that I strongly believed had significantly shaped or modified that language. Although there's room for debate, women haven't been in the mix quite long enough for one of them to have written such a score. But I'm as sure as I am of my own breath that one of them soon will. In fact, I'd go so far as to say that the full inclusion of female composers is essential to the growth of the craft.

The film music trade, like the priesthood, boardroom, and laboratory, is in great need of new perspectives. I intend to keep seeking, and writing about them. So, too, do I hope to do musical "exegesis" on works by such composers as Patrick Doyle, Mychael Danna, Bruce Broughton, Alexandre Desplat, and Howard Shore, all of them stars in the film music firmament.

MUSIC PERMISSIONS

HOW TO TRAIN YOUR DRAGON
By John Powell
Copyright © 2010 DWA Songs
All Rights Administered by Almo Music Corp.
All Rights Reserved. Used by permission
Reprinted by permission of Hal Leonard LLC

INCEPTION (Score)
Composed by Hans Zimmer
Copyright © 2010 Warner-Olive Music LLC (ASCAP)
All Rights Administered by Universal Music Corp. (ASCAP)
Exclusive Worldwide Print Rights Administered by Alfred Music
All Rights Reserved
Reprinted by permission of Alfred Music

JAMES BOND
Composed by Monty Norman
© 1962 United Artists Music Ltd. Copyright Renewed by EMI Unart Catalog, Inc.
Exclusive Print Rights Controlled and Administered by Alfred Music
All Rights Reserved
Reprinted by permission of Alfred Music

JENNIFER EIGHT
By Christopher Young
Copyright © 1992 Sony/ATV Music Publishing LLC
All Rights Administered by Sony/ATV Music Publishing LLC,
424 Church Street, Suite 1200, Nashville, TN 37219
International Copyright Secured. All Rights Reserved
Reprinted by permission of Hal Leonard LLC

LA PIEL QUE HABITO
By Alberto Iglesias
Copyright © by Union Musical Ediciones S L
International Copyright Secured. All Rights Reserved
Reprinted by permission of Music Sales West

L'HISTOIRE DU SOLDAT
Composed by Igor Stravinsky
Libretto by Charles Ferdinand Ramuz
Music © Copyright 1924, 1987, 1992 Chester Music Limited Worldwide rights except
the United Kingdom, Ireland, Australia, Canada, South Africa and all so-called
reversionary rights territories where the copyright © 1996 is held jointly by
Chester Music Limited and Schott Music GmbH & Co. KG, Mainz, Germany.
Libretto © Copyright 1924, 1987, 1992 Chester Music Limited.
All Rights Reserved. International Copyright Secured.
Reprinted by permission of Music Sales West

THE MATRIX (Score)
By Don Davis
Copyright © 1999 Warner-Barham Music, LLC (BMI)
All Rights Administered by Songs of Universal, Inc. (BMI)
Exclusive Worldwide Print Rights Administered by Alfred Music
All Rights Reserved
Reprinted by permission of Alfred Music